Reflections on
the Appalachian Trail

Reflections on the Appalachian Trail
One Woman's Journey of Faith

Beth Eden Abel

XULON PRESS

Xulon Press
2301 Lucien Way #415
Maitland, FL 32751
407.339.4217
www.xulonpress.com

© 2022 by Beth Eden Abel

All rights reserved solely by the author. The author guarantees all contents are original and do not infringe upon the legal rights of any other person or work. No part of this book may be reproduced in any form without the permission of the author.

Due to the changing nature of the Internet, if there are any web addresses, links, or URLs included in this manuscript, these may have been altered and may no longer be accessible. The views and opinions shared in this book belong solely to the author and do not necessarily reflect those of the publisher. The publisher therefore disclaims responsibility for the views or opinions expressed within the work.

Unless otherwise indicated, Scripture quotations taken from the Life Recovery Bible, New International Version (NIV). Copyright © 1973, 1978, 1984, 2011 by Biblica, Inc.™. Used by permission. All rights reserved.

Unless otherwise indicated, Scripture quotations taken from the The Message (MSG). Copyright © 1993, 1994, 1995, 1996, 2000, 2001, 2002. Used by permission of NavPress Publishing Group. Used by permission. All rights reserved.

Unless otherwise indicated, Scripture quotations taken from the the Holy Bible, New Living Translation (NLT). Copyright ©1996, 2004, 2007 by Tyndale House Foundation. Used by permission of Tyndale House Publishers, Inc

Sarah Jones Decker
Photography Copyrighted by © SarahJDecker can not be reproduced without permission from Sarah Jones Decker

ATC Photos and Maps used Courtesy of the Appalachian Trail Conservancy

Materials provided, including the photos and map linked above, are authorized only for use in the publication previously described (*Reflections on the Appalachian Trail, One woman's journey of faith*, by Beth Eden Abel) in print and/or ebook form, and cannot be used in another publication in any medium without additional permissions provided by the Appalachian Trail Conservancy. The Conservancy maintains the copyright and/or ownership of the photos, files, and all other assets marked as "With Permission: ATC"

From: Ben Montgomery benmontgomerywrites@gmail.com
You have permission to use the whole of "The Reward of Nature" with attribution to Emma Gatewood.

Paperback ISBN-13: 978-1-6628-4536-9
Ebook ISBN-13: 978-1-6628-4537-6

Endorsements

"There are plenty of guidebooks that tell how to hike the Appalachian Trail, but this is the first I've seen that blazes the path for a spiritual thru-hike. Using her own experiences and those of legendary AT pioneers like Grandma Gatewood and Jennifer Pharr Davis, Beth Eden Abel invites us all on an important and inspiring journey." **Ben Montgomery, author of *Grandma Gatewood's Walk***

"Beth Eden Abel quotes Eleanor Roosevelt: For it is not enough to talk about Peace, one must believe in it. And it is not enough to believe in it, one must work at it." Beth makes the Appalachian Trail the setting of talking, believing and working on her spiritual journey. This book is her invitation to join her on the trail of spiritual flourishing". **Rev. Dr. Kim Cape, PhD candidate in Practical Theology, Cambridge, UK**

"Luke 1:45 tells us that we are blessed when we believe that the Lord fulfills His promises. God promises that He is always there no matter what the circumstances are. That by trusting Him, you can do anything. This devotional book is full of His promises. It will help and guide you along life's journey in more ways than you can imagine". **Marcia Roland, "Smasher", Beth's beloved Trail companion**

"This devotional book is a beautiful collection of Beth's faith journey and experiences from hiking the Appalachian Trail. She reflects on the beauty and ruggedness of God's nature, the interesting people she meets, and relationships formed, as well as what it means to her life struggles and future directions. The scriptures and life lessons help the reader relate their own life experiences and inspire growth in their own faith journey. **Jeri Hilsabeck, faith friend, Austin, Tx.**

"There could be no better companion on the trail of life than Beth Abel! As she chronicles her Appalachian Trail hikes — complete with challenges, adventures, joys and fears — she not only reveals an intimate exploration of her faith journey but equips all of us for our own spiritual quest, aided by relevant, thought-provoking devotionals". **Cathy Cochran-Lewis, Writer, Seeker, Hiker, Austin, Tx.**

"I have known Beth for many years as a friend, counselor, hiker, and fellow follower of Jesus Christ. Through this book of devotional reflections may you also get to know her and more, the One who walks this journey with us". **Rev. Dr. Lynn Barton, Austin, Tx.**

"This book is an inspirational guide for those looking to find a renewed sense of God's presence in their lives. Beth's writing comes from a place of personal and professional experience. Her words are deeply profound while being genuinely relatable. Don't miss the opportunity to take this powerful journey!" **Amy F. Butler, LMSW, MDiv, Mentee and friend of the author, Tuscaloosa, Alabama**

DEDICATION

To all the wonderful AT Trail Maintainers who volunteer their time to make the expansive display of God's Nature more accessible for everyone. And to all the behind-the-scenes and unknown Trail Angels making recreation on the AT become Re-Creation moments with God's Love through strangers. The publishing of this book celebrates the first 100 years since the proposal of the Appalachian Trail with the hope and prayer that we will continue this good stewardship of God's land. Beth Eden Abel, Trail name - "Spirit"

This book and the experience on which it is based were influenced by many people who know my faith in Jesus Christ. These people of faith helped me to answer God's calling that I bear witness to His loving presence and guidance in my life. I am deeply grateful for their prayers and their talented support to create this book.

My dear husband and faith partner of forty-four years, Tim Abel. He has labored beside me birthing this book as my dedicated editor-in-residence.

My precious Trail Buddy, Marcia Roland, Trail Name "Smasher." A steady pilgrim in faith, she walked beside me through 15 hiking trips over thirteen years, always aware of God's Grace and loving presence and eager to share this Truth with me. Smasher has contributed to my recollections in many parts of the book.

A Trail Angel on the writing of this book, Cathy Cochran Lewis. When I prayed for urgent expertise in book writing, Cathy stepped forward from a social acquaintance into deliberate servanthood on this need. Cathy gave hours and hours of editing assistance and overall conceptual scope to the book.

A Trail Angel on scripture integration with life experiences, Lynn Barton. A dear family friend and clergy colleague to Tim, my husband, Lynn has been a dedicated contributor by helping me bring Trail experiences into scriptural references. When I was floundering with the faith message, Lynn's prayerful and thoughtful contributions helped me focus on God's light.

Adrianne, my daughter, for her graphic designs and most importantly, for her prayers and support.

RW, my son, videographer for the final 10 miles and a great hiking companion.

Epigraph

"God writes the Gospel not in the Bible alone, but also on trees, and in the flowers and clouds and stars."

Attributed to: **Martin Luther**

Contents

Copyright iv
Endorsements vii
Dedication ix
Epigraph xi
Foreword xvii

Introduction xix
A Concise History of the Appalachian Trail 1
AT Hiking Trips Lead To A Spiritual Pilgrimage 11

Chronology of 20 Faith Journeys

Introduction 21
Hiking Partners 23

First Steps: 1997 to 2002

1997 June – Damascus, Virginia northbound to
    Grayson Highlands 27
2000 July – Damascus, Va. Southbound on NC/TN
    border to Erwin, Tn. 29
2001 May - Wallace Gap, NC northbound to
    Fontana Dam, NC. 32
2001 September - Pinkham Notch, NH southbound to
    Mt. Lafayette, NH. 35
2002 May – Shenandoah National Park, Virginia:
    Compton Gap southbound to Fishers Gap 38

Hiking with Smasher: 2002 to 2008

2002 September – Grayson Highlands State Park,
  Virginia northbound to Pearisburg, Virginia 42
2003 May – Springer Mountain, Georgia northbound
  to Neels Gap, Georgia 46
2003 September – Pearisburg, Virginia northbound
  to the James River, Virginia. 50
2004 September – James River, Virginia northbound to
  Compton Gap, Shenandoah National Park, Virginia 54
2005 September – Standing Indian AT shelter, NC
  southbound to Neels Gap, Georgia 58
2006 September – Shenandoah National Park, Virginia:
  Compton Gap northbound to Pen Mar Park, Maryland 62
2007 June – Great Smoky Mountain National Park 68
2007 September – Roan High Knob Shelter, NC
  southbound to Erwin, TN. 42

Onward from Mt. Katahdin: 2008 to 2012

2008 July – Mt Katahdin, Maine southbound to Rangeley, Maine. . 79
2010 September – Pen Mar Park, Maryland northbound
  to Swatara Gap, Pennsylvania. 87
2011 September – Swatara Gap, Pennsylvania
  northbound to Bake Oven Knob Rd., Pennsylvania. 93
2012 September – North Carolina/Tennessee border
  to fill in the Trail mileage gaps 99

New Beginning Steps: 2013 to 2015

2013 September – Bake Oven Knob Rd., Pennsylvania
  northbound to Bear Mountain bridge, NY. 105
2014 August and September – Vermont/Massachusetts
  border northbound to Maine/NH border. 110
2015 August and September – Vermont/Massachusetts
  border southbound to Bear Mountain bridge, NY. 117
2015 September - Final Steps: Bear Mountain State Park,
  Tye River near Dutch Haus, Montebello, Virginia 126

Natural Fibers in the Weaving of a Faith Journey

Moments of Grace

Spirit	137
Fellowship	142
Grace	146
God's Gifts	150
Hospitality	154
Unexpected	159
Trail Angels	163
Beauty	168
Fun and Recreation	172
Sanctuary	178
Giving	182

Moments of Belief

Storms	189
Diligence	195
Pacing	200
False Summits	204
Grieving	213
Hope	219
Joy	223
Shelter	227
Soul Food	232
Strength	236
Asking	240
Chosen	246
Trusting	250
Living Water	255

Moments of Faith

When Nature Calls	263
Closeness To Christ	269
Freedom	273
Healing	279
Holy Matrimony	282

Lost	285
Outcast	291
Suffering	295
Transitions	300
Truth	305
Faithfulness	309
Forgiveness	314
Peacemaking	319
Encouraging	323
Celebrating	327

Living a Spiritual Pilgrimage

A Well Lit Path Has Life Direction **335**

Appendices	343
List of Volunteer Appalachian Maintaining Clubs 1921 – 2021	345
List of Abbreviations	347
Bibliography	349

Foreword

When Beth told me that she was going to hike the Appalachian trail I thought that she was nuts. It all started in 1996 when we were on a family vacation along the East coast from Gettysburg, PA, through Washington DC and eventually to Disney World to let out teenage children see something of the United States other than Texas. This was before GPS's and Google Maps. We had to use a paper map to navigate through this unfamiliar territory. Beth was THE navigator.

I clearly remember when she asked, "What's that dotted line on these maps?" I looked and quickly realized that it was the AT. I had hiked about 30 miles of the AT in Smoky Mountain NP as a Boy Scout. Her response was 'Oh, Hmmm…..." Her silence was deafening. When we got home, she announced. "I am going to hike the AT!" I knew that talking her out of something once she made up her mind rarely proved to be fruitful.

Beth had a difficult life as an adolescent. She contracted an infection in her digestive tract that prevented her from athletic activities until after her first year of college. Her strength of character and will far exceeded her physical strength. I knew how difficult the AT was based on my experiences of long distance hiking as a teenager.

The rest is history. It took three years for her to build the strength and endurance needed to meet her goal. Every morning she got up at 5 am, put on her 20 to 25 lb. pack and walked four miles. On Friday's she increased this hike to 10 to 12 miles. Her dedication was an inspiration to all. Even though I continued to think that she had lost her mind!

After her first three or four treks on the Trail, I came to embrace and celebrate her achievements. But I didn't anticipate what else was going on in her life while she walked those difficult miles.

Beth and I met in a church. She was another alto in the church choir I was directing as I attended a seminary in Dallas TX working on a degree path to ordained ministry. Our decision to get married was based on a solid foundation of faith. I was accustomed to her being my partner by singing in the choir, leading children's choirs, teaching Sunday School, and being my spiritual council and support. Yet as she hiked the AT, each step she took was a step toward an ever-deepening spiritual relationship with Jesus Christ.

Beth's professional background is in Social Work. After years of working in the juvenile justice system as well as youth treatment centers, she began to transition to a private practice in guiding and counseling women in life transitions. Seeing the changes in her client's lives as a result of her work was an inspiration to all.

Yet I had no idea about the transitions that were going on in her own life as she physically and spiritually matured through her experiences hiking the Appalachian Trail. This book is a testimony to that journey of faith. She has been an inspiration to me and to those who have been her cheerleaders and to many other people as she walked those 2000 miles. Our lives have been enriched by her experiences and testimony. It is my hope and prayer, that these words she has to share will be a guide and a companion to each reader in their journey to a personal relationship in Jesus Christ.

Rev. Dr. Tim Abel – aka Beth's Husband

Introduction

Ephesians 3:14 *When I think of the wisdom and scope of God's plan, I fall to my knees and pray to the Father, the Creator of everything in heaven and on earth.* NLT

I went to the Appalachian Trail (AT) looking for something new in life to capture my attention and energy so that I could passionately find a respite from struggling with midlife transitions. What I found on the Trail was far more than my low-expectation prayers requested. Ephesians 3:17 states *"May your roots go down deep into the soil of God's marvelous love"*. God's Nature in the wilderness brought this balm of Truth to me and I was saved from my own demise. By spending time in God's Nature and away from ordinary distractions, the AT hiking trips became annual faith journeys that refueled my life purpose both in my personal life and in my counseling practice relationships. Eventually I was no longer a wounded healer, I have found peace and joy in being a viable Christian, wherever I am.

Immersion in recreation and travel adventure were the primary motivators that led me to the AT. But once I experienced God's Nature touching my soul and rejuvenating my spirit, the AT hikes became a series of faith journeys. As I embraced the presence of the Holy One within those faith journeys, my enjoyment of the recreational time and the travel adventures naturally increased.

Fear was contaminating my ability to have a vision of a good future for my family and for me. My years as a professional counselor guiding women through bumpy life transitions as well as major emotional disturbances had contaminated my hopeful worldview. I had become a wounded healer, no longer able to grasp my need for the Savior, Jesus Christ. I had succumbed to the humanistic approach that I must be in control of life. This fear and angst of lacking control over life was troubling me more each day.

There were many challenges on the AT. Time away from family and work, finding a compatible female hiking partner, becoming physically fit for backpacking and living on the Trail. Unanticipated were three hurricanes, a moose encounter, and meeting a variety of personalities including a Santa Claus.

Many Trail acquaintances inspired me with stories of their life journeys. Each year the AT hiker community taught me that people are inherently good and care about others.

I hiked 2,000 AT miles! There were 2185.3 miles of Trail on the AT the year I completed my hike. I was unable to complete those miles due to Trail closures in Maine because of washout conditions. More importantly, I found the answers to my quest; a life grounded in Jesus Christ. God's Creation became a hospitable space to seek and trust God's love, and to let faith grow.

Whether fear plagues you in personal life changes or the fear mongers in this world are getting to you, I assure you this reflection devotional book will guide you away from fear and into the loving arms of Jesus Christ Our Savior. He will provide and protect you while walking beside you. And your life purpose in Him will be fueled with Love and strength that will not fail you ever.

In this book, you will find 40 reflection devotionals that describe Trail experiences applicable to life in general. Each devotional contains a relevant scripture passage, a narrative about my recollection of a Trail experience that relates to the scripture passage, and a closing prayer. After the prayer, you will find a question for you that provokes further thoughts and optional writings about the devotional topic.

The 20 hiking trips over two decades became a pilgrimage of wonderfully anticipated faith journeys. By reading the faith journey accounts, you will experience the ebb and flow of my meandering spiritual pilgrimage. This contextual background will provide a helpful back drop to those reflection devotionals. By sharing the devotional topics intertwining with my faith journeys, I believe that you will find your well-lit path as you walk with Jesus.

In these reflection devotionals and the faith journeys, I share the intimacy of my struggles to let go and to turn to our trustworthy and faithful God more frequently. I also share the immeasurable joy and peace that comes from Jesus Christ being my Guide and Companion in daily life. My hope and prayer is that you will find this reading experience an inspiration to seek a deepening relationship with Jesus Christ.

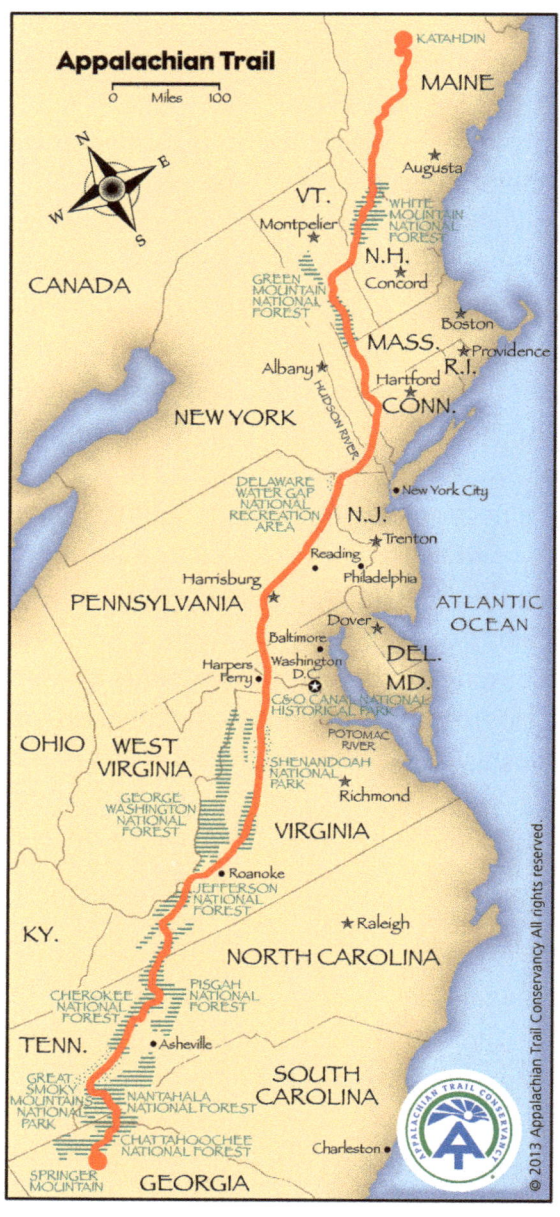

Appalachian Trail: 2,168 Miles from Springer Mountain, Georgia to Mt. Katahdin, Maine

Courtesy of the Appalachian Trail Conservancy

A Concise History of the Appalachian Trail

My interest in the Appalachian Trail (AT) began with a family vacation where I first realized that this gem of God's Nature existed. It was the summer of 1996 when our family embarked on a two-week summer vacation to the East Coast. Our Texas teenagers, Adrianne and RW, had never been to the East Coast and the timing seemed ideal to explore this part of the USA. We chose a trip itinerary plan that would educate our children about the nation's history. The plan was to visit the Gettysburg Civil War battlefield, Washington DC, and then Williamsburg, Virginia. Just before leaving on the trip, we added Disneyworld in Orlando, Florida to the itinerary. My husband, Tim was the primary driver, and I chose to be the navigator because of my love for maps and choosing road directions through unfamiliar territory. That is how I discovered the Appalachian Trail. I was studying the Rand McNally large scale Road Atlas for the next step of the trip and exploring the regional information imbedded in the giant-sized maps. There it was in the form of a faint red slash-mark line as we neared Gettysburg, Pennsylvania. And later, there it was again, that same faint red slash-mark line as we headed southward through Virginia, North Carolina, and Georgia on our way to Orlando, Florida. When I found the words "Appalachian

Trail" along the red line in one state after another state, my curiosity was really tweaked. When I shared my curiosity with Tim, he told me of his experiences on Boy Scout trips from Wisconsin to areas along the AT where the Boy Scout troop was camping and enjoying hiking excursions. After the family vacation, I started reading AT books that focused on its origin and history. I found the AT history to be fascinating. I soon became equally enamored with the people who chose to hike the AT for countless reasons. Within a year of immersion in AT reading, I realized that I had become an "armchair quarterback" with all kinds of opinions about the AT and how to hike it. Oh my gosh, I was looking forward to becoming an AT hiker enjoying the adventure for myself!

The Appalachian Trail historical material that I use in this narrative comes from the book, *The Appalachian Trail: A Visitor's Companion*, by Leonard M. Adkins. Over years of reading various books about the AT, this author is my favorite because his approach is a wide overview of the Trail using interesting topics. In addition to history, the author's coverage of the AT flora and fauna is a captivating narrative, giving the reader a visual experience of the AT's extensive variety in Nature.

In October 1921, the AT vision was born to the public eye when Benton MacKaye's article "An Appalachian Trail: A project in Regional Planning" appeared in the Journal of the American Institute of Architects. As this reflection devotional book manuscript is preparing for publication, it is 2021, the 100th Anniversary of this magnificently planned vision of the Appalachian Trail. In 2021, AT enthusiasts are also celebrating additional milestones. The two milestones are the extraordinary celebration of the oldest as well as the youngest age of hiker completing the AT. Both occurred in 2021. Nimblewill Nomad (Trail Name) at age 83 became the oldest AT Thu-hiker to complete the 2,193 miles of the AT in one year. M.J. "Sunny" Eberhart lives in Flagg Mountain,

Alabama and has been a long-distance hiker since he retired as an optometrist in 1993. His first major hike coincided with a search for peace after lugging emotional baggage that involved a divorce and losing the respect of his children. He eventually found peace, and forgiveness. *"You can seek peace. That doesn't mean that you're going to find it. I persevered to the point that the good Lord looked down on me and said you're forgiven, you can be at peace. It's a profound blessing,"* said Nimblewill Nomad. *"It's as simple as that,"* he said. [1] Nimblewill Nomad recently met "Little Man" (Trail Name) while traversing the AT. Little Man is a five-year-old boy, Harvey Sutton, from Lynchburg, Virginia. In a matter of months, Little Man completed the AT miles in August 2021 on a thru-hike with his parents. Four-year-old, Juniper Netteburg, also finished the AT in 2020 with her missionary parents.

When Benton MacKaye shared his regional planner vision in 1921, he was immersed in the post-World War I era in America that was becoming rapidly urbanized, machine-driven, and further removed from the world of God's Nature. [2] MacKaye obviously envisioned recreational opportunities but his vision also addressed the need for *"cooperation replacing antagonism, trust replacing suspicion, and emulation replacing competition."* MacKaye spread the word of his vision to anyone who would listen, including officials of the National Park and National Forest Services.

Especially receptive to the trail concept were members and officers of already existing trail organizations such as the Green Mountain Club of Vermont, the New England Trail Conference, and the Appalachian Mountain Club. In October 1923, just two years after publication of his article, the first few miles of trail to

---

[1] "'Nimblewill Nomad,' 83, is oldest to hike Appalachian Trail", November 7, 2021, Fox News and Associated Press.

[2] The Appalachian Trail: A Visitor's Companion, Leonard M. Adkins.

be built specifically as a part of the AT were opened to the public around Harriman and Bear Mountain State Parks in New York. New York-New Jersey Trail Conference, a hiking club that was recently formed, built these trail blazing miles of the AT.

In 1927, with the establishment of the Potomac Appalachian Trail Club, construction of the AT began to rapidly accelerate. Myron Avery, a founding member of this AT trail club, took it upon himself to recruit volunteers and to spread the word about the AT. Myron Avery also went out into the field scouting practical routes for the trail and building and blazing multiple miles of the pathway. He was so successful at inspiring volunteers that 1200 miles of the AT were completed in 1931 and increased to 1900 miles by the end of 1934.

The Shenandoah National Park (SNP) inclusion of the AT miles furthered federal support of this primarily non-governmental volunteer effort. During the 1930s Great Depression, the federal funded Civilian Conservation Corps (CCC) built major parts of the Trail pathway and many AT shelters. These first improvements happened in SNP, but expanded to all federal lands involved with the AT pathway. Skyline Drive in the SNP is a notable example of the federal involvement through the efforts of the CCC labor. Let us give great thanks for the CCC work and labor! There are many AT shelters and Trail miles that were built with their manual labor which are standing and remain sturdy to this day.

On August 14, 1937, the last section of the Trail was constructed on a ridgeline connecting Sugarloaf and Spaulding Mountains in central Maine. In less than sixteen years from the publication of Benton MacKaye's original article, the AT was a reality, a continuously marked 2,045-mile footpath from Maine to Georgia. This feat is even more remarkable since most of the work on the Trail was done by volunteers whose only motivation was a love of the outdoors and whose sole compensation was the satisfaction of having contributed to the successful completion of the AT.

The US Congress was slow in recognizing the importance of the AT in the eyes of the American people. Recognizing the fragility of the Trail route, Daniel Koch (a member of the ATC board of managers, president of the Blue Mountain Eagle Climbing Club of Pennsylvania, and an elected member of the US Congress) introduced legislation in the House of Representatives in 1945. This legislation was crafted to protect a system of federally protected footways, but the bill never made it out of committee.

Just when the solidarity of the AT's future seemed bleak, a hero in AT history emerged. His name was Earl Shaffer. In 1948, Shaffer became the first AT "Thru-hiker" by walking the entire 2,050-mile route from Georgia to Maine in a continuous four-month trek. Shaffer, an unassuming man from Pennsylvania, did not undertake the journey to set any records, but merely to enjoy time in the mountains and to put his memories of World War II in perspective. Armed with just road maps and no guidebooks, Shaffer found a Trail with few blazes and signs, its way blocked by hundreds of tree blowdowns, and its route forced onto roadways because of timbering operations or disputes with landowners. Earl Shaffer's accomplishment of thru-hiking the AT became a national news item and inspired many people who volunteered to help the Trail's development in a variety of ways.

In 1955, Emma "Grandma" Gatewood, who walked in sneakers and carried her gear in a duffel bag slung over her shoulders, became the first woman to solo thru-hike the Trail. She would make history again by becoming the first person to hike the entire length of the AT three times. Grandma Gatewood did not seek publicity, but the well-known TV program, the Gary Moore "Today Show," found her traversing the AT and insisted that she leave the Trail and make a live appearance on the program. Through Grandma Gatewood's popularity, national recognition of the AT as a gem in God's Nature was catching on and becoming a popular form of recreation. People took to the AT for backpacking, hiking, camping, or as a volunteer Trail maintainer helping the fledgling effort to thrive. You may choose to read the reflection devotional "Outcast" that centers on the life of Grandma Gatewood as you read this concise history of the AT.

As you might imagine, the 1950s became a decade of protecting the AT's pathway, then a fragile fledgling of volunteerism spirit. There were powerful forces encroaching on this grass-roots ground swell of American people striving to create cultural space and recreational time away from the mechanization of their lives. Throughout the whole of its Trail length, the AT was threatened by numerous developments such as mining and timbering operations, ski resorts, housing projects, communication and utility towers and lines, and new roadways.

In 1964, Senator Gaylor Nelson of Wisconsin introduced a bill to federally protect the AT and eventually the National Trails System Act was passed and signed into law by President Lyndon Johnson in 1968. The Appalachian Trail and the Pacific Crest Trail were designated the country's first two national scenic trails. This act gave the National Park Service (under the Interior Department) the primary responsibility for administering the AT and authorized the agency to protect the pathway through easements, cooperative agreements, land exchanges, donations or purchases, and acquisition of the land through eminent domain. Additionally, the act authorized agreements between the Interior Department and the Appalachian Trail Conservancy (ATC) and its affiliated hiking clubs to "operate, develop, and maintain" the AT.

The backpacking boom of the late 1960s and early 1970s had a major impact on the national interest and use of the AT. After years of public pressure to procure long term sustainability for the AT, Congress passed what became known as the Appalachian Trail Act, March 21, 1978. The act appropriated 90 million dollars in federal funds to purchase the acreage needed to move the final 900 miles of Trail pathway off roadways and private property. By 1982, the land acquisition program was no longer dependent on the federal government because the ATC had implemented its own monetary resources. The volunteer and philanthropy base of the ATC wisely foresaw that the AT's future depended on self-sufficiency, not the government. The ATC established its headquarters near the AT in Harper's Ferry, West Virginia where it remains to date. In 1982, the ATC also established the Trust for Appalachian Trail Lands, which are private funds used for purchase of land to protect the corridor of the AT experience. It is the provision of these private funds that protects the Trail experience including the viewsheds and the exposure to Nature's wilderness.

Because of the makeup of this organization, the Appalachian Trail Conversancy (ATC) relegates most of its responsibility for care of the footpath to the volunteers of the local trail and hiking clubs. Volunteers have always been the backbone of the AT, and, in many ways, may be more valuable to the trail than the ATC itself. It is the volunteers who undertake the bulk of trail maintenance, devoting weekends and other spare time to relocating and rebuilding the pathway and keeping it clear of undergrowth and blowdowns. Volunteer efforts also provided advocacy for the AT through local and regional decision making. Through their efforts, monitoring of the Trail lands for any problems such as encroachment, development, or illegal usage by motorized vehicles keeps the AT in its pristine condition for all of us.

Today, there continues to be an increasing number of people seeking a lengthy trail experience in the wilderness yet hoping to find a getaway opportunity easily accessible from their urban lifestyle. If you do internet research on my hypothesis about this cultural trend, you will find that citizens continue to coalesce locally and create additional long-distance trails in the USA. The Great

Eastern Trail (GET) is a planned network of trails from Alabama to New York passing through nine states. This new trail will rival the AT and hikers hope that it will take some of the heavy usage burden off the AT.

From the beginning of my curiosity about the origin of a 2,000-mile hiking trail on the East Coast, I have been inspired by the resilient spirit of ordinary Americans uniting to create and maintain a massive outdoor recreation space for generations of Americans and all people. From the beginning of quenching my thirst of curiosity by reading AT books, my spirit was uplifted through the awareness of kindred spirits who made the AT a reality. You and I share that same resilient spirit that envisioned and created the AT. This resilient spirit causes us to instinctually seek God's presence in our lives through Nature. We inherently know that God will remind us through His Nature that we were made in His image, and we are His children. Through regularly immersing ourselves in God's Nature, we will be refueled and inspired to seek more of Him. My curiosity, fueled by this desire to seek God, led me out of challenging times in my life, and charged me with changing my life through embracing a spiritual quest.

The number of people hiking the entire Trail has risen dramatically over the years.[3] From 1936 to 1969, only 59 completions are recorded. In 1970, the numbers began to rise. Ten people completed the Trail in 1970, including Ed Garvey, whose thru-hike was well-publicized. The trend was further fueled by the release of Garvey's popular book, Appalachian Hiker: Adventure of a Lifetime. *The term "2,000-miler" was coined in the late 1970s to help identify this growing group of hikers.*

---

[3] December 31, 2021, Excerpt from the Appalachian Trail Conservancy website, www.AppalachianTrail.org

2,000-Milers by Decade

1930's	1940's	1950's	1960's	1970's	1980's	1990's	2000's	2010's
5	3	14	38	793	1,438	3,346	5,970	9,946

Hikers of a wide range of ages have completed the A.T. While about half of all thru-hikers are in their 20s, many people in their 30s, 40s, and 50s have thru-hiked the A.T. About 750 people in their 60s have completed thru-hikes, but only about 50 people aged 70 and above have completed thru-hikes. Two people in their 80s have completed a thru-hike; the oldest was 82. Teens comprise about four percent of thru-hikers; a very small number of children have completed the A.T. with their parents. Section-hikers tend to be older, with a median age of 40. Their ages at the time of their hike completions have ranged from 15 to 86.

A full listing of the numerous hiking clubs and trail clubs called the Appalachian Trail Maintaining Clubs is printed in the Appendix.

AT Hiking Trips Lead To A Spiritual Pilgrimage

We go hiking in search of refreshment from Nature and a temporary hiatus from life's burdens. We often seek more from Nature than overcoming our current stressors of the moment. The beauty of natural surroundings shifts our awareness to the grandeur picture of life. We are often seeking a closer walk with our loving God, and we hope to find this balm through being in Nature, God's world. If your life is in a state of transition and you are exploring your life direction while walking with the Lord, these devotionals can be a powerful aide to your exploratory journey.

My Trail name is "Spirit," and I finished hiking 2,000 miles of the Appalachian Trail (AT) in 2015. I chose to hike the AT during September whenever possible and averaged 15 days on the Trail during each of the hiking trips. My first hiking trip was in 1997 when I was 47 years old.

The northern end of the Trail, or terminus, is in central Maine and the southern terminus is located just north of Atlanta, Georgia. The AT is a diverse trail that meanders through fourteen states with a variety of forests, magnificent vistas above tree line, pastures in the farmlands, small towns in the mountains and even urban sidewalks. There are Trail miles in the mountains with underground springs spilling forth to create bubbling brooks. Here the hiker's thirst is quenched, and rest comes easily while listening to the soothing sounds of Nature.

Over the years of hiking and backpacking, the scenery along the majestic landscape of the AT opened my eyes to the diversity of Nature's beauty. In a comparable way, I came to a sense of celebration about the holy uniqueness of every individual's faith journey, including my own.

I stumbled onto long distance hiking as a setting to get away from the pressures of my hectic lifestyle. Initially, I chose this form of recreation for the sole purpose of finishing necessary conversations with myself. My complicated lifestyle did not allow "me time" to acquire an inner peace. It takes time! As I hiked and pondered unfinished conversations with myself, there were three life problems that emerged that clearly needed resolution. One of the three problems was despair about the pending changes of my family-focused lifestyle. Our children were launching from home into their independent lives, leaving me with feelings of a lost life purpose. How could I ever find a new purpose and lifestyle with equal passion and meaning? The second problem was my lack of physical fitness. I felt disgusted with my body. Building body endurance required energy and motivation that I did not have. The third problem that quietly haunted me was a stale spiritual life. This spiritual problem turned out to be the most important one of the three unresolved problems - my "baby trust and faith" in God.

During the first years of the annual AT hiking trips, I longed for a new way of living which would put the "empty nest" family life stage and its drudgery into my rear-view mirror. I wanted to blindly focus on the road in front of me, seeking to urgently create a positive future. With anxious anticipation, I embraced a year-round physical fitness routine ensuring that I would be ready for the hiking trips. My childhood years were laden with a chronic illness that kept me from participating in sports or attempting any fitness and stamina. At age 19, I underwent major surgery that brought health for the first time in my life. Now I was healthy, yet I entered adulthood with little experience and confidence in my physical being. So, I jumped on this opportunity years later, to take on physical fitness for my new interest in hiking and backpacking. However, this obsession to become a physically fit backpacker did not fill the "empty-nest" hole in my life. I still felt really lost. As my zeal about the physical fitness and sport of hiking dwindled, the increasing time in Nature due to frequent hiking experiences was slowly kindling a fire in my soul, and spiritual needs were increasingly being fed. As a professional therapist, I came to instinctively know that counseling was not what I needed during this time of transition. I needed a deeper belief in Jesus Christ. Looking back on the early years of preparatory physical conditioning hikes and then the annual lengthy hiking trips, the increasing exposure of time in Nature induced a spiritual transformation despite my rocky life transition.

    Spiritual journaling while on the Trail and in everyday living helped deepen my faith. Writing to God in this way about my life became the cornerstone for overcoming my confusion and a better understanding of where I was headed as I passed through life transitions. Journaling was a way to shed light on the life trail ahead. It helped me to understand times that I was stuck dead in my tracks, and to accept a pace of one step at a time. Only after I finished walking the AT did I realize how the spiritual journaling helped to create a narrative about my faith journey. As you will learn, the journaling informed many of the reflection devotionals. During my years of AT hiking trips, my faith journey passed through life problems and multiple life transitions. In this book of reflection devotionals, I share experiences related to the three life problems that were previously listed; the empty nest, my physical conditioning, and a stale spiritual life. I share with you how my growing faith helped me to address them. You will find additional common life issues addressed in the devotionals such as grief, loneliness, building courage, letting go, feeling shame and being easily misled by others.

As the years went by and these vacation hikes transformed to walks with Jesus, my trust and faith matured. In this new season of my life, the vacation hiking trips transformed into intentional faith journeys and other reflection devotionals were written. Yes, there are more stumbling blocks in the latter years of a faith journey. A growing Christian faith eventually addresses issues like pride, greed, idolatry, and jealousy, to name a few. Life has many obstacles to address as a believer leans into a closer relationship with Jesus, Our Savior. The good news is that never again will you walk alone through life's troubles. Writing the reflection devotionals amplified God's presence in my life, and my faith in Him. Hopefully, the reflection devotionals will relate to some of the life issues that you need to explore during your walk with the Lord. It is my prayer that your relationship with God will deepen from reading this book, and your faith in Jesus as your Guide will grow.

When I began long-distance hiking, I was happily married, with teenagers at home. I was excelling in my well-established business as a licensed counselor and life coach in Austin, Texas. A casual observer of my life would have assumed that I was a contented woman full of self-satisfaction. But my life was far from ideal and complete. At that time, all my energy was focused on helping everyone else find personal growth and self-esteem. But the meaning of life is not all about helping others. Practicing this life focus of helping others over two decades, I was weary of the tremendous weight on my shoulders from the role of being a helper, both in my personal life and professional life as well. The meaning of life seemed so futile as I recognized the truth that the human condition inevitably includes imperfections and limitations. Clients came to counseling with idolized expectations, innocently imagining me as a perfect person. They often expected perfection in their lives as the outcome of my professional services. It took me far too long to acquire the spiritual wisdom to understand this Truth. Finally, I accepted that practicing Humanism, the foundation of the counseling profession, did not bring true mental health.

As I realized my own human imperfections and limitations, despair took over my personal life as well as my professional role. All areas of my life were unfulfilling. It was time to reckon with this. After a time of self-examination and searching for an answer, I took the unresolved burdens to the hiking trail. I hoped to escape my troubling responsibilities, but the troubles remained, residing in the fiber of my being, my soul. Through desperate prayers, I began to realize that I could not be the savior of this world, and not even the savior of myself. Uninterrupted time with God during the initial annual hikes was the balm that I needed. Over time and with baby steps, I resolved to live in this Truth every day, that the one and only Savior is Our Lord Jesus Christ.

God has a way of loving us through His creation of Nature. When we take in the beauty of Nature, we experience God's majesty. When we gaze at a sunset from the grandeur of a remote mountaintop vista, God's sovereignty over all of creation is unquestionable and unfathomable. God's love is raining down on us constantly, whether we are standing on a city street or in a mountain forest. We call this Grace. Whether we notice Grace happening or miss it in the moment, our faith grows as we learn to seek God's love. Grace! In a daily lifestyle that is filled with the surroundings of God's Nature, there are fewer distractions away from God's Grace and therefore more opportunities to be caught up in it.

The 40 reflection devotionals seek to take you on a deep journey into Nature with me as your personal guide. Pointing out some of the God moments that happened on the Trail and how these experiences enriched my faith. The journey goes beyond Nature experiences that provide a break from regular living and on to Nature experiences that become a doorway through which you grow more aware of the presence of the Creator of Nature. I will guide you into Nature experiences that are transformed and witnessed as a grace-filled holy doorway that leads to individual experiences of a loving relationship with God. Here is my experience of these faith journeys.

As the hiking trips continued, I began seeking the hospitable space of Nature where I would hold dialogues with God. Over hours upon hours of walking the Trail immersed in private conversations with God, I began to trust God with my precious burdens. Though I proudly held onto these burdens as if they defined me, I also wanted to be free of them. I deeply sought our Gracious God to take my burdens as He promised to do through my belief in Jesus Christ, My Savior.

By reflecting on the AT journeys over time, I came to see that I wanted to move from Grace Moments to Belief Moments, and then on to growing Faith Moments.

After such a walk-with-the-Lord Trail experience, I would return to everyday life increasingly centered on Christ, and enthusiastically ready to take His companionship with me into everyday living.

A spiritual pilgrimage is a life-time journey without an earthly destination. Once I came to that understanding about the purpose of my life, I no longer become overwhelmed with times of life transition and the life changes that are outside my control. God provides me with the peace that surpasses all understanding as I walk beside Him. This is my spiritual pilgrimage.

Faith Journeys Became a Spiritual Pilgrimage

DO NOT FOLLOW WHERE THE PATH MAY LEAD GO INSTEAD WHERE THERE IS NO PATH & LEAVE A TRAIL

-RALPH WALDO EMERSON

Chronology of 20 Faith Journeys

Introduction

A backpacking trip on the Appalachian Trail (AT) that started as an adventurous getaway with other middle-aged women does not instantly transform into a personal faith journey. My faith journey became a lengthy process of personal insights intertwined with transformative God moments. I believe that faith journeys, by their very nature, are a crooked path. Faith journeys include times when we are not able to walk with the Lord, despite His loving presence. I hope to reassure your journey of faith by pointing out the crooked trail of my own journey. Faith journeys are like the Appalachian Trail's rugged terrain of two steps up, three steps down, then multiple switchbacks, then the Trail loops on itself, and so on and on. This reality was discouraging until I gained understanding about a typical faith journey. Accepting this reality about the AT terrain required management of my expectations as well.

Gradually, as I prepared for the hiking trips, I anticipated these spiritually vulnerable experiences with joy. The joy came from anticipating God's deep presence on each Trail excursion. The setting of a long walk-through God's Nature for progression in my faith journey was an essential factor. God's Nature was a punctuation mark, or a Trail Marker, so evident to me when I reflected on the settings of millions of steps in growing closer to God.

These chapters guide you through some incremental steps of my faith journey using my annual AT hiking trips to distinguish the increments. In each description of a specific Trail section hiked, you will find:

- A reflection on my personal life situation at the time.
- A description of the AT terrain including the flora and fauna in that season while also sharing interesting events and Trail stories.
- You will learn my post-trip reflections concerning my faith journey and life.
- Specific Reflection Devotionals are mentioned when the Devotional relates to the Trail section narrative.

I chose to hike the AT in multiple annual trips, also described as section hikes. Since I live in Texas, a long distance from the east coast setting of the AT, all road trips required a minimum of four days driving time for a round trip. My work schedule would not accommodate months away for a "thru-hike" trip of the 2,000 plus mile Trail. With marriage and family life a high priority for me, the annual two-to-three-week hiking trips were the best solution. As you read the chronology of the 20 hiking trips, you will see that I did not choose to hike the AT in sequential miles. For example, I did not choose to hike from Springer Mountain, Georgia northbound to Mt. Katahdin, Maine. Instead, I chose a specific Trail section of the AT each year to fit into my personal needs and opportunities.

Hiking Partners

1997 - Teresa Johnson Connell, Brenda Barker

2000 – Robert Wilson Abel (RW)

2001 – May: Margret Mills, and two female seasoned hikers
Sept: Two female seasoned hikers

2002 - May: Tim Abel
Sept: Paula Wiesner, Marcia Roland (Smasher)

2003 - May: RW Abel
Sept: Marcia Roland, Stan Miller (Millerman)

2004 - Marcia Roland, Stan Miller

2005 - Marcia Roland

2006 - Marcia Roland, Cheri Cantu

2007 - June: 8 Teen-age Girl Scouts from Central Texas
Sept: Bann Evensen plus a solo hike

2008 - Marcia Roland, Jana Jones

2010 - Debra Barnett

2011 - Marcia Roland, Lois Arnold, Haskell Davis (HAD)

2012 - Marcia Roland, Haskell Davis (HAD)

2013 - Marcia Roland, Stan Miller

2014 - Marcia Roland, Tim Abel

2015 - Marcia Roland, Tim Abel, RW Abel, Jana Jones, Haskell Davis, and our hosts, Lois and Earl Arnold

FIRST STEPS: 1997 TO 2002

June 1997 Wild Ponies in Grayson Highlands
© SarahJDecker

1997 June – Damascus, Virginia northbound to Grayson Highlands

After a year of preparing my family to exist without me and preparing myself with physical conditioning and obsessive levels of food and gear planning, I temporarily escaped all responsibility for my loved ones and headed out for adventure.

Damascus, Virginia was the chosen spot to launch this first hike because of its reputation as a hospitable Trail town. A good place to go for help. Like-minded Austin female friends were my companions, all of us seeking Trail adventure away from the daily surroundings of Texas. We eagerly sought the change of terrain and the beauty of the Appalachian Mountains. The wide variety of deciduous trees in the forests quenched the thirst of my everyday existence on the grassland plains of home. In June, the massive groves of Rhododendron and the blaze azaleas were in bloom with breathtaking splendor on the mountainsides. It was here that I first experienced how underground mountain springs spill forth to frequently puddle the Trail. Using a stile over a fence was another first-time experience. AT stiles are small ladders built to climb over a fence line. Throughout Virginia, as hikers follow the Trail they approach a fence stile, climb over the fence using the stile and are on their way again. Each fence stile is a unique design. In the Grayson Highlands State Park, wild ponies graze on the mountain ridges, creating open pastoral ranges. The ponies are known to be friendly to hikers along the AT. One foggy afternoon we walked through rainy mist on the Highlands, petting and feeding the ponies along the Trail.

It rained throughout this initial trip and the summer heat and humidity were awful. One hiking partner became ill with a virus three days into the backpacking trip. She was so sick that the other hiking companion accompanied her off the Trail to obtain medical assistance in a nearby town. Abruptly I was alone on the Trail overnight, guarding the campsite and all our gear.

My Trail journal records the experience as *"I discovered for the first time that I could get past the scary feeling of being lonely and into the experience of solitude in the forest. This was a comforting realization. My spiritual strength got me through it."*

On the long drive home, I reflected on this first experience of long-distance backpacking. The desire to return to the AT for more hiking trips was in my heart, stamped with indelible ink. I felt better about myself because I had accomplished an adventure outside of my comfort zone.

Reflection Devotionals: Grace, Strength, Truth, Closeness to Christ, Spirit

July 2000 Hot Springs, NC from AT
©SarahJDecker

2000 July – Damascus, Va. Southbound on NC/TN border to Erwin, Tn.

The second AT trip comprised 52 scattered miles of backpacking where the Trail path meanders along the North Carolina and Tennessee border. The trip started in Damascus again, this time headed southbound with RW, my 17-year-old son. It took three years to return to the AT because of multiple family events that needed the attention of every family member. Our oldest child, Adrianne, graduated from high school one month prior to this trip, and RW was on course to complete high school just one year later, in 2001. There were several empty nest issues haunting my daily thoughts, and I took those ponderings with me on the Trail.

Once again, the humid heat depleted my energy as I tried to adapt, having come from the dry climate of Texas. Even more difficult was RW's hiking pace which was incompatible with mine. Being a young and experienced backpacker, he was leaving me in the Trail dust as I continually tried to catch up.

The forests were thick with ground vegetation and mountain laurels bloomed everywhere. We enjoyed an abundance of wild blackberries on sunny mountain ridges along the Trail. One late afternoon we looked down from a ridgetop into a gap at an AT shelter that was our intended destination for the night. Overmountain Shelter is an exquisite large barn shaped structure that sleeps 20 people. It was donated to the AT after its construction by a movie crew for the movie "Winter People". RW went ahead of me at his normal rapid hiking pace to the shelter. When I caught up, he insisted that we hike on and find a primitive campsite for the night. I was sorely disappointed about the change of plans, but he convinced me that a mentally ill man was hanging out at the shelter and would not be good company for the night.

The most challenging part of the Trail section was the 1,000 feet climb to Roan High Knob Shelter. My body reacted to the over exertion with hypothermia. We stayed overnight at the Roan High Knob Shelter where RW used his Boy Scout skills to give me first aid treatment. My predicament of being the patient was quite humbling. However, this hiking trip bonded our relationship beyond the roles of mother and son as we shared the epic adventure.

One night a surprise thunderstorm left us with waterlogged tents and gear. The following morning, we decided to break camp, leave the Trail, and hitch hike to a nearby town, Hampton, TN. While staying in Braemar Castle hiking hostel, we dried out gear and refreshed our bodies. Further southbound on the Trail, we enjoyed a lengthy stay at the infamous Uncle Johnny's Nolichucky Hiking Hostel.

What little stamina I had at the beginning of this trip was depleted. Resting at the Hostel for several days allowed time for renewal. My physical weakness was destroying all motivation to become a backpacker. I was ready to quit the AT quest, but the hiker fellowship helped me through my self-doubt. "Braveheart," an advanced long-distance backpacker with bowed legs as a result of childhood polio, was so helpful to me at this pivotal time. He shared his history of overcoming his disability and the happiness of life on the trail. My self-perception changed. [4]

At the end of this two-week trip, we spent an overnight at the equally infamous Elmer's Place in Hot Springs, NC. The down-home Hot Springs Spa brought luxurious relaxation for our tired backpacking bodies.

There was an overabundance of lessons from this hiking trip. I had personal insights that were bubbling slowly to my consciousness. There were family life stage lessons surfacing as our children transitioned into adulthood. At the time, I could not see these important lessons, both life lessons and faith journey steps. At least I was aware of the significance of the life moment, unprocessed as it was. I was skating through life, making decisions without prayer time or forethought. A lesson learned for future hiking trip plans was finding a female hiking partner. I needed a female hiking partner who was interested in annual hiking trips in September to get out of the summer heat and humidity. And the chosen female hiking partner needed to be someone who hiked at a pace like mine. I also realized my weak endurance for long-distance backpacking. Even so, the AT hiking bug had bitten me, and I was determined to keep on going.

Reflection Devotionals: *Grace, God's Gifts, Suffering, Transitions*

---

[4] Read more on this story in the Devotional *God's Gifts*.

AT Marker on Big Bald Mountain
© SarahJDecker

2001 May - Wallace Gap, NC northbound to Fontana Dam, NC

After the July 2000 hiking trip, I constantly thought about my current state of multiple life transitions. With both children launched into their adult life choices, home life felt empty and boring, like a dry bone. My loving husband tried to comfort me about the rapid changes in our lifestyle. However, only I could address the inner unrest dwelling within me. My solution was letting the counseling practice absorb all my energy. Eventually I would recognize that the counseling of other people with their own needs was depleting my life. As important as it was to the lives that my business touched, the absence of work/life balance was not sustainable. As I counseled clients to create this well-being in their lives, it was obvious to me that I was not practicing what I said as a life coach. As I wrestled with myself, the uncertainty increased.

Seeking enjoyable annual Trail time was my immediate solution to the uncertainty and stale lifestyle. I found two female hiking partners by placing an *AT Journeys* magazine ad. One woman was from Florida and the other from New Jersey; both women had completed hundreds of Trail miles. We agreed on a trial hiking trip to see if we were compatible for future AT trips together.

Wallace Gap to Fontana Dam is a sterling example of the beautiful southern AT. In this region, trail switchbacks occur frequently, creating a friendly up and down the mountains. Let us thank the volunteer Trail maintainers for their labor on our behalf. Coming from Texas big sky country, I am accustomed to open plains and big sky views. Walking this Trail section under the giant tree forests that obscured a sky view was a spectacular contrast for me. I thought of this forested mountain trail setting like the experience of being in a holy cathedral. The cathedral's stain glass windows were the foliage variations in the tree canopy, as the sunlight danced in patchworks on the forest floor and on the Trail. In the southern AT, spring flowers are abundant in May, such as pink and yellow lady slippers, Dutch iris, mayapple, trillium, and dogwood tree blossoms. There is a monumental climb from the Nantahala River at 1,500 feet elevation to the Cheoah Bald at 5,062 feet elevation. The eight-mile climb was a big challenge. There are few road crossings in this remote area. The nights were much colder than I had anticipated for the month of May, so I learned to layer my sleepwear.

When the hiking trip was over, my reflections were of little use to me. My reflection thoughts and prayers focused on my human compulsion to succeed as a backpacker. I did not realize that I was not making a good decision concerning my new hiking partners. We were not compatible due to my inexperience and their advanced skills. I was too quick to follow their lead. I desperately sought an escape from boredom, causing me to wrongfully trust these women. I ignored all internal signals to distrust them. I also ignored the perspective of Margret Mills, my Austin friend, who accompanied me on the backpacking trip to hike with these seasoned strangers. God was with me even though I was not listening. I sure did want an escape adventure!

Reflective Devotionals: Outcast, Transitions, Beauty, Pacing, Lost, Asking

Ascending Mt. Lafayette on AT
Courtesy of Appalachian Trail Conservancy

2001 September - Pinkham Notch, NH southbound to Mt. Lafayette, NH

Trail enthusiasts consider this section of the AT in New Hampshire, the Presidential Mountain Range, to be the most difficult Trail section. It was the wrong thing for me to attempt. I allowed the advanced hiking partners to persuade me, a novice backpacker, to take on this challenging Trail section for a six-week backpacking trip. I insisted on a September hike and fortunately the hiking partners accepted it. This hiking trip in September was much more enjoyable due to the cooler temperatures and I resolved to plan all future hiking trips in September.

The terrain of this Trail section is granite rock bouldering, not the dirt trail of the southern AT. Fast changing weather elements leave trekkers exposed to safety issues because the Trail is frequently above the tree line. In contrast to the southern Trail with green tunnels of dense vegetation in the mountains, the mountains of New Hampshire are magnificent open sky views with alpine vegetation. God's Nature has countless forms of beauty. The autumn colors frequently uplifted my troubled spirits as I carried a backpack over the challenging terrain. My first experience of seeing a moose in the wild occurred one evening as the large creature rumbled through the woods and emerged into the campsite. Moose are really large creatures, but are GIANTS, when sitting around a campfire. After the moose stared at our shocked presence, he slowly sauntered away and disappeared.

The hiker fellowship in the AT Huts was a fun memory about this trip. Along the Presidential Mountain range, the Appalachian Mountain Club maintains six huts for trekkers. The terrain for the huts is above tree line and frequent sudden storms make it a dangerous area to be exposed to the weather. The huts are full service lodges where hikers can enjoy shelter from storms and prepared meals.

Though I diligently prepared with physical conditioning for this difficult terrain, I did not have the necessary physical endurance for the Presidential Mountain Range. The Trail quickly informed me of this reality. After completing ten days of a six-week planned trip, with God's help I broke away from the hiking partners who refused to hike at my slower pace. I left the Trail and returned to Texas.

By avoiding an awareness of my physical limitations and my distrust of the hiking partners, I had left home on a romanticized escape adventure. The awareness of pending greater physical injuries if I didn't stop was difficult to accept. But the faith lessons learned made this shortened hiking trip a pivotal empowering life-changing event. From my broken self-image emerged a humble pilgrim gratefully walking with Jesus, my merciful gracious Savior. My immediate reflections about this trip were glaring reality checks, unlike the previous trip in May. Informed by the recent Trail experiences of knowing Jesus as my Savior, I began looking at reality without my previous fears.

As you later read the reflection devotionals, you will find that the September 2001 hiking trip is referenced more frequently than any other trip. Several devotionals carry a story from that trip that hold a "growth nugget" for me. Yes indeed, the September 2001 hiking trip was a pivotal experience that ultimately turned me toward a new chosen life path. Walking with the Lord God Almighty. Don't be surprised by these repetitions. Instead, note that this pattern in my faith journey is an attribute of how God is with me. I believe this pattern may be true for you as well. The devotionals where this May and September 2001 stories occur are: *Storms, Grieving, Trusting, Lost, Faithfulness, Forgiveness*

Reflection devotionals: Beauty, Pacing, Outcast, Grieving, Trusting, Lost, Forgiveness, Faithfulness

25th Wedding Anniversary Trip SNP

2002 May – Shenandoah National Park, Virginia: Compton Gap southbound to Fishers Gap

To say that I returned home from the September 2001 trip in a bruised and broken-down state is an understatement. Not only was my body bruised from trying to keep up with my hiking partners, but I realized that I did not have the stamina and strength to do what I was trying to do. I had a bruised ego. God's presence was with me on Mt. Lafayette, at Greenleaf Hut dining table where I found the help to get me down the mountain, and later at my home for recuperation. God renewed a right spirit within me, and I healed! Thankfully, I journaled while on this hiking trip and when I returned home. Through the journal writing, fervent prayerful times, and deep conversations with my loving husband, Tim, the unrest, and confusion within me began to fade away. As I reflected on all that I had learned, I could see that my defeated mood did not mean that I was a fragile person. Finally, at the age of 52, I was leaning on God's guidance more than my own understanding about the path forward in my life.

Because faith was healing the "empty nest blues," my marital relationship improved. 2002 was our 25th wedding anniversary year so Tim and I began searching for a special vacation trip. After looking at our options, we chose to vacation in Virginia and North Carolina, enjoy the countryside and touring Civil War battlefields. Tim proposed that we include a three-to-four day AT backpacking trip, because he wanted to experience what I talked about with so much passion. I could not believe that he wanted to share the AT experience with me, but he finally convinced me that it was true. What a guy! The backpacking portion of our vacation centered on use of a Bed and Breakfast in Front Royal, Virginia as a luxurious base camp. Skyline Drive passes through the center of Shenandoah National Park on a north/south direction that parallels and frequently crosses the AT. We arranged a plan with the BNB lodging host to drive us to a Skyline Drive crossing of the AT. Backpacking the AT in the Shenandoah National Park is great for beginners because of the easier rolling hills rather than the mountains. After enjoying nights on the Trail, our host picked us up at another crossing with the AT and we returned to the BNB.

Shenandoah National Park in the month of May is bursting with new beginnings in life that the Spring season brings. It was a romantic setting for celebrating our wedding anniversary! The deciduous forests were mostly leaf bare, and we lingered on the mountain top vistas. Wildlife was abundant with their newborns tagging along. Spring wildflowers were bursting out from the grayness of winter, bringing a message of hope. Though we encountered day hikers, very few people were like us, backpackers on the trail. We did get acquainted with a retired female Navy officer who appeared to be in her forties. She was on a solo backpacking excursion that began in the Florida Glades and then moved northward to Springer Mountain in Georgia, the southern end of the AT. She had already hiked 1,000 miles and intended to finish the entire AT that year. We admired her stamina and great attitude when we stopped to chat on the Trail. Tim and I seized an opportunity to share a meal with this inspiring backpacker at one of the National Park lodge restaurants. This AT portion of our vacation proved to me that Tim and I really enjoyed being together, and we did not need our children involved to make this true. Returning home from this vacation trip, a renewed spirit within me was seeking future AT trips. Feeling so motivated, I began correspondence with future hiking partner prospects, now clear minded about what I needed in a hiking partner.

Two essential lessons were immediately learned from reflections about this trip. My marriage is the primary cornerstone in the lifestyle that I want. God gave me a specific marriage partner, Tim, as a sacred covenant with Him. And the second lesson was about choosing a hiking partner for future Septembers on the AT. God helped me raise the bar of my standards and expectations and reminded me to seek the faith centered companionship that I was willing to cultivate in a hiking friendship. I committed to finding a female hiking partner that would be a faith friend as well.

Reflection devotionals: Holy Matrimony, Trusting, Chosen, Transitions, Living Water

Hiking with Smasher: 2002 to 2008

Sprit and Smasher become AT Buddies

2002 September – Grayson Highlands State Park, Virginia northbound to Pearisburg, Virginia

I have never forgotten how Jesus mercifully guided me off the Trail in 2001 when I was nothing more than a bruised basket case. God provided all that I needed to move forward with future steps of my faith journey supported by time on the AT. Through prayerful requests, a stranger appeared in my life and became the lasting faith friend and Trail partner for the coming years of an AT spiritual pilgrimage. Her name is Marcia Roland, trail name Smasher, from Franklin, North Carolina, a mountain town close to the AT. Through an *AT Journey Magazine* ad connection, we bonded on our shared priorities of taking time away to backpack, and camp along the AT each September. We shared the priority of growing our faith life as we shared the Trail experience of God's Nature. This unique beginning of our friendship through a magazine ad did not seem strange to us because of the faith sharing in our first phone conversations. It seemed very natural. We met in Damascus, Virginia for this September 2002 hike after months of getting acquainted through email correspondence and land line phone conversations.

You should note that communication technology did not arrive to the AT's remote areas until 2006. In 2002, there were few cell phone towers, limited internet availability, and no ATM's in the rural communities along the trail. In the small mountain towns, to be sure I could receive service, I used cashier's checks and an ATM machine when it was available. To have phone conversations while out in these remote settings, we used pre-paid long distance calling cards in public pay phones.

Smasher arrived in Damascus, Virginia from North Carolina and I drove in from Texas, and we met for the first time. Over the previous months, we had planned with detail the Trail miles and campsites for a two-week backpacking trip from the southern border of Virginia northbound into the state that claims the most mileage of all 14 states. My impression of Smasher that immediately deepened our bond was her patriotism. Like me, she was passionate about remembering the national tragedy of September 11, 2001, when our country underwent a terrorist attack and thousands died. Smasher arrived with US flags on her backpack and even had an extra one for me. Throughout the following fifteen Septembers on the AT, we continued to memorialize the importance of 9/11.

As we left Grayson Highlands State Park, we noticed that our plan for water sources on the AT was not dependable, counter to information from our resource book. The further north we went, the drought conditions were more evident. We looked for mountain underground springs noted in the *AT Data Book* and often found streams completely dry. We accepted that carrying more water in our backpacks was a necessity. Whenever we found water on the AT, we topped off our water supply, keeping our pack weight heavy. Extra pack weight does not make for a happy backpacker. Then a 'lightbulb' moment came to us. Why not hide jugs of water in the forest near the AT road crossings, and then backpack from one parked car to another parked car? This was a winning solution. We met a retired Marine who left the AT pathway to hike the creek beds hoping to find water. Even though he was off the Trail, this thru-hiker needed to do what was best for him. As they say, "You hike your own hike."

A favorite AT shelter, known as Partnership Shelter, is in this section of the trail near Marion, Va. Lovingly constructed by the family of a former AT thru-hiker in his memory, it is known as "The Palace." The three-sided Shelter is a beautiful two-story log structure that can house about 15 hikers. Most shelters can house about 6 hikers. This shelter has a solar powered shower, privy, picnic tables, firepit and a fantastic water source. A Ranger Station near the shelter with a pay phone (remember those?) which allowed hikers to call home or place an order at a nearby restaurant for delivery. No cooking tonight! Ahh, the luxuries. As we settled into this beautiful spot, suddenly there was rustling in the woods. Alarmed by the sounds, we saw two hunters emerge from the woods brandishing rifles and laughing. There was no time to confer what we should do as they walked up the trail toward the shelter and us. Our fears were soon diminished after talking with these men who were courteous outdoorsmen. They were out hunting and heading home. On that luxurious night at Partnership Shelter, we enjoyed a great meal delivered from a pizza place in Marion. We were revived.

We passed through mountain terrain covered with the expansive southern hardwood forests that include fifty distinct species of trees in the typical elevations of 2,000 to 3,500 feet. You will find white ash, buckeye, sourwood, holly, Fraser magnolia, sugar maple, basswood, black walnut and more. As we approached an old apple orchard, we saw our first deer. That night Smasher and I slept under the star filled sky in our sleeping bags.

Our relationship, grounded on our shared faith throughout the months of planning and the shared daily trail experience, brought a hopeful peace to me. Through the initial bonding of friendship in faith, and then the daily devotional practice on the Trail, Smasher and I found the pace of our journey to be supportive to both of us and to our budding friendship.

Pearisburg, Virginia nestles against the magnificent New River. On the outskirts of Pearisburg, we found superb hospitality at the Holy Family Church Hostel where we spent our last night.

On my two day drive back to Texas, I reflected on feelings of great enthusiasm to make these AT section hikes occur every September. The 110-mile hike informed me that my body could build up endurance and I also realized my strong will and determination to continue. Most important, my time away with the Lord was renewing my right spirit about life.

Reflective Devotionals: Soul Food, Chosen, Trusting, Shelter, Asking, Fellowship, Storms

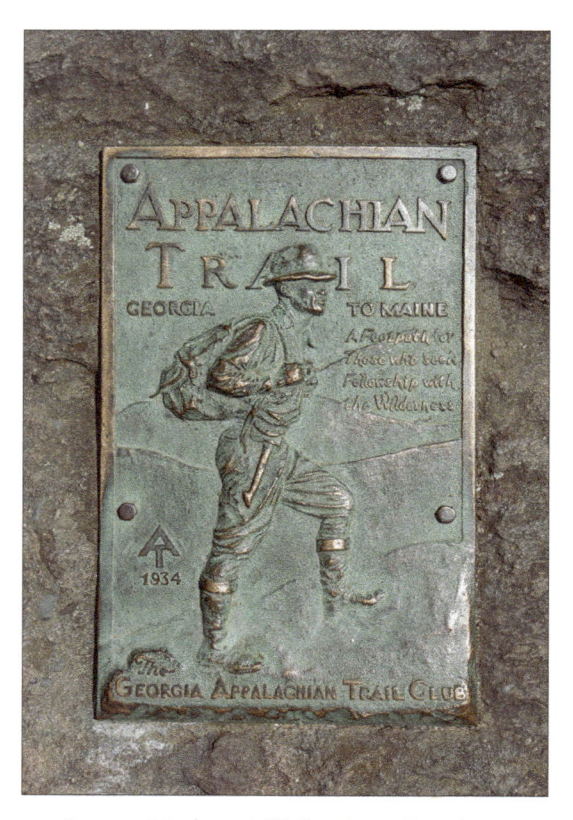

Bronze Marker at AT Southern Terminus

2003 May – Springer Mountain, Georgia northbound to Neels Gap, Georgia

Having accumulated a total of 315 AT miles, I began to feel a groove of experience and capability in backpacking skills. Not long after the September 2002 hike, I released that the condition of my varicose veins needed to be surgically addressed. I was not disappointed with the post-surgery results. The increased blood circulation invigorated my leg muscles giving stamina and endurance that I had never known.

From the start of 2003, I was daily preoccupied with life changes around me and inside me as well. My empty nest issues were slowly resolving, but not without a lot of bumps in the road. Most importantly, trusting God required consistent effort on my part. As I prioritized time with Jesus to reach out and to then listen, trust was building because He was there. I also improved with my attitude! No longer was I feeling bored with life. Listening to Christ's guidance through prayer times, I resonated with Jesus' words of encouragement to be His servant. This kept me alert and curious about daily life as it unfolded. My physical fitness and endurance increased throughout my daily lifestyle. To enjoy the hiking trips, this discipline of regular physical conditioning was necessary. Without a doubt, time on the Trail was positively impacting the whole of my life.

With both young adult children immersed in college campus lives, my energies continued to focus on building my business practice. I began developing of a life coaching curriculum for women in life transitions who sought a goal-directed lifestyle to enrich their future lives. Because the women's goal setting program was so interlocked with my personal future goals, over the next several years, the life coaching business increasingly pumped energy into the whole of my life. The Lord was guiding me to live with a faith-based cornerstone from which all accomplishments in life would steadily grow.

As RW, our son, completed the second year of college, he decided to take a college break and embark on an AT goal of backpacking the entire 2,168 trail miles in one trip, a thru-hiker. RW invited me to accompany him in the beginning miles at the southern terminus, Springer Mountain, Georgia. I jumped at this opportunity and said "Yes!" As parents we were not thrilled that he was making this decision, but it was time to cautiously support RW's decisions.

The Georgia AT is surprisingly mountainous with deciduous woods and thick turf on the forest floor. In the 31 miles of this backpacking trip, RW demonstrated his autonomy and independence by hiking with newfound friends and expecting Mom to "hike your own hike". This time, unlike four years earlier when I first hiked with my son, "Spirit" (that's my trail name) was more confident, and enthusiastically ready to take on this challenge. The Trail community was out in force, so the camaraderie motivated me to finish the day with a shelter stay and a warm campfire chat. "Millerman" (his trail name,) a retired Army lieutenant colonel from Huntsville, Alabama, became a lifetime friend through the campfire chats along this Trail section.

Blood Mountain, elevation 4,458 feet, is the highest point on the AT in Georgia. There was a long straight up climb to the peak in 2003, but I understand that AT trail maintainers have built a series of switchbacks that now eliminate this climb. There are several legends about how the mountain got its name. The one I prefer comes from a mountain top battleground between Cherokee and Creek tribes. Many died in this battle hence its name, "Blood Mountain."

Neels Gap was the end of this AT section hike and an oasis in the wilderness for all. At the Neels Gap road crossing of the AT sits a vintage store and hiking hostel owned by legendary Winton Porter. The Mountain Crossing store and hiking hostel is built of stone and uniquely includes an archway where the AT passes through the building. Porter and his staff are dedicated experts who guide novice backpackers to be equipped for the long journey ahead. Their trail experience and knowledge of latest equipment is priceless at this first stop on the Trail, about a three-day journey from Springer Mountain. [5] Winton Porter's book, *Just Passin' Thru,* is a great read about this region of the AT

---

[5] Porter, Winton. *Just Passin' Through*

and the history of the community that is centered on this rural store named "Mountain Crossing."

On the front steps of the Mountain Crossing building, RW and I parted ways. He launched the AT thru-hike pulling up his forty-pound backpack, and I drove off headed for home. I made that long drive back to Texas alone. A satisfaction with life emerged. God is with me, and God is with RW on his journey without me. God was holding me as I saw both adult children as independent persons. I enjoyed the solo time of this trip filled with long and uninterrupted talks with Jesus that decreased the worry about the changes in life. Leaving the empty nest stage of life was becoming okay.

Only through my faith and trust in God was I going to find a meaningful future. I felt the first glimmers of hope that the current mysteries of the pathway would lead to my resilience and joy of purpose.

Reflection Devotionals: Spirit, Joy, Shelter, Soul Food, Transitions

Hiking in the Hemlock Trees during Hurricane Isabel

2003 September – Pearisburg, Virginia northbound to the James River, Virginia

Smasher and I met at the Holy Family Church Hiking Hostel where we had parted ways in September 2002. Using our prior year's hiking trip experience, we improved our plans through evaluative conversations over the twelve months. In this way, we established a daily trail routine at the beginning of this hike. With this second year of hiking in Virginia, it became apparent that the AT in Virginia was going to require several hiking trips.

AT hikers call it the "Virginia Blues" because 500 miles of the AT are in Virginia. This southwest Virginia Trail section runs for miles along the western border of Virginia with West Virginia. The area is known for magnificent rocky mountain outcroppings that are popular photo scenes and spectacular views, particularly McAfee's Knob. The AT traverses Dragon's Tooth and Tinker Cliffs, which are great spots for rock climbing and relaxing on scenic mountain top vistas. Along this trail section, we humbly witnessed Civil War history everywhere, with abandoned homesteads of freed slaves as well as Confederate cemeteries in the wilderness. Frequently small country churches emerged from the forests as the Trail connected with remote road crossing. We walked through century old apple orchards. From these mountain vistas, we frequently viewed tobacco farms in the valleys. Open doors displayed tobacco leaves hanging to dry inside the barns.

We came to love the abundant yellow and orange wildflower bush, jewel weed, that cured insect bites and briar scratches. Just break off a clump of Jewel Weed leaves and rub it on the irritated skin. It is a forest pharmaceutical!

After the previous year of drought conditions, this September in southwest Virginia was a complete change. Hurricane Isabel drove us off the trail for two or three days due to wind as well as rainfall. Using an AT annually updated resource book, *AT Trail Companion*, we found The Dutch Haus B&B and hiking hostel in Montebello, Virginia. We weathered the storm safely with the owners, Lois and Earl Arnold. They became lasting friends to the end of our 2,000 miles on the Trail.

My new AT friend from the previous hike, Millerman, joined us on this hiking trip which made for more fun and additional methods of getting the most miles hiked each day. With three vehicles, we had lots of choices on how to approach a basecamp usage, do day hikes and still enjoy backpacking as well. Surprising a hiker with a gift is called Trail Magic! Though Trail Magic usually comes from a stranger doing a good deed for random hikers, we also enjoyed leaving Trail Magic for each other. Millerman planted Peppermint Patty candies for Smasher and me. We often left smiley faces in the Trail dirt just to bring a bit of laughter to Millerman.

My client caseload was so demanding that I could not completely close the door on the business for multiple weeks. Therefore, I arranged phone counseling sessions on scheduled evenings during the trip. Looking back on my trail journaling, clearly God's grace in the Trail time rescued me from the stressors of a counselor. Upon returning to Texas, my refreshed spirit was a good influence for those lives that I touched.

An additional abundance of grace came towards the end of this trip. Millerman, Smasher and I had settled into a campground for basecamp alongside the James River. We were exploring what Trail miles to hike in our last few days of the trip when I decided to use the campground payphone to call home. Unexpectedly, I was urgently needed at home with the stark purpose of helping my 22-year-old daughter, Adrianne, through an acute emotional breakdown. Within twelve hours, I booked an airline ticket and flew home and Millerman drove my truck from Virginia to Austin, Texas with his small truck in tow. He is forever a Trail Angel! Adrianne needed me to be emotionally present and most importantly, she needed me to be secure in my faith to help her find hope.

All praise to God's presence through the hiking trip. I had no doubts in Christ's redeeming grace and I was able to fervently help Adrianne embrace salvation, despite how much she dwelt on her imperfections.

Reflecting over the years on this important family event, without a doubt, the practice of daily devotionals and the lengthy private walking conversations with God surely prepared and grounded me. Trail time prepared me to be at Adrianne's side with Christ's healing presence that was so necessary.

A growing faith is essential to my own stability and happiness. With a growing faith, I can be a steady witness to the grace and peace of Jesus, especially when it is unexpectedly needed.

Reflection Devotionals: Diligence, Forgiveness, Storms, Spirit, Sanctuary, Unexpected, When Nature Calls

Black Bear in Shenandoah National Park

2004 – September, James River, Virginia northbound to Compton Gap, Shenandoah National Park, Virginia

Millerman, Smasher and I gathered on the James River banks to launch our annual hiking trip. What a gorgeous river it is, and we all enjoyed taking photos on the impressive AT pedestrian bridge over the James River. As we headed northbound on the AT, once again we crossed intersections with the Blue Ridge Parkway. Within the first few Trail days, the Blue Ridge

Parkway transformed into Skyline Drive as this scenic quality roadway entered the boundaries of Shenandoah National Park (SNP). There are 28 crossings of Skyline Drive and the AT in the SNP. This was the second time for me to enjoy the SNP and the AT having celebrated my 25th wedding anniversary AT backpacking excursion in 2002. Smasher, Millerman and I hiked the entire 107 AT miles in the SNP on this hiking trip.

This year's hurricane season brought two hurricanes up the east coast and pushed thunderstorms westward into central Virginia. The first hurricane, Frances, came at the beginning of our hiking trip. Once again, as in 2003, we sought shelter with Earl and Lois Arnold's hospitality at the Dutch Haus, escaping the fierce winds and rain of Hurricane Frances. Our friendship with the Arnolds deepened and Lois' great home cooking was a total delight. Earl provided shuttle service for three day hikes and we conquered a grand mountain climb, known as The Priest. By now, Earl had nicknamed us the "Hurricane Hussies," because we kept bringing hurricanes into their regions each September. While we sheltered at the Dutch Haus during Hurricane Frances, we met Sweetfish, a thru-hiker.[6]

Later, when we were established in the Shenandoah National Park, Hurricane Ivan hit the Park area. We chose to rent a Park cabin for one night to weather the storms from that second hurricane.

We returned to the SNP after the hurricane passed and established a Park basecamp at the Lewis Mountain campground with a winning strategy of day hikes using Skyline Drive to easily leave parked cars and hike between those locations. A typical day of hiking in the SNP section was easier than the backpacking approach to the Trail. We ate breakfast at our tent camping site

---

[6] Read the Devotional *Fun and Recreation* to enjoy the story of Nigel and the Gnome Sherpa.

enjoying water spigots, restrooms with showers and parked cars nearby. Once we set up the parked cars for a day's hike, we could accomplish 12 to 15 AT miles in one day without carrying full pack weight. The hiking day started by 8:30am and did not stop until sunset. Then we drove back to basecamp, ate dinner, cleaned up and planned the next day's hiking miles. Not only did we enjoy the luxury of less weight on our backs, but there was also no need for water filtration at a stream, no placement of a bear bag in a tree, and no setting up and taking down a campsite. What a luxury!

There were few AT hikers on the Trail immediately after the first hurricane passed, and the Park Rangers at the south AT entry station were glad to see us and asked for our help. They asked us to count the number of trees blown down onto the AT within SNP and to deliver this information to the north AT station as we exited the Park. Wow! We climbed over one or more blowdown trees every mile!

On the numerous open ridges, we met birdwatching club members with binoculars watching the skies for hawks. They stood in the parking lots along Skyline Drive in mass, enjoying their outdoor fellowship while counting hawks flying south for the winter months. We came to discover that this is a common activity along the entire AT every September as the hawks fly over the Appalachian Mountain ranges southbound.

We finally saw a bear towards the end of the SNP Trail section, but only because we decided to change our ways. Smasher and I constantly talked on the Trail, and this habit caused bears to scurry away when they heard us coming. Knowing bears to be nocturnal creatures, we decided to start our hiking day in silence, hoping to see a bear. Sure enough, minutes later we saw a whole family of bears!

This year was filled with life transitions in the individual lives of my family, making the year a chaotic one. For Tim and me, there was a similar chaotic theme developing around new callings from God in our work settings.

Tim had been an ordained minister for 12 years when he left the ministry in 1990. He spent the following years as a successful businessman until 2005 when he felt called once again to return to local church ministry. His calling came from business acquaintances expressing to him the hollowness of their lives without a faith. Tim returned to ministry in 2005 to answer this calling.

During 2004, my counseling business began to shift into life coaching. I wanted to practice my calling from Christ. I wanted to openly address the spiritual lives and faith journeys of my clients. I did this by including faith-based questions in my group coaching settings including the written materials I authored. This group coaching curriculum, *Lifestyle Goal Setting Journey for Women*, became the principal source for groups of eight to ten women. I shared personal illustrations based on my AT experiences of spiritual growth in Nature to inspire these women along their own goal setting journeys.

This was a time of transformation. Something more than a life transition. No longer was I a lonely bird in an empty nest. My life was shifting in priorities toward a fuller relationship with Jesus Christ. My time alone on the trail with the Lord guided me to understand and embrace these changes. As our young adult children flew away from 'The Nest,' I was learning to trust God's presence in their independent lives rather than attempt to control them. The story of this transformation with its ups and downs became the impetus of this book of devotional reflections.

Reflection Devotionals: Fun and Recreation, Transitions, Storms, Soul Food, Celebrating, Hospitality, Strength, Closeness to Christ, Spirit

Laurel Falls on AT © SarahJDecker

2005 September – Standing Indian AT shelter, NC southbound to Neels Gap, Georgia

"God is good, all the time!" In the Spring of 2005, Smasher was diagnosed with breast cancer and underwent a mastectomy. Months later she had hysterectomy surgery. As often occurs for women, this news came to her abruptly. The reason I say 'God is Good' in this instance is due to God's timely provision of our established faith friendship. As Spring flowed into Summer and Smasher was recuperating from the second surgery, we prayed in our phone conversations that she would be well enough to do a September hiking trip. As September grew close, we chose a plan of hiking AT miles near Smasher's Franklin, NC home, if the doctor permitted this activity. At the last minute, Smasher's doctor released her to backpack two Trail sections, one of them on the NC/Georgia border. These were Trail miles that Smasher repeated because I had not hiked this section of the Trail. On this hiking trip, we both felt the answered prayers of God's presence through Nature around us and the blessing of being immersed in this place so soon after her surgery. I too knew the blessing of my Trail buddy's presence at my side.

Having this September hike in Smasher's "AT neighborhood" was an unfathomable provision of Grace through the beauty of God's Nature. Standing Indian Mountain (5,498 feet elevation) is nicknamed "Grandstand of the Southern Appalachians." Catawba rhododendron dot the mountaintop with purple during June, while the paler blossoms of great rhododendron burst forth in July. We walked through these massive thickets on the Trail in September, experiencing the green tunnel once again. Tray Mountain (4,430 feet elevation) was another magnificent climb on the Trail to the south end of the Trail section journey. Tray Mountain has a wild and ragged look because of the weathered sheets of the mineral mica in this mountain. I celebrated crossing the NC/Georgia border as we journeyed southbound to Neel's Gap. Finishing the trip at Neel's Gap was a life transition memory. My son RW launched from there in 2003 on his thru-hike attempt.

You might ask, what is a gap? This Texan gal sure did! A gap is a low area between two mountains, like a mountain pass. My flatlander perspective of gaps compared to passes is another regional difference in vocabulary. The Appalachian Mountains are very different from the Rocky Mountains.

We made a second short backpacking trip to an area north of Smasher's home, near Laurel Falls, on the TN/NC border. Laurel Falls is a spectacular waterfall beside the AT and viewing it was worth the entire trip. Also of note is the extensive volunteer trail maintainer's construction project of stone steps leading to the waterfalls. The entire project was accomplished by a women's trail crew. Yeah!

Also of note in this beautiful area is the legendary Kincora Hiking Hostel. The Bob and Pat Peoples family owned this year-round hostel on the AT for several decades. It was known for its robust accommodations of kitchen, bunkroom, showers, tent sites and shuttle services. It was especially known for friendly hospitality to all.

My faith and trust in God continued to be tested and my comforting internal experience of resilience in Christian character was the result. During this year, I often looked back over the previous four years to recall how different I felt when I was retreating from marriage, family, and self because I did not like the life changes that I could not control. I was maturing because my faith was growing.

This hiking trip and my general lifestyle kept fueling my personal relationship with Jesus as I expectantly looked for Christ to be with me, and He was. I was becoming an individual disciple in all walks of my life, independently facing many midlife challenges with Jesus at my side. Cancer had returned to my elderly mother, a widow, and I wanted time to be with her. As I made trips away from home to visit Mom, I reflected on how her faith was an inspiration to me. Tim had returned to ministry. By serving Industry United Methodist Church, our home and my business were too far apart to allow us the blessing of living together. But Tim's calling was so evident, as was my own, that I strongly embraced living apart four days a week to make our Christian discipleships happen.

My life coaching practice continued to inspire me as I saw women claiming personal responsibility for spiritual growth in their efforts to construct life enrichment. Some women clients used the setting to find new steps forward in Christian faith. And I enjoyed sharing my AT journey with the women.

Reflection Devotionals: Healing, Strength, Living Water, Trusting, Grace, Beauty, Spirit, Transitions, Feelings

Cheri & Smasher on AT near Bear's Den Hostel

Near Harper's Ferry hiking the AT/C&O Canal Towpath

2006 September – Shenandoah National Park, Virginia: Compton Gap northbound to Pen Mar Park, Maryland

In September, we returned to the AT. Being a little further north, allowed for more autumn color in the leaves of the forest. A delight of Nature that I do not have in central Texas.

Mom passed away in May of 2006. My grief journey was a heavy load to carry into this hiking trip. I always thought of Mom as my greatest cheerleader, and over time I realized that she still is cheering me on, right beside Jesus.

Matthew 28:20 *"Lo, I am with you always, even to the ends of the earth."* NRSV

My faith journaling at the time recorded the precious comfort I received from Christ's tender loving care during my months of grieving. Just four months after Mom's death, I was able to function on the Trail only because of the comfort of my faith in Christ. A faith deepened from being in Nature. I eagerly looked forward to this time with God on the Trail, in the provision of His Nature, further absorbing God's grace and love.

A young woman, Cheri, joined Smasher and me on this backpacking trip. Cheri was a member of Girl Scout Troop 961 where I was the Troop Leader throughout my daughter's years in public school. Though it was a blessing to share Girl Scouting memories with Cheri while on this trip, she was preoccupied with rumbling private thoughts that needed processing on the Trail. Cheri had recently finished cancer treatment and her prognosis for remission was not hopeful. Cheri's pensive concerns about cancer reoccurring in her future certainly added to the Trip theme – "Humans have limitations." In her 20s and otherwise a healthy young woman, the reality of life and death was walking the Trail with me in the form of Cheri. I was feeling very blessed by my excellent health and stamina at age 56. With Smasher's two surgeries in 2005, we both praised the Lord God Almighty for getting us out on the Trail one more September.

The three of us began our journey north of Shenandoah National Park, (SNP) backpacking through the rolling terrain appropriately named the Roller Coaster. Soon we discovered the pristine accommodation of Bears Den Hostel, managed by the

Potomac AT Hiking Club. Located near Bears Den Rocks and the AT, the hostel is a restored stone mansion with many rooms and amenities. Weekend hikers from Washington DC enjoy this hostel as do the long-distance hikers like us. The hostel's lounging room invited hikers to relax at the end of the day in the company of like-minded trekkers and share stories of the AT. The Bears Den Hostel live-in host, Lori, initiated deep discussions about faith with us. Like the Dutch Haus, we found another AT home base at the Bears Den Hostel and the live-in host Lori.

We saw an abundance of wildlife on this section of the Trail – deer, snakes, asps, and a hornet's nest. Often, we walked in the rain and if it was not raining, it was frequently misty and foggy. We seized an opportunity to attend Sunday church worship with a small congregation in Bluemont, Virginia near the AT. About twenty miles northward, we arrived at Harper's Ferry, West Virginia. Finally leaving Virginia after 500 miles of trail over a total of four annual hiking trips.

It is a beautiful vista as the AT tops a mountain ridge and overlooks Harper's Ferry in the valley at the confluence of the Potomac and the Shenandoah Rivers. After touring the Civil War site of Harpers Ferry National Historic Park, we climbed the steep streets to the office headquarters of the Appalachian Trail Conservancy. Warm greetings from volunteers and staff plus a tour of the AT memorabilia there made for a worthwhile short respite from the Trail. Cheri left us in Harpers Ferry and picked up a train into Washington DC for a whole different part of her vacation getaway.

Smasher and I crossed a pedestrian bridge over the Potomac River and entered Maryland. Here the C&O Canal Towpath was converted into the AT pathway. For three miles this flat surface is the AT. This path was used for mules towing barges on the Potomac River until 1924. As we traveled on the short mileage through Maryland, only 40 miles, we were amazed by the well-maintained AT shelters in this area.

For two nights we curiously viewed a mountain top that was covered with floodlighting. As we passed local hikers on the Trail, no one could explain what this hilltop location was. We stopped in Frederick, Maryland for a bite of lunch at a café and a female hiker and military soldier finally exposed the community secret. The extremely well-lit mountain top was the US President's Camp David. She explained that for safety precautions, the community honors the importance of not broadcasting this information to strangers, and maybe AT hikers especially!

In this area, there were more Civil War sites along the AT in addition to the sites in Harpers Ferry. We spent an afternoon viewing a Civil War enactment in a local park. We also crossed the Mason – Dixon line just before arriving at the Pennsylvania border with Maryland, our place to stop for this year.

After that 2006 AT trip, I had much to reflect on about my life. My reflections covered both my current life issues and the after-life too. I wrote these words to capture my thoughts at the time:

---❋---

The morning air has been heavy with fog that encourages introspective ponderings as I walk and climb. Moving from the focus on my internal thoughts as I walk to the new focus on the mountain top vista is like my life journey of the last six months. In this transition time, I am reminded of a lesson Mom taught me. Mom was an artist in oils and watercolors. She usually created landscape scenes. Mom would say that to paint well or live life well, we need to practice perspective. The artist cannot create a landscape without viewing both the up close and the far away and the contrast between these places. Likewise, we cannot live life well without viewing life in its wholeness, which includes death. Life has daily patterns and there is connectedness of these two parts. To live life well is to know that life is multidimensional with a spiritual thread holding together the reality we create each day. And so, I stepped off that vista having enjoyed that contrasted moment away from the fog. I stepped back into the fog and the forested trail, and I thanked God for my life. My faith gives me perspective that always leads to hope, to healing, to purpose in life.'

This quote from my journaling captures the essence of my reflections as I left the Trail and drove home. For months after this September 2006 trip, I carried these deep spiritual thoughts.

I made it through the first anniversary of Mom's passing. For months I had worried about May 2007, because my experiences as a grief counselor informed me that the first anniversary is often an unexpected resurgence of grief. I prayed consistently for Jesus to save me from this pending doom and gloom, and to give me joy and laughter instead. Oh, my goodness, my prayers were answered with more joy than I could have imagined. I was belly laughing on the first anniversary of Mom passing away. We have such a fun and clever God.

On the anniversary day of Mom's passing, I came home to an empty house in the late afternoon after a long day of work but dreading hours of being alone. I opened my email Inbox to find a message from Cousin Bill who never corresponds with me. When I opened the message, I found a photo of Cousin Bill and his wife. They were standing next to my husband Tim's cousin Sandy and her husband. The four of them were holding up wine glasses making a toast. Bill explained that they met during a happy hour time at a Louisiana Bed and Breakfast. Through a get-acquainted conversation, they discovered their connection through the marriage of Tim and Beth. There is more bewilderment coming! Tim's cousin lives in Wisconsin and my cousin lives outside of Houston.

Now, add to God's "magical mystery tour," the clincher, which captured my full attention and turned me away from grieving and towards the impressive and captivating surprise. Tim's cousin and my cousin have another rare connection. It so happens that Sandy's mother is the twin sister of Tim's mother. And Bill's mother is the twin sister of my mother! Both cousins are special to us because they are the offspring of our mothers' twin sisters!

Folks, that is not a coincidence! That event on the first anniversary of Mom's passing away is God's Nature; it is His way of showing me how deeply my prayers are heard. Only God can take me where I experience unlimited joy and a happiness with buoyancy beyond my measure. In His serendipity ways, God is always present and engaged with us, and I love watching His provision with wonder and awe. This "gift from God experience" was an uplifting launchpad for me to move on with life. But God was not finished with me!

Reflection Devotionals: Healing, Suffering, Grieving, Sanctuary, Unexpected, When Nature Calls, Chosen, Closeness to Christ

Texas Girl Scout's 1ˢᵗ Backpacking Trip

2007 June – Great Smoky Mountain National Park

The month following the anniversary of my mother's death, I embraced leadership of an AT trip for Central Texas Girl Scouts. Eight Central Texas Girl Scouts registered and prepared for the backpacking trip with multiple weekends of skills training and weekend backpacking. The group was comprised of four adults with the eight teens who had varying degrees of experience prior to the required training weekends. We divided into two groups once we hit the Trail. One group was the older teens who had a fast pace and were more experienced. My group was the younger middle school age girls, and this trip was their first long distance backpacking experience. We proudly called ourselves the "Turtles" because of our slow hiking pace!

The AT passes through the center of Great Smoky Mountain National Park (GSMNP) from the southern boundary at Fontana Dam and following the NC/TN border north to Davenport Gap. There are 75 AT miles within the Park. We used the AT shelters instead of carrying the added pack weight of tents. By using the AT shelters for the overnights, we could cook breakfast and dinner at the shelter, and we had convenient access for filtering water from a stream. Keeping the backpack weight to a minimum was a priority so that beginners would not be discouraged as the Trail miles accumulated.

The Smokies are an infamous and spectacular mountain range, and June is a beautiful time to be there. The temperatures ranged from the 30's at night to the 70's for daytime high. The AT path climbs an overall elevation shift from 1,700 feet at Fontana Dam to Clingman's Dome at 6,643 feet elevation. Descending from Clingman's Dome, the Trail is 2,600 feet elevation at the north boundary, Davenport Gap. 400 to 600 bears were Park residents where we backpacked the Trail, so the safety procedures for food storage at night were particularly important. We met a park ranger along the Trail carrying a rifle, and he stopped to talk with us about a 'friendly bear.' When people feed the bears, they become dangerously friendly and must be removed from the Park.

The AT path follows the mountain ridgetops throughout most of the Park, so the most challenging parts were the climbs up to the ridge and the descent from the ridge. My group enjoyed the thick forests and well-worn Trail itself. We enjoyed the Trail community gatherings at the shelters each evening. There were even large families that included children as young as six years old backpacking together on the AT through GSMNP. And there were thru-hikers on their journey to complete the whole AT.

Our Girl Scout patrol of six people, the Turtles, enjoyed the chosen slow pace and readiness to stop and notice spectacular things. We examined bizarre mushrooms hanging on tree trunks, weird bugs crossing the Trail and beautiful vistas from the mountain tops. Favorite spots on the AT were Charlie's Bunion and Clingman's Dome. [7]

Using our leisurely pace, the 'Turtles' patrol abruptly changed our hiking schedule when we discovered a Music Festival in the Park. And we were glad that we did. The teenage girls giggled like eight-year-olds as they danced and sang at the Festival. After the Festival, we scurried back onto the AT and hiked and danced through the Rhododendron blossoms that abundantly blanketed the Trail.

The spiritual experience of this trip furthered the joy and laughter that God was using to refuel my soul and further transform me. I loved the fun and laughter of this female group. We prepared for adventure and recreation in the outdoors, and we faced the adventure with determination. And when the 75 miles were behind us, I absolutely saw a greater self-confidence and maturity in each of the Girl Scouts.

Smasher intended to participate in the June backpacking trip through GSMNP with the Girl Scouts, but she was ill with multiple symptoms, primarily unexplained fatigue. Though I missed her presence on the Trail, she pitched in to shuttle vehicles around and create a food fest celebration at the trip's end. We Girl Scouts sure appreciated her Trail Angel role. Unfortunately, Smasher's fatigue persisted, and she began a series of medical appointments with specialists, seeking a diagnosis. As September 2007 approached, I worried about losing Smasher as a hiking buddy because of her unknown medical condition.

Reflection Devotionals: Freedom, Shelter, Fun and Recreation, Beauty, Spirit, Grieving, Strength, Soul Food, Fellowship

---

[7] Reflection Devotional *Freedoms* about our bear family encounter

Blaze Azalea in Bloom on Roan Mountain

2007 September – Roan High Knob Shelter, NC southbound to Erwin, TN.

Without Smasher knowing, I planned a September AT hike. It was designed to finish gaps of Trail miles near her North Carolina home. These were Trail miles Smasher had already completed. The two-week trip was planned for hiking two separate parts of the Trail. The first Trail part I enjoyed with an adult Girl Scout friend, Bann. The second Trail part I planned as my first solo backpacking trip.

Bann and I started at Roan High Bluff, elevation 6,267 feet, the spot where I left the Trail in 2000. Roan High Knob Shelter (originally a fire warden's cabin) was where my hypothermia developed quickly after a day of over exertion and poor pacing on my part. My son RW cared for me in the Shelter through the night, but I had to leave the Trail the next morning due to my weakened condition. Revisiting this sight where I was a novice backpacker caused informative reflections about my journey over the previous seven years. [8]

As we hiked southbound on Roan Mountain, the AT followed a ridge crest with spectacular views interspersed with plunges into the woods. In this area, Catawba rhododendron grow in profusion as the Trail tunnels through this dense vegetation. The purplish-pink blossoms reach their fullest point about the second or third week of June. Here the forests include evergreens, the Fraser and Balsam fir, and some red spruce. Bann and I noticed how vegetation on the forest floor was hanging low, clearly indicating drought conditions. It became alarmingly true to us as we continued down the Trail that the region was in severe drought condition.

At the end of our three days together, Bann and I spent the night at Uncle Johnny's Nolichucky Hostel. Overnighting here was another reminder of the year 2000 and my novice backpacker history when I lacked stamina and physical endurance.[9]

Bann and I parted ways the next morning as she returned to Texas, and I embarked on seven days of solo backpacking. Hemlock Hollow bunkhouse was my base camp as I traversed AT miles south of the Nolichucky River. The mountains are covered with rhododendron thickets and the Trail tunnels through them just as the previous section that I hiked with Bann. And once again, the drought conditions were evident. Occasionally a rock outcropping emerged from the thick growth on the forest floor. Walking alone through this forest was a comforting pastoral experience as if God's Nature's comforting arms were wrapped around me. The Trail follows the TN/NC border through the Cherokee National

---

[8] Read descriptions of 2000 hiking trip

[9] Read Reflection Devotional – *Unexpected* which focuses on the solo trip

Forest and the Pisgah National Forest. In this dense forest area managed by the US National Forest system, September is always marked by hunting season. I remembered to wear something flaming orange for this reason. On this trip, as was often the case with September AT trips, hunting dogs barking in their pack could be heard from a distance in the forests. I never saw another hiker during my solo trek which was not unusual given the remote location, and the fact that over the years of September hikes, we found the Trail and the shelters to be sparse with hikers. That was particularly true during the weekdays.

Hiking alone, I carefully followed a plan that addressed the basic concerns for safety, and I left the route plan with the owners of Hemlock Hollow. Due to the drought conditions, I validated reliable water sources with the local people. As the owner of Hemlock Hollow shuttled me to set up the backpacking trip over multiple days by leaving my car parked at the destination and dropping me off at my starting spot, he revealed to me a new concern unfortunately at the last minute. He informed me that Park Rangers from the nearby Smoky Mountain NP had recently moved bears out of the Park and into the local vicinity, where I would be. The relocated bears were a safety concern because the bears were too interested in people food. I am not one who usually carries fear of wildlife, but this safety concern did impact my psyche. Between the drought conditions and the last minute warning about bears, ultimately, I chose to shorten my solo trip.

This solo time in God's Nature was filled with resonating and transforming time with Jesus. Over years of reflection about AT hiking trips, I have noticed that a deep fiber of my identity as a loved child of God was formed during this walk of multiple days alone with God. You should know that my deep faith journey growth came from anticipating this opportunity and preparing for this time with God. In preparation for this trip, I wrote the lyrics of favorite hymns and sang the songs as I walked. Songs like "Pass It On," "A Mighty Fortress Is Our God," "How Great Thou Art," "Surely the Presence," "He Leadeth Me" and a favorite that I memorized, "Oh God, Our Help in Ages Past." Hearing my voice resound in Nature's wilderness affirmed my identity – I am a follower of Jesus Christ. Other songs that I sang on the Trail were "Happy Wanderer," "Shenandoah," and "This Land is Your Land."

Another preparation for this quality time with God was carrying my spiritual journal and my Upper Room Daily Devotional booklet. Reviewing the writings from this solo trip, I was wrestling with complex life issues that only faith in God would give me the peace that I sought. Outside of business hours, my lifestyle had returned to the social role of a pastor's wife; I did not want to be pigeon-holed by the role that occurred 20 years earlier, when I was less mature in my faith. I felt that my maturing faith had finally incorporated the role of a life coach and a psychotherapist. I sought a similar gift from God about my role as a pastor's wife. As you probably know, life only gets more complex as we age! The solo-hike experience grounded my identity on the rock of Jesus Christ and sanctified the non-conformist part of me as an important trait that Jesus would call into use. As He had in the past. All my life I have been attracted to the periphery of social groups.

While writing this book, I was re-reading my journaling from this time, and I recalled my struggle with life and death in general. I was in the final stages of grief about Mom's passing away, but I was also struggling with letting go of responsibility for Adrianne's mental illness. At 26, she needed to feel my expectations that she take responsibility for her mental health. Though I wanted her to have a resilient Christian faith, I grappled with the reality that I did not have a resilient faith at age 26. The fact that my brother's mental illness brought him to suicide as a young adult added to my troubling thoughts and prayers.

On the Trail in this solo-backpacking experience, I addressed these troubling thoughts through complicated conversations with Jesus. I accepted God's truth that a maturing faith begins with hope and baby steps of trusting God. It became clear to me the importance of my faith witnessing with Adrianne on those specific experiences of trustworthiness and faithfulness of Jesus Christ's presence in my life. Folks, at the writing of this book, Adrianne is a woman of faith and maintains her mental health as she takes on the responsibilities and stressors of young family life with two children. Adrianne and her husband Bryan have named their daughter Hope! Praise God!

Reflection Devotionals: God's Gifts, Beauty, Healing, Hope, Sanctuary, Spirit, Pacing, Grieving, Trusting, Faithfulness

Onward from Mt. Katahdin: 2008 to 2012

Climbing Mt. Katahdin

Girl Scout Friend Jana bravely crosses a swift stream on the AT Pathway

2008 July – Mt Katahdin, Maine southbound to Rangeley, Maine

Smasher and I sought to take on the challenges of Maine before our bodies became too old to do it. Despite our well-intended plans, this trip was not about our fitness success. It was a trip constantly reminding us of God's unfathomable provision sustaining us despite new health concerns and unexpected Trail flooding conditions.

As Smasher and I planned this trip, I was concerned about my physical limitations despite the years of building my physical endurance through the annual hiking trips. In early 2008, I hired a fitness coach to prepare me for the infamous remote wilderness Trail section of Maine. The physical condition planning addressed the reality that there would be no day hiking options on this section of the Trail because road crossings were rare. I was building my endurance and stamina for backpacking multiple days in a row on challenging terrain over a four-week trip schedule. Meanwhile, I had learned to approach the AT trips with a spiritual discipline as well. As we neared the July trip, I was looking forward to the challenge with confidence and ease.

Then I received a phone call from Smasher updating me on the outcome from her medical specialists visits over the prior months. The doctors had ruled out some of the major medical conditions that would explain her chronic symptoms, but it had been an arduous journey for Smasher to undergo. May 2008, Smasher was diagnosed with Multiple Sclerosis (MS). With only two months before our July 5th departure, Smasher was determined to not cancel the hiking trip but to begin treatment needed to minimize the chances of a MS outbreak while on the Trail. She was given medication to be administered by injection every other day, and she promptly learned to give herself the shots. Her medical condition was newly diagnosed and a concern to both of us. Smasher's determination and courage was a huge inspiration to me.

A Texas adult Girl Scout friend, Jana, chose to accompany Smasher and me on this Trip. We contracted a wonderful and reliable shuttle service man, Buddy Ward, who drove the three of us from Bangor, Maine airport to Katahdin Stream Campground at Baxter State Park. Once we arrived at the campground which is at the foot of Mt. Katahdin, we established a base camp and prepared to summit Mt. Katahdin the next day. [10]

Mt. Katahdin (elevation 5,267 feet) is the northern terminus of the AT and has historically been the end of a 2,126-mile journey

---

[10] Please read the Reflection Devotional False *Summits* for the in-depth account of this epoch day of all days on the AT as we climbed up Mt. Katahdin and came down, 14 hours of hiking.

for the AT thru-hikers. Therefore, most of the hikers we met on our first day were celebrating the end of several months on the Trail. There were a few thru-hikers embarking on the long journey south by choosing Mt. Katahdin as their launch pad. "Ranger" and "Barefoot" were thru-hiker Trail friends in this category, south-bounders. Not only did they step in to help us on Mt. Katahdin, but these young men also chose to be our companions for the next several days, giving us great comfort with their presence.

The AT in Maine is 281 miles long. The northern trail section is the area north of Monson, Maine and the first AT steps southbound from Mt Katahdin. The terrain is a multitude of wilderness lakes and ponds. This area is the largest forested timberlands on the East Coast. AT enthusiasts call this section the 100 Mile Wilderness. The forests are predominantly dark green spruce and fir trees.

After our Mt Katahdin experience, we left Baxter State Park and backpacked to Abol Bridge Family Campground. Our lovely campsite was adjacent to a small lake. We were awestruck with the magnificence of a Bald Eagle nest beside the lake. As we relaxed around our campsite, we were rewarded with the entertainment of the Bald Eagle catching fish from the lake and feeding the baby birds in the nest.

Traveling further south bound, we consistently crossed fast flowing streams and rocky terrain. I was surprised by the frequency of bogs or swamps whenever we were in lowlands. The volunteer Trail maintainers of Maine have a particularly challenging job keeping the Trail accessible because of the short summer season and the swampy areas. Throughout Maine, we hiked on Trail paths made from lengthy wooded planks to traverse the Trail over these swamps. When you slid off the wooden planks, your leg was submerged in water to the knee cap.

The rock outcroppings on mountain ridges were marked by trail cairns, a tall pile of rocks stacked upon each other with the AT white blaze marking the Trail through sparse foliage. One surprising and scary rock formation that we traversed was Chairback Mountain.[11]

Camping in this terrain was distinctly memorable. For the first time, I experienced a Loon, an aquatic bird singing at night with the moonlight over the expansive ponds in the forest. The mosquitos were aggressive and use of a head netting even inside my tent was helpful for sleeping. The dark sky of Maine made for magnificent star gazing nights at our campsites.

Moose are prevalent in Maine, and I came to know their habitat and ways. Bless these creatures for they really are not very smart and are easily spooked.

One of the unusual events of the AT in Maine is the ferry crossing of the Kennebec River by canoe. Though the AT crosses countless large streams and rivers over the 2,000 plus miles, most of the crossings use a bridge. The Indian word "Kennebec" means long, quiet water. After a thru-hiker drowned trying to cross the Kennebec River in 1983, and many other trekkers had a narrow escape when fording the Kennebec River, the AT headquarters finally declared the official river crossing would be a free ferry ride by canoe. I had read about this fact in AT books and long anticipated this unusual treat in the middle of nowhere. It was sheer fun to step into a canoe, hold onto my backpack and enjoy the ride!

Hanging out at Shaw's Lodging in Monson, Maine was a highpoint of this trip. There we developed friendships with AT trekkers moving north and south. I found the quaint town of Monson to be a peaceful and friendly respite from life on the Trail. One evening we happened upon an impromptu gathering at the local

---

[11] Be sure to read the devotional, *Closeness to Christ* for the full story.

general store. In the small quarters of the store, four or five string musicians gathered for a Hootenanny of sorts! Lots of townsfolk and hikers poured in. What a delightful evening of music, singing and fun. [12]

We meandered further southbound with our backpacks loaded. The Trail followed the Piscataquis River and was not a mountainous area. I recall the beauty of pristine waterfalls in this area.

When we arrived in Caratunk, Maine and moved into our reserved canvas cabin, we were so thankful to enjoy some luxuries again. At this point, we were two weeks into the long outdoor journey and beginning to realize an unanticipated surprise. We had arrived in Maine for one of their heaviest rainfall seasons. Over several days, a heavy rain fell and somedays we remained indoors rather than venture into the dangerous weather. When we heard from northbound trekkers that the AT was washed out where we wanted to traverse, we hired a shuttle service and traveled to our next reserved lodging further south. We hiked a few days north of Rangeley, Maine before the heavy rainfall returned. It was scary to hear their stories of strong young men fighting to survive flooded stream crossings of the Trail only to discover that the AT could not be located on the other side of the rushing water. We then shuttled to one more reserved lodging south in Andover, Maine and tried to find a section of the AT to safely hike. No luck. We were discouraged and strangely, we were feeling cabin fever staying indoors after so many days on the Trail.

I wrote the following while sitting indoors on one of those heavy rainfall days in Maine:

---

[12] *Fun and Recreation* Devotional

Matthew 7:24-25 Anyone who listens to my teaching and obeys me is wise, like a person who builds a house on solid rock. Though the rain comes in torrents and the floodwaters rise and the winds beat against that house, it will not collapse, because it is built on rock. LNT

I stepped out into a swift moving mountain stream with vigor and confidence. A beautiful day and I was ready to "take on the trail!" Step, step, wobble, wobble – "WHOA. Do not fall! Think first. You know how to safely cross a stream with a strong current." Approaching this with the attitude of "best foot forward" will not be successful or safe. I quickly turned and faced the oncoming water with my feet spread to my shoulder width. Solid footing. After slowly crossing the stream in this stance, reflections on my initial approach and then quick regrouping, I recalled the scripture. I could see how spontaneously we use a centered on oneself approach of my best foot forward. This may be good in a short-term way, like secular living. But eventually I will need solid footing as the current of life causes an "on my own" strength approach to be wobbly at best. Let us be quick to claim our need for Jesus and turn head-on to Him as the swift waters required solid footing.

Sitting down once again to problem solve another plan for our predicament was necessary. Smasher and I were using all the perseverance and determination we still had. Our final solution was to stop the AT backpacking trip due to the Trail not being passable.

We became tourists! We rented a car, drove to the Maine coastline, and enjoyed the final few days eating lobster and sightseeing. We really enjoyed an expensive trip at the L.L. Bean headquarters in Freeport, ME.

A Husband's Perspective

While the challenges of getting through a water soaked Maine were going on for the hikers, I received three separate requests from Beth to reschedule her Southwest Airlines flight back to Texas. Which I did with the help of great service reps from the airline. When the fourth request to reschedule occurred, I was just short of climbing in the truck and driving to Maine to bring my wife home! As we problem solved, it was determined that Spirit and Smasher would get off the trail and enjoy being tourists, including a visit to the international headquarters of L.L Bean in Freeport, Maine. It made sense and saved me a long drive! Of course, the call ended with the final request: "Can you find us a rental car?" Finding a rental car in deep woods Maine was easier said than done. But I did it!!!

The 2008 AT hiking trip in Maine had a life context that bears mentioning to you. 2008 had an empowering theme of women friendships and women life coaching clients who were acting with courage and inspiring one another. Smasher had certainly lived with courage on the Trail and in the whole of her life. Women clients were frequently showing courage as they faced life changes, each in their own journey. The Lifestyle Goal Setting for Women groups were becoming a significant part of my life coaching business. I facilitated self-accountability agreements between the female clients which encouraged everyone to seek their future goals with support. I was serving as a role model for the women clients as I prepared for this AT Trip and afterwards as well. Thank you, God, I felt comfortable with my role.

It was months after the Maine trip before reflections on my faith journey became clear messages to me. This was a pivotal and transformative time that changed my life. The overarching feeling that I came to have, and still have, is Peace. I now know where home is. However, I am not in a hurry to go there, to Heaven. From this Trip experience, life was no longer making me be anxious, reactive, and scared. I have a peace that surpasses all understanding.

Reflection Devotionals: Purifying Water, False Summits, Closeness to Christ, Lost, Fun and Recreation, Storms, Pacing, Shelter, Faithfulness, Chosen

Privy at Deer Lick Shelter, Pennsylvania © SarahJDecker

2010 September – Pen Mar Park, Maryland northbound to Swatara Gap, Pennsylvania

2009 was absorbed by multiple demands on the home front for both Smasher and me. It was so full of demands that we chose to forego our September, 2009 hiking trip.

On my home front, big changes were in the works. My faith and trust in God were tested and strengthened as Tim and I made decisions concerning our church ministry location with the priority of what was best for us as a married couple. We felt God leading us to serve Him while once again living together full time.

We expected the Methodist church system to accommodate our calling for a local church ministry closer to our Austin home so we could live together again. The Methodist church system responded to our request positively. I believe this happened because we asked for God's provision.

Our lives in 2009 focused on a new church appointment. Leander United Methodist Church was a reasonable commute from our Austin, Texas home allowing life together 24/7. This was another affirmation that God is listening to our needs as we desired to serve Him. Within the first few months of our arrival at Leander UMC, the tragic and deadly motorcycle accident of Kris Klein, a key faith leader of the congregation, threw his family and the whole congregation into despair and grief. Understandably, the church milieu became a robust ministry on grief recovery through faith in Jesus Christ. Do you see how God prepared me to help this congregation through my Trail time with Him? God is good, all the time! God had further blessed me with full time togetherness in marriage. The servanthood felt like a heavy load, but Christ's yoke is easy because of Him. Leander UMC congregation leaned on faith in Christ and healed. With the Holy Spirit flourishing in their midst, an unexpected membership growth over the next few years occurred. Praise God!

When the new year of 2010 arrived, and I suddenly realized that I had become a 'couch potato!' So I got back into God's good self-care discipline of regular physical conditioning as well as quiet time with the Lord. I was eager and fit to go by September. Balancing "love your neighbor with love yourself" is so challenging in the long journey of faith. I hit the Trail singing the hymn tune "Leaning on the Everlasting Arms."

Unfortunately, Smasher was having another difficult year that interfered with a September hiking trip respite from her lifestyle. The good news was that she no longer suffered additional health problems as in recent years. Managing the newly diagnosed MS was going well because she consistently adhered to the treatment plan. The sad news was a nasty pending divorce that she did not anticipate. After several decades of marriage, her husband left Smasher with a cascade of financial woes which had a lasting impact on her lifestyle. Once again, Smasher's faith journey sustained her through a dark valley and difficult life transition. In 2010, Smasher remained home to protect her limited assets during these divorce proceedings.

Debra, a neighbor and adult friend through Girl Scouting joined me for this September hiking trip through Pennsylvania. Debra's daughter, Cheri, hiked with us in 2006.[13]

To quickly capture the kick-off spirit of this hiking trip, read the *Hospitality* Devotional where the first Pennsylvanians we met welcomed us to their state and to their home with precious hospitality. [14]

The state of Pennsylvania has a bad rap among AT enthusiasts because of its grand variety of rocky terrain throughout the 230 Trail miles in the state. The rocks are small and often slippery, perfect for causing a twisted sprained ankle. Therefore, Pennsylvania is often referred to as "Rocksylvania." Debra and I completed 118 miles in Pennsylvania over a ten-day time on the Trail.

As Debra and I traveled northbound from the Pennsylvania/Maryland border, we were immediately educated about the state's iron and steel industry. Large deposits of iron ore, an abundance of trees perfect for converting into charcoal, and streams to harness for power enabled Pennsylvania to supply more than half of America's raw iron during the late 1700s and into the 1800s. The Trail passed by disturbed areas where wood

---

[13] 2006 September, SHP, Virginia to Compton Gap northbound to Pen Mar Park, MD.

[14] Read the Reflection Devotional *Hospitality*

was burned to produce charcoal, which was used to fuel the iron furnaces. We saw the ruins of the Caledonia Iron Works furnace as the Trail passed through Caledonia State Park and later Pine Grove Furnace State Park.

We enjoyed miles of Trail with a pleasant mix of walking along a low ridge and then into open fields. The small village of Boiling Springs was especially scenic. Boiling Springs is the location of the AT mid-Atlantic regional office where we checked in to receive Trail condition, information, and a weather forecast. The AT Shelters were well maintained in this area, and we used them frequently.

There is a lengthy and memorable rock scramble along the mountainside where the Trail approaches the south bank of the Susquehanna River. After the Trail crosses the River bridge, we entered the town of Duncannon. Carrying our backpacks through the city streets, we entered our planned overnight lodging, the historic Doyle Hotel. More than 100 years old, Debra and I experienced a stark contrast to our outdoor sleeping by staying in an old hotel room with a shared bathroom down the hallway. The Doyle Hotel is one of the original Anheuser-Bush hotels which included a ground floor corner tavern with an excellent dinner and beer on tap.

Using a local car shuttle service for AT trekkers, we positioned our car several Trail miles ahead and then had the shuttle service drop us off before we backpacked the next few days back to our car.

I loved this southern and central Pennsylvania section of the AT. Though the rocky pathway slowed us down, we maintained a good pace enjoying the picturesque views along the way. Debra and I decided to enjoy one full day in Lancaster, Pennsylvania as tourists. The short drive from the AT brought us to the Pennsylvania Dutch communities where the Amish communities use horse drawn carriages for transportation, and the farms operate without modern amenities like electricity. We enjoyed the organic fresh food of this culture, especially the yummy fruit pies! Debra and I even rode a horse drawn carriage for the fun of it!

At the end of our trip, we discovered the AT 501 shelter, a fully enclosed cabin with a parking lot area nearby. As usual, there is no fee for using the AT shelters. It has 12 bunks, table, and chairs, a privy and a solar shower and a water spigot nearby. We used the 501 shelter for two days of day hiking and enjoyed its amenities tremendously.

As we stood in the parking lot at 501 Shelter, packing our car to head home to Texas, a new Trail Angel appeared, driving his large Chevy Suburban into the parking lot. "HAD", his Trail name, is a retired elementary school teacher from North Carolina. He was continuing his AT journey of annual hikes and bird watching. He cheerfully greeted us by offering his free shuttle services which he had enjoyed doing for years. We took his contact information to use for 2011 and assured him of our gratitude for his volunteerism to hikers on the AT.

When the trip was over and the long drive home began, I realized once again how richly blessed I was to have multiple weeks away from work. To be immersed in God's presence through His Nature, thereby renewing my faith. Sometimes I felt guilty because of His favor in my life, as if I had control over God's ways. Ha Ha! Overtime I learned to see the falsehood of this guilt and instead fully relish in His goodness. As a tourist seeing the Pennsylvania Dutch faith-based culture with stark lifestyles that proudly revealed their faith-centered lives, I was further convicted to own my faith journey. I celebrated how Christ speaks to us and relates to us individually, not just in a faith group or any other form. We believers are not part of a Borg collective like in

Star Trek! I had used the Trail time well to finish conversations with Jesus and I felt "it is well with my soul."

Reflection Devotionals: Shelter, Hospitality, When Nature Calls, Encouraging, Trail Angels, Chosen

The Knife's Edge is one of the Scariest Spots on the AT
Courtesy of Appalachian Trail Conservancy

2011 September – Swatara Gap, Pennsylvania northbound to Bake Oven Knob Rd., Pennsylvania

An opening prayer: *Thank you, God, for giving me the gift of long, deep, and completed conversations with You. Amen.*

As my 2011 life events unfolded, I was developing a better understanding of God's ways. God was comforting me and affirming me with His trustworthiness. A journey that began on the Maine 2008 trip. The deepening of an individual relationship with Jesus Christ was preparing me for a time when Tim would need to lean on me more than ever before.

Our 2011 hiking trip kicked off like a large traveling party group when contrasted to any of my previous hiking trips. The Girl Scout trip experience in 2007 is the exception to that blanket statement! Our group included Lois Arnold, co-owner of Dutch Haus BNB in Virginia, as she hiked with us for about five days. "HAD," an irreplaceable ever-smiling Trail Angel, joined us as well. Smasher returned, thank God, and she was in good health. And me! We created a base camp setting at the 501 AT shelter and began with day hikes northbound.

As we were settling around the shelter's picnic table for an evening meal, an elderly married couple arrived carrying their backpacks ready to overnight in the shelter. This Maine couple were on their second AT thru-hike and celebrating their 50th wedding anniversary year on the Trail. The happy couple were in their 80s and 'fit as a fiddle.' Their first AT thru-hike occurred on their honeymoon! I was inspired by their love of life and love for each other.

On the first day hike, Smasher tripped over a log, fell, and hit her head on a rock. After a quick trip to a minor emergency clinic, we were assured that she was okay, except for a gigantic black eye. We made up horrific stories about her black eye to entertain the hikers that we passed along the Trail.

The magnificent rocky ridgelines mark this portion of the AT in Pennsylvania. The AT meanders along the Blue Mountain ridge with pastoral vistas allowing you to peek out into the valley below as you watch hawks soaring above the ridgeline. Pulpit Rock (elevation 1,582 feet) is one of several spots along this section of the Trail to stop for a snack with a view. We enjoyed breaks to sit down among the forest ferns and drink-in the quiet and the friendship time. Sometimes we added a short devotional to our break. The

Trail surface in this area gives merit to the name "Rocksylvania." Grapefruit-sized stones that twist ankles and scrape shins were constant on the Trail. Over these Trail miles, hiking boots do not touch soil, only rocks.

Our Trail Angel, HAD, gravitated to this Trail section over past years because of his interest in birdwatching, specifically hawks. Because of the nearby hawk nesting areas, Hawk Mountain Sanctuary was established near the AT. When HAD was not busy with dropping us off or picking us up at the Trail road crossings, he was enjoying the busy fall season of watching hawks soar through the sky.[15]

Port Clinton is the next Trail town headed northbound. As we left the wooded mountain ridge and followed the Trail downhill into town, this friendly town grabbed our hearts right away. We had read in an AT resource book about the town's open-air pavilion available for shelter. The sprinkle of rain turned into steady rainfall, so we located the pavilion and moved our gear under its shelter just in time. The rainfall remained steady for two or more days which made the pavilion a huge blessing to us. When we got off the Trail at the end of the day, we were comforted by tents already set up inside the pavilion, where we ate and relaxed at the picnic tables. We relished the dry comfort and cautiously watched the nearby Little Schuylkill River rising and overflowing its banks. It was another cool and rainy September on the AT. This Texan was only glad that the weather was not hot and rainy.[16]

One of the scariest Trail surfaces to traverse is the Knife's Edge which is northbound on the AT from Port Clinton. There is another AT Knife's Edge near Mt Katahdin, Me. which is also difficult. I

---

[15] Read Reflection Devotional *Encouraging* to become more acquainted with HAD's servant heart.

[16] Read the Reflection Devotional *Shelter* for more details

haven't hiked the Maine Knife's Edge, but the one we crossed on this Trail section required 30 minutes of crawling up its difficult and potentially hazardous rocks.

The following narrative comes from my journaling after crossing the Pennsylvania Knife's Edge on the AT.

---※---

After much mental jousting with my fears, I realized my choice must be to believe. The Knife's Edge was a ridge of rock slab just wide enough to walk or crawl down. It went on and on as I looked out at the vast rock outcropping that was the AT summiting the mountaintop. If I had known the difficult level of this part of the Trail, I surely would have by-passed it somehow. But the best chozice I could make was to face my fear, use my years of experience in similar situations and ultimately <u>believe.</u>

Daily life is often like this. Fear and anxiety come at us unexpectedly. When we are surprised by our fears, it is doubly hard to act out on our beliefs and our faith. We humans want to react in fearful situations. But when we do find the courage to face life using our faith in God, faith is fortified and our trust in Him grows.

After slowly crossing the Knife's Edge, I turned and looked back at the intimidating obstacle. I made it! But, before I got too full of myself and self-confident, I amended my victory self-talk right away. Thanking the Lord, my Great Comforter and Guide, for calming my fears, helping me to focus as well as move forward into action. I sang a song of praise and I danced!!!

---※---

The 2011 Trail miles were fewer than past annual hikes. Our trip ended shortly after the Knife's Edge crossing, due to a phone call from Tim. Unlike ten years earlier when pay phones were the method of staying in touch, in 2011, my cell phone was able to receive a signal in most AT areas that were not massively remote, like the national forests. My husband Tim's medical concerns were continuing to expand, and I needed to return to Texas.

Tim had two throat surgeries for an esophagus problem before I left on the hiking trip in 2011. Unfortunately, a nerve in his voice box was injured during one of the surgeries and Tim lost his voice. As a pastor without a preaching voice, Tim was understandably struggling. I was stressed as well watching Tim go through multiple medical procedures without an end in sight.

On my two-day drive home from the Trail, I carried so much peace because my stress was released, and I had returned to trusting that God would provide. The AT had once again wrapped me in God's Nature and given me the pervasive all-encompassing reminder that I needed. God is in control. Not Tim. Not Beth, thank God! God is in control; thanks be to God. A journaling from this time contains a note that is relevant to share - *"I am walking for spiritual renewal more than AT miles."*

Within a couple of weeks upon returning home, Tim underwent stress tests to ascertain if his heart could undergo another surgery on his throat. I cannot find enough words of gratitude to God for preparing me for what came as unexpected additional medical challenges for Tim. The heart stress tests were recommended, only as a protocol based on his age and the recent surgeries. They revealed the immediate need for triple bypass heart surgery. Tim had a heart condition known "the widow maker." This heart condition is usually found on an autopsy table because it is not easily diagnosed. We would not have known of Tim's heart condition if he had not lost his voice and medical procedures were being planned to address that condition. During his heart surgery, I sat with my son RW in an empty waiting room late at night and prayed for God's provision once again. I prayed for God's protection and comfort as this jolting surprising situation surrounded me. I am thankful that my relationship with God was already in place and ready for me to be within His comforting arms. I had learned to pray without ceasing, keeping Jesus at my side.

Tim came through the heart surgery in good health even though he continued to adapt to life with a limited voice. We began to have conversations about whether it was high time to retire.[17]

Reflection Devotionals: Shelter, Encouraging, Faithfulness, Holy Matrimony, Trail Angels, Transitions, Living Water

---

[17] In December, 2011, Tim had surgery on his larynx which allowed him to regain a speaking voice and to continue his ministry until his retirement in July, 2014.

The Infamous Max Patch on a Stormy Day © SarahJDecker

2012 September – North Carolina/Tennessee border to fill in the Trail mileage gaps

Tim had started calling me an athlete! As he typically does in our loving marriage, he was half teasing me and half pointing out a new reality. Slowly I was coming to terms with my new physical fitness. Though I questioned my athlete status, I totally trusted the feelings of a resilient Christian faith. My belief in the nature of God and my relationship with Him were clear to me. I was beginning to accept God's plan that the AT miles would be completed, and that God had more life chapters ahead for me, after completing the AT. But those plans were still a mystery to me. Tim and I often talked about his long-time commitment to help me finish the AT after he retired. We were walking towards the retirement reality for both of us and completing the AT miles would be the first vacation trip of that new lifestyle. I felt peaceful and held happy expectations.

2012 was a short mileage year. But the short milage was necessary to complete the southern Appalachian Trail miles that had been left unattended for years. Two separate trips occurred. On one trip, Smasher day hiked with me. The second Trail trip became a short backpacking trip. Trail Angel HAD joined us in his encouraging and supportive role. Smasher's divorce had finalized, and its resolution left her busy with emptying the family home, preparing to sell it. We decided to day hike the magnificent Trail miles near her home in Franklin, NC., AT territory that was Smasher's beloved home turf. I was grateful for the opportunity to be present with my precious Trail buddy for a brief time during this pivotal change in her life.

Where the Trail traverses near Smasher's home in Franklin, NC, there is a captivating view of the mountain ridge. This ridgeline view includes the spectacular profile of Albert Mountain (5,220 feet elevation) on the AT. The ridgeline sits to the south, close to the NC border with Georgia and, on the north, close to the southern boundary of Great Smoky Mountain NP. As the Trail leaves Georgia and enters NC, the Trail maintains an altitude of more than 4,000 feet and stays above that height for the next 26 miles. Zigzagging in several directions, it first swings around the headwaters of the Tallulah River and then the Nantahala River. The Trail then climbs above 5,000 feet on the bald summit of Standing Indian Mountain (5,498 feet elevation).

The next 75 miles northbound, the Trail traverses a series of jumbled ridges – the Nantahala, Stecoah, Cheoah, and Yellow Creek Mountains. Albert Mountain also sits within this jumble of mountains. Those who have hiked the AT in New England refer to this stretch of the Trail in NC as a training ground for hiking in New Hampshire and Maine. This is true especially for the steep, rock-scrambled ascent of Albert Mountain. Hikers have speculated that there are more steep ascents and descents per mile between Cheoah Bald and the southern boundary of Great Smoky Mountain NP than any other stretch of the AT. When Smasher and I climbed the Trail up Albert Mountain, I truly felt like I was back in New Hampshire.

Our three-day backpacking trip was on the Trail section north of Great Smoky Mountain NP. On this trip we once again saw infamous locations on the Trail. Max Patch (4,629 feet elevation) is a well-known site with its broad, open, and grassy meadow mountain top view. Standing on this mountain top, we saw the East's most formidable peaks, including Mount Mitchell (6,684 feet elevation,) the highest peak in the Appalachian Mountains in North America. As we traveled further northbound, we crossed many other mountain tops and eventually dropped to the French Broad River at Hot Springs, NC. In 1795, hot springs were discovered and plans to commercialize it began with a road access. The elegant Mountain Park Hotel, which could accommodate 1,000 guests, opened in the 1890s, and for the next two decades visitors soaked themselves in the hotel's bathhouse, built on the springs. The hot springs were also used as a bubbling beverage for its healing water properties. Though I had thoroughly enjoyed the "down-home" hot springs bath at the end of my 2000 AT trip, this Hot Springs visit did not allow time for the pleasure of the therapeutic mineral baths.

Our last night out on the AT, we backpacked to Davenport Gap on the northern boundary of Great Smoky Mountain NP. We stayed at Standing Bear Farm hiking hostel for the primary purpose of enjoying hiker camaraderie on this short AT trip. We certainly accomplished that purpose when we slept in a bunkhouse with seven men! I am so glad that I had my ear plugs on that night!

On the two-day drive home to Texas, once again I used my alone time to reflect on this AT trip as well as the 16 other hikes that had occurred over years. I left the year 2012 with a pleasant rear view mirror image. My faith journey was becoming more predictable because I was relying on my tried-and-true beliefs about 1) Who God is! 2) Who Beth "Spirit" was becoming! And 3) The Nature of my ongoing relationship with God!

Reflection Devotionals: Discerning, Strength, Grieving, Trusting, Transitions, Chosen, Pacing, Fellowship

New Beginning Steps: 2013 to 2015

AT White Blaze Marker on Rock with Millerman and Smasher Leigh Gap

2013 September – Bake Oven Knob Rd., Pennsylvania northbound to Bear Mountain bridge, NY

As 2013 began, I was aware that my business of life coaching was flourishing and my private talks with God helped me to understand why. My soul invigorated the business. The Holy Spirit was moving individuals and groups, transforming their lives, and allowing me the joy to be a witness to this transformation. The business was booming due to *The Lifestyle Goal Setting for Women* book that I wrote for group life coaching. It became the backbone of my business and publishing this group coaching Workbook allowed these groups to form quickly, and enabled clients to sustain a life enriching journey without my presence.

A successful surgery allowed Tim to regain his voice and allowed him to continue pastoring his church. 2013 began with

Tim and I making a commitment to God's calling once again and to establish retirement plans. It was time to trust God to fulfill our lives with new purposes as His servants. People were resisting our plans to retire, but another life transition was ready to launch.

This September 2013 AT hiking trip is best known for the outstanding Trail miles accomplished in very few weeks – 155 miles! A great returning team of Millerman (Trail Name), Smasher and I was successful in making long mileage days happen with three vehicles accommodating a leap-frog method of shuttling between them. If my memory serves me well, this trip was the origin of the creative option for quick set up for day hiking between parked cars at road crossings with the Trail. Smasher and I parked a car and hiked south while Millerman parked his car and hiked north on the same day hike section. When we passed each other on the Trail, we switched car keys, so everyone had a ride back to the base camp as a parked car destination was reached. Clever!

An initial Trail attraction northbound was the steep climb out of Lehigh Gap, Pa. The three of us gingerly approached the loose rock mountainside because it was so steep, but also because it was our first day on the Trail. It was a windy day looking down on the historic coal mining of Lehigh Gap.

Choosing from a variety of shelter options was an additional ongoing feature of the hiking trip. Initially we chose to stay in AT shelters and small hiking hostels usually operated by families. As we moved further north on the Trail and into more urban areas, we gravitated to inexpensive motel rooms that were conveniently located near the Trail.

At the Pennsylvania border with New Jersey, there is a spectacular mountain overlook of the Delaware River. We enjoyed the panorama of this location, Delaware Water Gap, while eating lunch on a relaxing Trail break. The forests of this region are different from the southern Appalachians which is in keeping with the monumental variety of vegetation throughout the AT terrain. The northern hardwood forest in this area includes the maples, beeches, and birch, along these ridges.

We knew that the urban areas were approaching as we continued northbound and came upon the Interstate 80 overpass. What a jolt into the alternate reality from walking in the ever-changing forests to walking the AT pedestrian overpass of the Interstate! There is a retreat center near the AT, operated by the Appalachian Mountain Club (AMC) which we noticed just a few miles further on the Trail. Trekkers can shelter at this center, a place particularly known for excellent outdoor training programs.

As we continued northbound on the Trail into New Jersey, Smasher, Millerman and I noticed the urban neighborhoods becoming more prevalent. It was not unusual to observe children playing in their backyards as we moved onward down the Trail.

I was fascinated by the state boundary lines creating a 90-degree angle on the northern tip of New Jersey called High Point. New Jersey State Park High Point has the state's highest elevation, a mountain top of 1,803 feet. The AT passes through this landmark on a steep uphill climb as we furthered onward northbound.

In low areas of New Jersey are what Texans might call a swamp, but it is not. It is a bog! Like the Trail pathway in Maine, the New Jersey AT section addresses these hard to maintain footpaths with wooden planks, sometimes covering an expansive length of the Trail. One of these expansive bogs exists north of High Point, NJ in Wawayanda State Park. One of them, Pine Bog, has close to seventeen feet depth of peat accumulation.

After a few miles from the New Jersey/New York border there is another landmark, Mombasha High Point. Millerman, Smasher and I arrived on this ridge top on September 11th remembering the national tragedy of 9/11. We had a special opportunity to memorialize 9/11 at that location because we could see the New York City skyline. Furthermore, three men suddenly arrived and joined us on Mombasha High Point coming from the opposite direction. They were members of the Wounded Warriors project, ex-military, and thru-hikers commemorating the wounded soldiers from the Iraq War.

New York state has 110 Trail miles between Delaware Water Gap (NJ/NY border) and the Hudson River, our destination for this year's hiking trip. At this point, we were like horses who could smell the barn. We became day hiking machines. Frankly, I do not remember much of the final 40 miles because of the quick pace we enjoyed.

We passed through Sterling Forest, then Harriman State Park and finally Bear Mountain State Park which butts up to the western bank of the Hudson River. It is important to note that the area of Harriman and Bear Mountain State Parks is where the first section of the Appalachian Trail was opened on October 7, 1923.

Ending the Trail section on a totally fun note, having "Santa Claus," Millerman, with us on the Trail was an all-out constant fun time. When Millerman returned to hike with Smasher and me after the 2003 trip, he had taken up a career as a professional Santa Claus. A persona that he pulled out of his pack while on resupply trips into town. As we entered Bear Mountain SP, there was a weekend Octoberfest gathering with a polka band. Millerman pulled out his Santa Claus hat and began dancing. Within minutes he was the center of the festive event! Everyone laughed and cheered Santa Claus in the gathering and, of course, the children, and adults too, wanted a photo taken with him.

As I drove home to Texas over two long days, thankfulness to God for the great provision and protection that brought our success poured out of me through prayers and singing praise songs as I drove. God had been with us on all those AT miles covered.

But I was now looking ahead to 2014 and 2015, knowing that Smasher and I would hopefully complete the 2000 miles, with Tim as our Trail Angel. I felt compelled by thoughts of closure about completion of the AT, but other matters as well. Tim and I were deeply invested in proper closure with church ministry, and I was seeking ways to downsize my business to stay in tandem with our needs as a married retired couple. Gone were the days of dreading a major life transition because I now stayed close in my walk with Jesus. Through those long conversations with God while I drove home, I was able to throttle my tendency to jump forward and instead, practice the discipline to walk beside Jesus as I yearned for future aspirations. Now the life transition of becoming retired felt like a blessed and exciting adventure. Thank you, God.

Reflection Devotionals: Fun and Recreation, Pacing, Transitions, Joy, Shelter, Grieving, Trail Angels, Fellowship

Backpacking South from Mt. Washington Summit

2014 August and September – Vermont/Massachusetts border northbound to Maine/NH border

As 2014 began, I looked forward to the annual hiking trip, especially because it was a two-month vacation with Tim. Additionally, the Trail miles in New Hampshire were retracing 2001 steps that were pivotal in my faith journey of trusting God and discovering how His trustworthiness and love is limitless.[18] I was eager to share lengthy Trail time with Tim which would include shared faith experiences.

The 2014 AT trip totaled 264.6 Trail miles through Vermont and New Hampshire. I was very satisfied. We planned the trip for months ahead establishing a novel approach founded on our purchase of a camper trailer, a Rockwood Roo, which we used as a

---

[18] 2001 September Hiking Trip

base camp while Smasher and I optimized mileage by day hiking. The camper had three queen-size beds and a bathroom with a door. Tim was an all-purpose Trail Angel as the truck/camper driver and shuttle service, base camp boss, cook, and housekeeper. Without one doubt, we could not have accomplished this great mileage as well as enjoyed each day's luxurious evening without our Trail Angel Tim. We found four campgrounds that were strategically located near the Trail. The cost of motel lodging in New England is high and lodging near the Trail sections was problematic. This plan was surely a blessing. [19]

The trip began at the Vermont/Massachusetts border where we embarked on the Trail headed northbound into Vermont. After meeting Smasher in Bennington, Vermont and establishing base camp, we took to the Trail logging about ten miles each day. The first few weeks of our time in Vermont were challenging because of the steady light rainfall and cool temperatures. Within the first hiking days we met very few long-distance hikers even though it was still summer in mid-August.

One late afternoon, we were hiking through a lowland area where previous hurricane damage to the Trail thoroughfare was significant. A backpacking woman came up from behind us moving fast and immediately we knew she was a thru-hiker. "T-Bird," her Trail name, was closing in on her final weeks of a long northbound AT thru-hike. As we stopped to visit on the Trail, she shared feelings of despair and doubts as well as loneliness. Smasher and I invited her to stay with us at our campground site and to enjoy an evening of home cooked food and good fellowship. She jumped at the opportunity. We enjoyed our time together that evening

---

[19] Read Reflectional Devotional: *Trail Angels*

getting acquainted with T-Bird and hearing about her adventures on the AT.[20]

Part of our pre-planned routine with this trip was to take a day off the Trail each week and enjoy the surrounding tourist attractions. This practice is called a "Zero Day." We thoroughly enjoyed Robert Frost's humble family home in Bennington Vermont which had been converted to a museum about his works and the family life.

Further northbound a special treat awaited trekkers following the Trail over Killington Mountain. The snow ski enterprise on this mountain provides AT hikers their ski lift service for free. Killington mountain is a picturesque area for tourists and winter recreation enthusiasts. It was a message of hospitality as we enjoyed the luxury of using the ski lift to hike downhill on each shoulder of Killington Mountain.

In August and September, we found abundant wildlife in Vermont. One early morning on the Trail, we came upon a porcupine standing in the Trail which was a new experience in all our AT hiking years. Throughout the AT, there is an abundance of orange lizards. We saw another here. I think the lizard was a broadhead skink. The forest floor throughout Vermont is often covered with beautiful ferns. And the trees are frequently decorated with a variety of mushroom and scales. An unusual mushroom, named Indian pipes, was prevalent. We had seen this eye-catching white pipe growth in many parts of the Trail. The dampness of the forests is such a difference from my Texas hill country woodlands. Occasionally the AT left the forests and went through pastures and crop fields. At those points of change, we once again enjoyed a uniquely crafted fence stile aiding the hikers over a fence line on the Trail.[21]

---

[20] Read Reflectional Devotional: *Hospitality*

[21] Reference *The Appalachian Trail: a Visitor's Companion* for more information on area flora and fauna

As Smasher and I approached this final stage of completing 2,000 miles on the AT, we both felt a calling to share our love for God's presence in Nature with greater punctuation. We chose to give objects that conveyed that message to people we met along the Trail. Smasher gave the faith-based message of New Beginnings through a butterfly sticker. The butterfly is a Christian message of being born again like the chrysalis transforms into a butterfly.

I gave a faith-based message of peace through a small balsawood dove. The dove represents the Christian message of the Holy Spirit bringing peace to all. Throughout this hiking trip as well as the 2015 final trip, we gave the butterfly stickers and the doves to strangers we met along the Trail. [22]

In the White Rocks, Vermont area of the Trail, there are expansive displays of AT trekkers who created artistic rock sculptures, alongside the shoreline of the lakes that are adjacent to the Trail. What a spiritually uplifting message I received while admiring the patient time people enjoyed recreating in Nature. Smasher and I built a rock sculpture in this location as well commemorating our multiple years together on the Trail. We added our butterflies and doves to the rock sculpture making our celebration include gratitude for God's presence on our journey which was clearly a spiritual pilgrimage.

On August 24th, we moved north to Gorham, New Hampshire to traverse the AT in the Presidential Mountain Range, also known as the White Mountains. Hiking through this alpine region above tree line requires access to the protective enclosed shelter of AT huts. These huts are safe shelters in the likelihood of quick severe weather conditions catching hikers with little or no warning. We had to reserve lodging space in these five AT huts before they closed for the season, usually by mid-September. In 2001, I backpacked ten days through this region before exiting the 6-week trip

---

[22] Read Reflection Devotional: *Peacemaking*

plan, due to my poor choice of hiking partners. For the first time in our blessed hiking partnership, I repeated these AT miles to be Smasher's companion on a Trail section she had not covered. You should know my small contribution to Smasher happened because of her precious gift of companionship to me in the 2002 and 2003 AT miles. Those 300 miles were a repeat for Smasher so that likewise, I could have her Trail companionship.

To begin this six-day backpacking journey, Tim drove us to the top of Mt Washington, the highest peak in the Northeast (6,288 feet elevation). The average summertime high is 52 degrees. There is a weather station on the summit. On April 12, 1934, an on-land wind speed of 231 mph was recorded, which stood as the world's record until 1996 when it was broken in Australia with a velocity of 253.

Smasher and I made our way down the mountain on the Trail as it went over granite rock boulders, averaging about seven tough miles a day. We stayed at the following AT huts - Mizpah Spring, Crawford Notch, Zealand Falls, Galehead, and Greenleaf. At the Greenleaf Hut, I had a profoundly affirming experience by reading my AT Hut journal entry from September 2001 when I chose to exit the Trail and return home.

Following are the words I found in the Hut's archived journal of Sept. 26, 2001:

After hiking SOBO for ten days, I'm unfortunately getting off the Trail. Fatigue has set in beyond any short-term recovery. But I'll revamp my planning and come this way again because I'm not going to give up my goal, the entire AT. Your mountains are just gorgeous. I'll spread the word back home of their beauty and the hospitality of the local folk. "Spirit" Beth Abel, Austin, Texas

Reading my hand-writing thirteen years later was a sobering force of God's presence over all those years, holding my hand and walking beside me through life. Praise God!

As Smasher and I continued onward, we eventually came to a long and steep descent into Franconia Notch where Tim had been waiting in the parking lot. It was weirdly funny to me that the "Old Man of the Mountain" profile had broken off this mountain in the recent past. The rock formation of the "Old Man of the Mountain" is the iconic symbol of Franconia Notch. But Nature decided to change it![23]

When we returned to our Gorham, NH campground for additional AT day hikes north of the Presidential Range, I had another "God is present" experience. I will keep the story brief here by suggesting that you read the full story in the Devotional Faithfulness. I was still floating from reading my prediction in the Greenleaf Hut journal entry of 2001, when I met Trail Angel Joe. After giving him a dove and stating my faith message of Peace, Joe shared his faith story which was profound. And the next day Joe gave me a balsawood replica of an AT shelter which he handcrafted. It hangs in my family room at home to this day.

Towards the end of this two-month hiking excursion, Smasher and I were day hiking through a forest as usual, looking forward to eating lunch in Hanover. Suddenly, the forested Trail opened into the backside of a baseball field! It was bizarre. We had entered the town of Hanover, NH, home to Dartmouth College. We walked the streets of town as the AT white blazes on street light poles guided us. We found the Chinese restaurant right on the Trail where Tim joined us for a festive lunch.

---

[23] There are several poems written about the Old Man of the Mountain

The last story for 2014 Trail experiences is about finding a "restroom" among the Maple trees. Smasher and I were on the Trail deep in a Vermont forest when we realized there was rubber half inch tubing connecting to each tree in the forest. It was a dark area so it took a while for us to grasp that this tubing continued a great distance as far as we could see. As we were exploring the possible purpose of the vast network of tubing, I decided it was time for a "body break." I left the Trail and climbed over and under the tubing to find a private spot away from the Trail. I did my "body break" business, picked up my pack and hiking poles and discovered that I was disoriented. I could not remember the direction that I had come from when I left the Trail. Honestly, the vast maze of tubing confused my generally good sense of orientation. Fortunately, Smasher was within ear shot and heard my yelling. Once her voice led me back to the Trail path, we solved the mystery of the tubing. The Maple trees were in season for harvesting maple syrup and the tubing was a clever collection method for people to do so.

As we completed this two month trek though Vermont and New Hampshire, Tim and I were surprised and delighted by Smasher's gift of a delightful evening together. The three of us enjoyed a local production of the play, "Mark Twain Tonight," a one-man play based on the sayings and stories of Mark Twain's life.

Nearing the end of my journey on the Appalachian Trail, I felt conflicted by the multiple facets of an incredible life experience coming to closure. A major part of that conflict was the basic question, "What's next?" I was reminded of Ezekiel 37: 1-3, where the prophet was directed by God to a valley filled with dry bones! *"He asked me, "Son of man, can these bones live?" I said, "Sovereign LORD, you alone know." Vs 3.*

Reflection Devotionals: Fun and Recreation, Grieving, Faithfulness, Hospitality, Trail Angels, Holy Matrimony, Transitions, Peacemaking, Celebrating, Shelter, When Nature Calls

Balsawood Dove in Hand, Spirit says "Peace Be With You."

2015 August and September – Vermont/Massachusetts border southbound to Bear Mountain bridge, NY

The Beth, the "Spirit," that started the Trail so many years earlier was not the same person who found herself just a few weeks away from completing her epoch goal. I was ready to get the AT behind me and to move on with the next season of my life. But completion of the AT was like leaving a longtime friend.

The 2000 AT mile faith journey was all about creating and celebrating a meaningful ending to the twenty hiking trips and two decades of living. For me, the fiber of endings is totally wrapped together with the fiber of beginnings. My approach to life is oriented to God's participation, especially in life transitions. As the 2015 trip approached, I knew the Truth that God was somehow weaving all the beginnings and endings together. Also, I knew that God wanted me to write about this lifelong experience. I was to thoroughly describe God's presence, especially in times of life transitions. Now that I can reflect on the whole of this faith journey, I see how God changed my life from hiking the AT into a lifelong spiritual pilgrimage. For a long time, I just did not know how to get started. The challenge was not finding things to say, but to get started on the direction that the Lord was leading me.

It didn't help that this final leg of our trek through Massachusetts and Connecticut, was frankly one of the least interesting sections of the AT. Rolling hills, manageable obstacles and terrains, frequent small towns and villages replaced the challenges of high peaks and rock climbs.

The image that keeps coming to mind is a reflection on my senior year in High School! A desire to 'just get it done!' as well as savoring the high points of this part of my life while being deeply infected with "Senioritis." So, rather than write about the challenges or lack thereof of these final hikes, I am choosing to lift up the highlights of those last wonderful miles that I was able to walk with my hiking sister and faith friend, Smasher.

Our plan for 2015 was essentially the same as 2014 with Tim, Smasher and I setting up a base camp which allowed Smasher and I to do our day hikes while Tim, our Trail Angel, kept house.

Beginning the last hiking trip on July 28, 2015, was a bittersweet day and the weather appropriately matched my mood. We established our first base camp near the Vermont/Massachusetts border. The first day out Smasher and I launched our day hiking from the state line southbound on the AT to Mt Greylock. The weather was cool and misty when we arrived there, a dense fog engulfing the War Memorial Tower which honors those who died in WW I. At 3,491 feet elevation, Mt Greylock is the highest peak in Massachusetts.

As the AT wanders through the Berkshires, it passes through many small towns in Massachusetts. With the AT white blazes that mark the pathway placed on nearby objects like telephone poles, we navigated through many villages using sidewalks instead of a dirt path. Hikers on long or short journeys mingle with the townsfolk for another aspect of the diverse Trail experience. Some of the towns provide a hiker kiosk detailing a town map of hiker services available there.

The Trail in Massachusetts is quite gentle with few mountains which allowed us to comfortably average eight miles a day. Near the town of Pittsfield, the AT runs along lake frontage and through damp lowlands. We hiked over lengthy wood planks on the AT as it crossed bogs. Further southbound the Trail moved into forests with rocky streams and ponds. We also enjoyed Massachusetts's diversity on the AT as we crossed fence line stiles and crop fields.

With frequent urban area connections, Smasher and I saw an increased number of hikers on the AT over the previous year. Many of the hikers were from the local area. Over the past three or four years, Smasher and I had noticed a newly developing trend that we found exciting. More and more women were taking to the AT to hike or backpack a long distance. We noticed that more women were solo thru-hiking or taking on a long-distance backpacking trip with multiple women in the group. This was rarely occurring when we began our hiking trips together in 2002.

Near the Massachusetts/Connecticut border, Tim, Smasher, and I re-established our second basecamp location to access the AT more easily in that area. The Trail terrain continued to remain moderate elevation shifts and frequently passed through small villages. The AT shelters along this Trail section were well maintained and numerous. Trail magic from AT enthusiasts in the local communities appeared along our way daily. The communities next to the AT path surely embraced the trekking visitors passing through on the footpath. We found ice chests loaded with cold drinks and snack food as well as Trail magic in the form of welcoming greetings from the community that warmed our hearts. Trail magic sure does lift my spirits!

One of the joys that we found as we logged our miles with every step bringing us closer to our destination, was an ice cream stand near our campsite that specialized in giant banana splits. I recall that eating ice cream desserts as an "end of the day reward" got us through the many Trail miles of Virginia. This giant banana split reward was a repeat of that reward at the end of a long hike!

The newly released movie "A Walk in the Woods" based on the famous book by Bill Bryson was playing near our base camp site. The three of us seized the convenient opportunity for an evening out and laughed heartily. We enjoyed recognizing familiar AT terrain throughout the movie. Robert Redford and Nick Nolte were hilarious actors in the movie, helping us laugh at ourselves as older people, out on the Trail for life meaning and for adventure, just like these characters.

I pleasantly recall numerous days of excellent weather as we leisurely hiked the rolling Trail terrain along the Connecticut River. A hiker's delight! The easy terrain and manageable pace allowed us to maintain the 2014 practice of 'Zero Days.' We had a variety of activities on Zero Days, one of which was enjoying the fresh apples and other fall vegetables found in the local farms.

Before we left southern Connecticut for New York State, Tim and I were able to connect with one of his high school friends, Walt Galloway, and his wife, who live in Rhode Island. We enjoyed a wonderful lunch in New Haven, CT overlooking the shores of Long Island Sound.

We also toured the family home of Franklin and Eleanor Roosevelt in Hyde Park, not far from our AT location. The museum home and property sit on a scenic high bank above the Hudson River. What a pleasant setting for these famous people to find comfort in their private lives.

Crossing into New York State on the AT, Smasher and I were astonished to come upon the AT Railroad Station, adjacent to the Trail. On weekends, a commuter train leaves the platform for NYC Grand Central Station multiple times a day. And commuter trains return to this platform as well. I was impressed!

On Schaghticoke Mountain near the Connecticut/New York state line, Smasher and I met two young women who were thru-hikers. They were backpackers headed northbound nearing their end of several months on the Trail. The women shared their story of friendship through their college years and recent graduation. They were celebrating this milestone with an AT thru-hike together. The world of work was their next life step after completing the AT. We shared with them the joyful story of being extremely near the end of our 2,000 AT miles as well, after years instead of months to complete the journey. The four of we women celebrated our lives on the mountain top, a mountain whose name I cannot pronounce! Tears flowed as Smasher and I gave each woman a butterfly and a dove to send them on their way.[24]

---

[24] See devotional *Peacemaking*

I could see the end in sight! The last steps of our 2000-mile trek were to walk across the Bear Mountain Bridge where we would arrive at Bear Mountain State Park. It is the place where Millerman stole the show when he arrived at Octoberfest as Santa Claus in 2013. But there were still mountains to climb before we arrived at this goal. And God was not done with us yet!

Only a day or two after this special moment on the Schaghticoke mountain top, we were stepping onto the grounds of Graymoor Spiritual Life Center, marking the beginning of our last day in the New England states area of the Trail. Over the multiple decades of reading personal stories and information about the AT, this hospitality by Franciscan monks to AT hikers was of deep spiritual interest to me. Over a century ago, Father Paul Wattson founded the Franciscan Friars of the Atonement. In 1970, the Graymoor Spiritual Living Center opened at this location near Bear Mountain bridge on the Hudson River. The Spiritual Center offers people of many different religious traditions and all walks of life an opportunity to slow down and encounter the Spirit in their lives. Because of the monks' hospitality, for many years AT hikers found shelter within the walls of the Center. In recent years, their hospitality moved to year-round outdoor accommodations on the campus. Sometimes the hikers comprised a tent city of AT trekkers passing through the area. The Trail passes through the expansive well-kept grounds with the cross of Jesus Christ and other faith messages evident to all "Who will see." Both Smasher and I felt peace and calm resonating in our walking pace as we traversed the spiritual and holy grounds.

Overwhelmed with years of thoughts swirling in my mind as I walked the Graymoor Spiritual Center grounds, I finally sat down and attempted to let the thoughts and feelings intertwine and settle.

In preparation for the book's manuscript, I found the following journal entry from August, 2015. I was astounded by God's ever-present residence in my soul! I could see God foretelling the journey my life would take after the AT trip of 2015. I can now see how God weaves conversations with me into the journey of daily living, guiding me to author this devotional book years later.

"I used to think that I was bland – uninteresting. Now I know that others see me as calm. Pass the Peace/ Peace be with You and Be blessed with a New Beginning (my gift of a dove and Smasher's gift of a butterfly) These messages are being given to hikers we see on the Trail. Though it's what we convey, it is also what we yearn to embrace in our own daily life. Living life fully is not found in the luxury of frequent vacations or hiking trips escaping from the complexity of life. It is found in creating a weaving of interlocking threads of life that when practiced with discipline, create a fullness and beauty to life that is peace. That every day was a new beginning.

So, my challenge is to not just take the Trail back home to Austin, but to take Austin to the Trail and interweave into a lifestyle. That's why I am doing 2000 miles so I can master this approach and find fullness of life. It is also a positive influence to others who seek glimpses of what their life could be like through God's Grace. By living this way, I am a better person in all venues."

Finding the self-discipline to author this devotional book came from God's continued ever-presence persisting me. God kept reminding me of my promise to Him. Over the six years after finishing the Trail in 2015, I have been collecting my journals, writing the devotionals, and preparing to publish. Like finishing the AT, finishing the book is another life transition and therefore filled with mixed feelings. It is truly a case of 'senioritis.'

A friend who listens to God's voice contacted me with the following words of encouragement from Our Lord God through His Word, the Bible. These words encouraged me to 'Get the book written.'

Isaiah 30:8 *Now go and write down these words concerning Egypt. They will then stand until the end of time as a witness to Israel's unbelief. For these people are stubborn rebels who refuse to pay any attention to the Lord's instructions.* (NLT)

Back to the grounds of Graymoor Spiritual Center and my closing ponderings. I was not totally settled. But I got up, put on my pack, and walked on.

Once Smasher and I left the peaceful and reflective environment of Graymoor, we descended to the Hudson River and crossed the Bear Mountain bridge. This was a personal terminus for both of us to 15 years and millions of steps. It was a different type of experience for us to finish across that long and busy bridge over a truly majestic river. The different experience reminded me that the AT is a long journey with vastly differing experiences. Just like Life!

Tim was there waiting for us, taking a video of our last steps. Going back to my 'senior year in high school' reflection, it felt like putting down the pencil on the last final exam on the last day of school.

I was ready to move on to the next chapters of my life, the chapters that God was preparing for me. Since Tim's retirement in 2014, our lives were at a significant phase of our marriage. Both of our children had married, Adrianne in 2014 and RW in 2015. Tim's retirement and the scaling back of my private practice were new experiences for us. We were now together most of the time rather than going our separate directions. Being together all the time was peaceful and calming to both of us, but it is a life transition, nevertheless. This life transition was often bringing me unsettled feelings. Thank God that I was better at accepting God's help in transitions than I had been in the past. Fortunately, Tim's health challenges were behind us, but we both found from that challenging time that neither of us could no longer take our health for granted. Reflecting to this moment of the Bear Mountain bridge, I knew God had totally transformed my life which was becoming a spiritual pilgrimage.

But God was not finished with us yet! Three celebrations were still ahead. Expanding on the high school Senior year metaphor, these were "The Prom;" "The Graduation;" and the "Party!"

Smasher and Spirit at Bear Mtn Bridge, Hudson River

2015 September - Final Steps: Bear Mountain State Park, AT Headquarters in Harper's Ferry West Virginia, Tye River near Dutch Haus, Montebello, Virginia

The Prom: Bear Mountain State Park Inn - From the Graymoor Spiritual Center, it is a short hike to Anthony's Nose, a steep descent to the river's edge of the Hudson River. As we descended towards the mighty waters of the Hudson River and then crossed the waters on Bear Mountain bridge, the years of memories flooded my thoughts. Gratitude for God's never-ending presence was the most apparent thought and feeling. Tim captured photos of us as we reached the opposite river bank, ending all but 10 miles of a 2,000-mile journey of a lifetime.

Tim surprised us with overnight accommodations in the luxurious Bear Mountain Lodge followed by a magnificent meal in their formal dining room. After two months of living in a small camping trailer, I fell asleep enjoying the luxurious lodging with thoughts that I could not yet comprehend this ending was real.

Spirit and Smasher receive their AT 2000 Miler Patch

The Graduation: Appalachian Trail Conservancy headquarters in Harpers Ferry –

After our Bear Mountain Lodge experience, Smasher, Tim, and I drove to Harpers Ferry, West Virginia for an in-person acceptance of the AT 2,000-mile certificate and patch. The ATC office manager awarded Smasher and I our certificates and patches. We appreciated the woman's sincere interest in our section hiking completion of the AT. Our picture was taken, our names were posted on the bulletin board, and we celebrated the news that our names would be in the ATC magazine with others that completed their hikes in 2015! Even though it was two days after the Bear Mountain Bridge ending, the feeling of completion was still surreal.

After sheltering in place during the two hurricane seasons, (2003 and 2004,) in the warm hospitality of the Dutch Haus in Montebello, VA, Smasher and I were committed to finishing our last steps on the AT at the nearby Tye River, and holding a celebration at this treasured place with our hosts, Lois and Earl Arnold. Read the *Storms* devotional for more details.

Tye River Bridge: Our Final Steps on the AT
Courtesy of Appalachian Trail Conservancy

'RW', son and Backpacking Buddy, Celebrates with Spirit

The Party: Dutch Haus, Montebello, Virginia -

It was fitting and appropriate that the 'Hurricane Hussies" make their final encore experience in that place with those long time Trail friends.

Smasher's son Jeff and his family came from North Carolina. Our son RW, arrived from Austin, Texas along with our friend Jana Jones who joined our Maine hike 2008. Tim's cousin Sandy and her husband arrived from Wisconsin, and our AT Trail Angel "HAD" and his wife drove up from North Carolina.

On this celebratory weekend, Smasher, and I, with RW along for the walk with three bottles of beer and a cigar in his backpack, completed the last ten miles of the AT arriving at the Tye River. RW memorialized the last ten miles as a videographer and posted it on YouTube[25]. Following that day's hike, we feasted, we wept, we rejoiced and celebrated with Smasher's gift of a fireworks display on the Dutch Haus lawn.

We were two 65-year-old women overwhelmed with gratitude to have been blessed beyond measure with our friendship and the life lessons learned from God's Nature along the Appalachian Trail. I had gained wisdom from God's presence that would continue to guide my life beyond this special celebration time. This was, indeed, a peace beyond my understanding, guiding my life to new beginnings. My spiritual pilgrimage had launched some time ago, conceived and nourished by 20 faith journeys. To God be all the glory! Amen.

***I have fought the good fight, I have finished the race, I have kept the faith.* 2 Timothy 4:7**

Reflection Devotionals: Transitions, Celebrating, Hospitality, Fellowship, Chosen, Living Water, Trail Angels, Fun and Recreation, Peacemaking, Spirit, God's Gifts, When Nature Calls, Diligence

---

[25] "Beth's AT Final Day" https://youtu.be/xrvQkpQCNEg

Natural Fibers in the Weaving of a Faith Journey

I want you woven into a tapestry of love, in touch with everything there is to know of God. Then you will have minds confident and at rest, focused on Christ, God's great mystery. All the richest treasures of wisdom and knowledge are embedded in that mystery and nowhere else. And we've been shown the mystery! I'm telling you this because I don't want anyone leading you off on some wild-goose chase, after other so-called mysteries, or "the Secret."

Colossians 2:2-3 LNT

Introduction to the 40 Reflection Devotionals

As you approach the reading of these reflection devotionals, reread the last page of the opening chapter "AT Hiking Trips Lead to a Spiritual Pilgrimage." The devotionals are placed in one of three parts of my personal faith journey: Moments of Grace, Moments of Belief, Moments of Faith. This is an intentionally loose order, like a "woven tapestry of love." Each reflection devotional stands alone. There is no prescribed order. Find those which have the most value to you in your personal journey with the Lord.

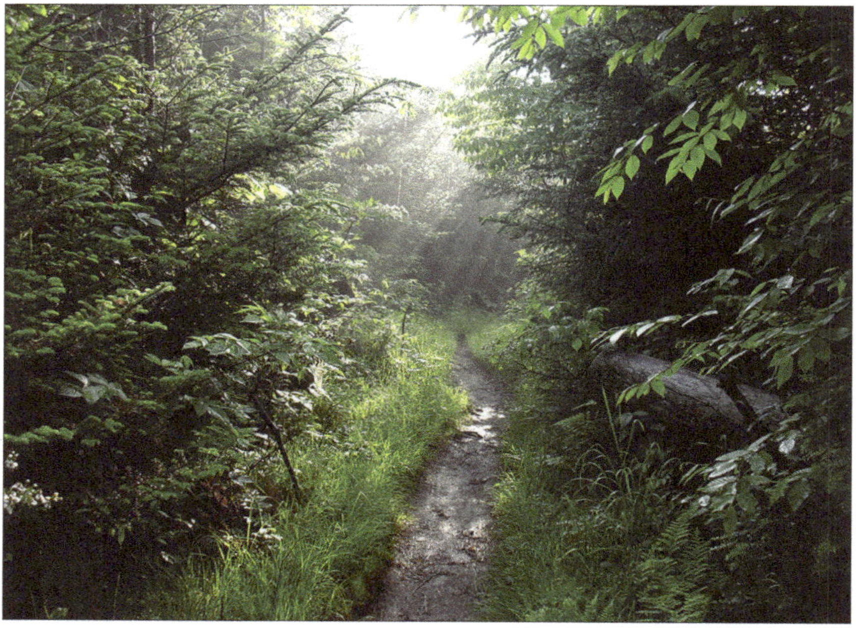

Moments of Grace

Spirit

A Step To Grace: We are not human beings having a spiritual experience. We are spiritual beings having a human experience. *Pierre Teilhard de Chardin*

Psalm 139: 1–10

O LORD, you have examined my heart and know everything about me. You know when I sit down or stand up. You know my thoughts even when I'm far away. You see me when I travel and when I rest at home. You know everything I do. You know what I am going to say even before I say it, LORD. You go before me and follow me. You place your hand of blessing on my head. Such knowledge is too wonderful for me, too great for me to understand! I can never escape from your Spirit! I can never get away from your presence! If I go up to heaven, you are there; if I go down to the grave, you are there. If I ride the wings of the morning, if I dwell by the farthest oceans, even there your hand will guide me, and your strength will support me. NLT

My trail name is "Spirit." A trail name is simply the name that a trail hiker uses with the hiker community while on the Trail, like camp names when you were a kid. Trail names are a great social equalizer and provide anonymity on the Trail. Using Trail names helps strangers become friends without the getting acquainted steps of normal living. Trail names are used in AT shelter log journals as hikers write the recent news of their journey and whereabouts.

Sometimes Trail names are given to a hiker due to unusual moments or irregularities that the hiker chooses to be known by, such as my Trail buddy's name of Smasher. Or a hiker may choose a Trail name because it correlates to something significant for the hiker as I did.

Smasher got her Trail name early in her long-distance backpacking adventures. Smasher has a propensity for tidiness such that I have called her "Martha Stewart of the AT". She is known to sweep out the Trail shelters upon arrival. Smasher got her Trail name when she traveled on a Canadian trail with several women. After dinner one evening while sitting around the campfire together, she noticed several tin cans cluttering the campsite. Smasher promptly collected the tin cans and proceeded to stomp them flat as the group of women watched her work in wonder. They were amazed by her interruption of their leisure setting as Smasher focused on tidiness and prepared to pack out all waste. One woman called out to the group "Let's call her Smasher" and the Trail name stuck. Smasher and Spirit were always a weird combination representing two older women on the AT.

Spirit is the trail name that I chose on my first AT hiking trip,[26] and I continue to cherish this name today. Looking back to that first hiking trip, I started the AT journey with an inkling of awareness that it would transform my identity into a spiritual being. The more that I explored my purpose of life, I left behind the human definitions of identity and embraced the gift God gives everyone - a spirit that relates to God, Our Creator.

My prayer group gave me a small cross before my first hiking trip knowing that I would wear it as a necklace while on the Trail. I have worn the cross necklace throughout the 20 hiking trips to complete the 2,000 miles on the AT. The words "Jesus Christ is Lord" are embedded on the cross.

Identity issues are a common topic of conversations with my counseling clients. Identity is directly tied to our mental health.

---

[26] 1997 June Hiking Trip

By guiding clients to grow in their understanding of how one's identity forms, this guidance to clients eventually encouraged me to seriously examine this identity search for myself.

As I assessed my identity formation process with a chronological approach, I saw a process that began with being a sickly child, then becoming healthy and fit. Being a social worker, a wife, a mother, and a grieving sister who couldn't prevent her brother's suicide. Becoming a born-again Christian, an empty nest questor, an AT hiker, and then the ever-evolving "Spirit." At the point of owning the Trail name and identity of Spirit, these earlier identities faded in their importance as Spirit rose to become the center of my life, lifting up the whole of my being up through a relationship with God.

Jean Deeds, author of *There are Mountains to Climb*, was an major inspiration for me to search for an expansion to my identity through AT adventures. Jean was a 51-year-old career woman with almost no wilderness or camping experience when she gave up a comfortable lifestyle to hike the entire mountainous AT in a six-month sojourn. I was enamored that Jean took to the Trail in 1994, just three years prior to my launch. She too was in search for new life beyond the adult experience of children leaving home. Over the years of AT hiking, I shared Jean's book with many women who were searching for a life purpose as they faced the empty nest blues. As I reflected on the development of my Spirit identity over time, the writing of this specific devotional caused me to re-read Jean's inspiring story searching for evidence of her faith journey transpiring during the time of her thru-hike. Sure enough, it was there! I didn't notice Jean's budding faith journey in the earlier years because I was so focused on our similar adult developmental stage. Jean's father passed away when she was a child and she clung to memories of him throughout her life. While traversing mountains day after day, Jean found herself talking to the spirit of her dad. In the book's Preface, Jean writes *"But I didn't realize the trail would become a pathway for spiritual evolution and a remarkable teacher of fundamental truths. Many lessons of the journey through life became clear to me on the Appalachian Trail."*[27]

The best image that captures my identity is the photo on this book's cover. I am standing on the infamous AT McAffee's Knob vista in Virginia. This image represents my identity of Spirit. Jean Deeds used the same location for her book cover.

Choosing the Trail name, "Spirit," it represents my intention to be tied to the Holy Spirit. During the last two years of hiking the AT, I chose to give others a tiny balsawood dove as I met them on the Trail. As I did so, I shared these words, "Peace be with you." To me, the dove represents the Holy Spirit moving among us. From my earliest AT hiking years, I chose to introduce myself to other hikers with the trail name "Spirit." By using this Trail name, I declared my purpose for being on the AT. Fellow hikers picked this first impression that I portrayed on the trail. In doing so, I chose to hold myself accountable by showing other people through my words and actions that aligned with my growing faith. Using Spirit as my Trail name, I also temporarily stepped away from everyday life roles associated with my given name. Through becoming "Spirit," an immersion experience of this identity occurred, and my intention of walking with Jesus materialized. I experienced a healthy detachment from my normal life roles and relationships. In this way, I began to trust God's counsel as the initial step in dealing with the world around me, rather than thoughtlessly deferring to others for decisions that I needed to address. By experiencing God's trustworthiness when I was so alone, my faith in Him grew and grew. Other people cannot

---

[27] Deeds, Jean. There are Mountains to Climb, page vii.

navigate the way of life for a loved one, and I needed to experientially learn this truth.

Prayer: Oh, sweet Jesus, You are the keeper of my heart and the lover of my soul. I have prayed these words countless times because it is so true and grounds me in who You are. You keep calling me to be Your child and to accept Your loving guidance in my life journey. I am so grateful for Your patience with my wandering ways. You always welcome me back home. My soul is deepened every time I return to You as the center of life. Alleluia! My Spirit soars in the grace and blessings of Your presence. My earthly existence depends on Your strength and guidance for the purpose of living. Amen.

A question to provoke faith journaling: Is your spiritual being called to a journey of faith in God?

Fellowship

A Step To Grace: Walk in Christian fellowship to amplify God's call to you

James 2: 1–4, 12. *My dear brothers and sisters, how can you claim to have faith in our glorious Lord Jesus Christ if you favor some people over others? For example, suppose someone comes into your meeting dressed in fancy clothes and expensive jewelry, and another comes in who is poor and dressed in dirty clothes. If you give special attention and a good seat to the rich person, but you say to the poor one, "You can stand over there, or else sit on the floor"—well, doesn't this discrimination show that your judgments are guided by evil motives? So whatever you say or whatever you do, remember that you will be judged by the law that sets you free.* NLT

I remember encountering a middle age male backpacker traveling alone on the Trail. He approached us unexpectedly from a thick underbrush as he joined us in a clearing on the Trail, where we were standing for a moment's rest. The spontaneous smile on his sunny face and the gentleness of his voice instantly proclaimed, "The Light." His scraggly straw hat, thread bare clothes, skin-and-bone body carrying a tote sack for a backpack ignited a yellow caution signal for me – homeless? My first perception of this man was therefore conflicted by the two opposing impressions. Then the man complimented the cross necklace I always wear on the AT and my gut told me that he was an authentic man of God. After years of wearing the choker cross necklace and introducing myself as Spirit, no one else had mentioned my necklace upon a first encounter.

On another AT hiking trip, we had just settled into a Virginia AT shelter at dusk when a man in his twenties walked into the shelter site to stay the night. Lucas was a friendly guy, and he was on the solo trek trying to sort out confusion in his life. Both his job and social relationships were not going well, and he hoped the Trail would bring him answers. After traveling with Lucas two or three days, Smasher and I came to really enjoy his companionship. When Lucas told us that he was searching for a Trail name that fit him, we offered our help to find a good one. One evening as we relaxed around a campsite, a Trail name for Lucas popped into my mind. Fellow-Ship. We are all "Fellow-Ships" on this journey of life and this Trail name speaks to that truth.

Immediately I went about persuading Lucas to accept "Fellowship," as his Trail name. I went on to say that this Trail Name would emphasize to fellow trekkers that he was ready to build caring community relationships with those whom he met, a fellowship. Lucas claimed this Trail name after I conveyed its meaning. [28]

I have been an active participant in many fellowships over my lifetime. I have benefitted from the ever-fluid AT community's fellowship twenty times over several years. In my lifetime, I have belonged to nine church congregational fellowships. I adore intergenerational and diverse fellowship which happens in countless settings. Fellowship happens beyond the AT community fellowship and church congregational fellowships. As much as I love good fellowship, I am impatient with a fellowship that I experience as unhealthy. There are two features of healthy fellowship that I deemed essential before I chose to belong to it. Here is what I look for:

---

[28] 2003 September Hiking Trip

- A shared awareness in the fellowship of individual relationships with the Holy Creator. We individually have a part in God's great plan.
- A shared vulnerability in the fellowship – a welcoming, hospitable attitude that demonstrates a caring presence ready to do what we can and to care for one another. We know that anyone may have an unexpected need of the fellowship, including self.

There is a natural precondition to the AT community that builds healthy fellowship even though we are often strangers to one another. Because AT trekkers are living in the wilderness and carrying only what is essential, each one of us is aware of heightened individual vulnerabilities. We count on each other in a pinch, so trekkers feel accountable to making healthy fellowship happen. An unsaid "oath of fellowship" happens when one steps on the AT for a long-distance trek.

In my tenured role as a minister's wife, I want to share how much I wish that local church congregations had the natural preconditions to build healthy fellowship like the AT community. A Christian songwriter, Dia Frampton, shares in her lyrics the statement "I'm losing my religion to be close to You." I understand the underlying meaning of this lyric. Too many congregations are more loyal to their religious affiliation than are loyal to maintaining a healthy fellowship of believers.

Let us remember that Jesus first brings us to him as an individual. And it is from that faith in Him that we have the courage to be vulnerable and therefore help to build healthy fellowships wherever we are. That is what I witnessed in ten minutes of fellowship with the man in the straw hat. And Lucas, trail name Fellow-Ship, demonstrated a readiness for fellowship with us in His name.

Prayer: Holy Creator of us all, help me to reach out to others in love that comes from knowing that You first loved me. My part is to know this Truth and to share this love. Like a campfire blazing at the end of a long trail day, help me to give myself as some of the wood that fuels the Flame which keeps fellowship warm and loving. When I drift away from You, help me to choose to return to the campfire blaze, to return to the fellowship where I will rekindle the fire of Your Love. Amen.

A question to provoke faith journaling: Where are you choosing to be in fellowship?

Grace

A Step To Grace: Always look for the Grace that is raining down on you

Acts 9: 2-15. *He requested letters addressed to the synagogues in Damascus, asking their cooperation in the arrest of any followers of the Way he found there. He wanted to bring them – both men and women – back to Jerusalem in chains. As he was nearing Damascus on this mission, a brilliant light from heaven suddenly beamed down upon him! He fell to the ground and heard a voice saying to him, "Saul! Saul! Why are you persecuting me?" "Who are you, sir?" Saul asked. And the voice replied, "I am Jesus, the one you are persecuting! Now get up and go into the city, and you will be told what you are to do." The men with Saul stood speechless with surprise, for they heard the sound of someone's voice, but they saw no one! As Saul picked himself up off the ground, he found that he was blind.*

So his companions led him by hand to Damascus. He remained there blind for three days. And all that time he went without food and water. Now there was a believer in Damascus named Ananias. The Lord spoke to him in a vision, calling, "Ananias!" Yes, Lord!" he replied. The Lord said, "Go over to Straight Street, to the house of Judas. When you arrive, ask for Saul of Tarsus. He is praying to me right now. I have shown him a vision of a man named Ananias coming in and laying his hands on him so that he can see again." "But Lord," exclaimed Ananias, "I've heard about the terrible things this man has done to the believers in Jerusalem! And we hear that he is authorized by the leading priests to arrest every believer in Damascus." But the Lord said, "Go and do what I say." LNT

My first hiking trip was June, 1997. We started in the town of Damascus, Virginia on the southern border of Virginia near the border of Tennessee and North Carolina.[29] I saw Damascus as a positive choice to begin hiking the AT because of its biblical reference but also because it is famously known as a mountain town friendly to AT hikers. Damascus is known as the favorite "Trail Town" because it hosts the premiere AT hiker gathering known as "Trail Days". In mid-May, thousands of AT hikers gather in Damascus to celebrate, enjoy the fellowship of other hikers, and to visit hundreds of vendor outdoor booths. With my first steps on the AT in Damascus, I was seeking a new beginning in life. Damascus' friendly townspeople easily handled all my newbie questions about the Trail. Putting on my backpack and leaving Damascus southbound on the AT, I experienced a new and different beauty in Nature. The drastic contrast of nature's beauty in the mountains of Appalachia compared to the open plains and big sky of Texas made me aware that this adventure was truly a new beginning. Due to a heavy June rainfall, the gigantic rhododendron and mountain laurel bushes bloomed with abundance. Later in my AT travels, I joined other hikers in naming this part of the AT the green tunnel. The Trail conditions were muddy, and the humidity was unbelievable. Even though the weather conditions shortened our plan, my new beginning in Damascus was deeply rooted in a newfound well-being on the AT.

Right away I was hooked on my AT adventures as a getaway from normal life. I had unknowingly approached life with a self-induced burden of perfectionism. I searched for quick fixes. Perfectionism took the form of expecting myself to unilaterally fix problems in the lives of loved ones. I had a self-expectation to be a perfect role model for everyone. My perfectionism trap was expanding within me because the worldview I carried put ME at

---

[29] 1997 June Hiking Trip

the center of the universe. I had to have The Answer. Perfectionism was my "Saul". When I first launched from Damascus, I thought the new beginning experience would be the last new beginning. I was wrong. New beginnings keep happening through the Grace of Jesus Christ, when we ask Him to be Our Savior.

Acts 9: 17- 18 *So Ananias went and found Saul. He laid his hands on him and said, "Brother Saul, the Lord Jesus, who appeared to you on the road, has sent me so that you may get your sight back and be filled with the Holy Spirit." Instantly something like scales fell from Saul's eyes, and he regained his sight. Then he got up and was baptized.* LNT

In this scripture passage, we learn about the moment that Grace transformed Saul to become Paul. Saul was the most well-known persecutor of Christians. When he committed his life to Christ and became Paul, he spread the good news to Gentiles as well as Jews. Few of us have had such a powerful conversion experience. Jesus Christ's presence on the road to Damascus transformed Paul through Grace. Before Paul accepted the saving Grace of Jesus Christ, he lived a rule-bound religion that cultivated perfectionism in himself and the same hopeless expectation of everyone. Through accepting the blood of Christ as salvation from his earthly sins, Paul experienced Grace. He experienced the first of many new beginnings for the rest of his faith-filled life in Christ.

Over time, I, too, addressed the true purpose of my life. Five years later, I returned to Damascus, where I began my spiritual pilgrimage. A journey that allowed me to relinquish the roadblocks of perfectionism, to lean on Christ's Grace of redeeming love. Before my 2002 return to Damascus, through months of prayerful guidance, I chose a hiking partner, Smasher, who shared my intention to use time on the Trail for focus on faith enrichment. Through embracing the truth that Grace has many "new beginnings", our journey over the coming years was a filled with blessings. One of these many blessings was reaching the goal of completing 2000 miles of the AT.

Prayer: Oh precious Jesus, my Redeemer and Savior, You are guiding me through daily life with Grace raining down on me every step of the way. Help me to see Your loving Grace as innumerable "new beginnings" that renew my soul and my life. Get me out of this self-induced center of this universe with its burdens beyond the ability of my human condition to bear. All glory and honor be Yours, sovereign Lord and King, for Your guidance is always trustworthy and good. Amen

A question to provoke faith journaling: In what ways are you ignoring God's Grace and instead holding onto needless control?

God's Gifts

A Step To Grace: Look for God's Love for you, especially through the talents and gifts of others.

1 Peter 4:8-11. *Most important of all, continue to show deep love for each other, for love covers a multitude of sins. Cheerfully share your home with those who need a meal or a place to stay. God has given each of you a gift from his great variety of spiritual gifts. Use them well to serve one another. Do you have the gift of speaking? Then speak as though God himself were speaking through you. Do you have the gift of helping others? Do it with all the strength and energy that God supplies. Then everything you do will bring glory to God through Jesus Christ. All glory and power to him forever and ever! Amen. NLT*

1 Corinthians 12:4;11. *There are different kinds of spiritual gifts, but the same Spirit is the source of them all. It is the one and only Spirit who distributes all these gifts. He alone decides which gift each person should have. NLT*

The second AT hiking trip was powered by my need to escape into the woods and away from the empty nest blues.[30] Our daughter graduated from high school that year and our son, RW, would leave the nest the following year when he also graduated from high school. My women hiking partners on the first hiking trip were unavailable, and months of searching for another female hiking partner had ended in failure.

With no where else to turn, RW kindly volunteered to be my AT hiking partner. Since I was anxiously seeking an escape from

---
[30] 2000 July Hiking Trip

my role in family life, I had mixed feelings about this arrangement, but God had a plan! As we walked the 45 miles southbound where the AT follows the TN/NC border, the ambivalence about my life became increasingly evident. It was quickly apparent that the life transition unrest would not be alleviated by my fantasy of instantaneous physical fitness. It was also apparent that my stale talents as a counselor would not be magically renewed. I was frustrated that a new lifestyle was coming, whether I liked it or not.

RW was an experienced backpacker, so the legs of this seventeen-year-old propelled him down the Trail ahead. Watching my son disappear ahead of me was a clear metaphor about my dismal perspective on life. In many ways, the AT was my son's element; his God-given talent was easily seen. Even at his young age, RW was already demonstrating some of his talents like instigating outdoor group recreation, creating hospitable community, and demonstrating a positive attitude of service to others. He is a "doer" for the Lord, not a talker or a writer like his mother. His God-given talents created an easy going and relaxed setting for our shared backpacking trip. His teen years were filled with examples of these spiritual gifts such as his enjoyment of church mission projects and Boy Scouts service activities. As an adult, he continues to joyfully volunteer for various service projects in whatever community he resides.

I needed this God-given talent from RW as my trail buddy despite my reluctance to accept his help. I especially needed it when I was sweating and fatigued and ready to quit. When frequently overwhelmed with my lack of endurance and the unexpected challenges within my inexperienced body, RW's servant heart was there for me. When I looked into my son's eyes with my total fatigue, I found God's grace and love. I was lifted from self-doubt and despair by his companionship. His cheerful spirit faced each peril with an attitude of fun and adventure. One night it rained with an unexpected gushing downpour as we tent camped deep in the woods. In the morning, we faced the grim situation of loading up our totally soaked gear and moving on down the Trail. I was ready to quit and go home, but RW was determined to lead us through the full two-week trip plan. Because of RW's right spirit, we carried on. As a Mom, I had expected the roles to be reversed with me leading my son, not my son leading me.

I was additionally depleted in my role as a professional counselor, a talent the Lord has blessed me with to serve others. By the end of backpacking this section of the AT, the Lord had fed my soul by pulling me out of the professional counselor role and bringing strangers in the form of hikers who cared about me. My spirit was renewed with so much love and encouragement through people who did not know me as a professional. These caring strangers knew me as a Mom or as a fellow hiker. We ended the section hiking trip at Nolichucky Hiking Hostel with Uncle Johnny and Braveheart as the hosts. This legendary hostel was a hiking fellowship that gave me a final dose of encouragement. By finding shelter off the Trail in the comfort of the hostel, I physically recuperated. I didn't feel like quitting my dream. Instead of being ready to give up all future hiking plans, I went home ready to tackle life and hike again.

No longer did I expect to instantly resolve all empty nest issues at one time. This AT trip showed me that God is always with me, especially through the spiritual talents of those around me. And today (twenty years later), looking back on this mother/son time together, I see God's presence still bonding us together, kindling a maturing love over the years. Through this AT trip with RW, I began to clarify the lesson of turning to my faith especially during the transition times in life. Examples of the future life transitions that eventually came: our adult children choosing marital partners, the needs of adult children to move away, and also the life transition of retirement.

Prayer: God of Grace, Your Holy Spirit gives talents to us so that we may use them in ways that will glorify You. Help me to cultivate and to share my talents knowing that everyone receives them as gifts from You. Help me to embrace a Servant Heart. When life gets confusing and I cannot find You, guide me to recognize Your love for me through the talents You gave those who are surrounding me. Amen.

A question to provoke faith journaling: How are you taking for granted the Love that God has for you through the presence of others in your life? Include strangers as well as loved ones in your thoughts.

Hospitality

A Step To Grace: Give and receive the grace of hospitality

Genesis 18: 1–10. *The L*ORD *appeared again to Abraham near the oak grove belonging to Mamre. One day Abraham was sitting at the entrance to his tent during the hottest part of the day.* ² *He looked up and noticed three men standing nearby. When he saw them, he ran to meet them and welcomed them, bowing low to the ground. "My lord," he said, "if it pleases you, stop here for a while. Rest in the shade of this tree while water is brought to wash your feet. And since you've honored your servant with this visit, let me prepare some food to refresh you before you continue on your journey." "All right," they said. "Do as you have said." So Abraham ran back to the tent and said to Sarah, "Hurry! Get three large measures of your best flour, knead it into dough, and bake some bread." Then Abraham ran out to the herd and chose a tender calf and gave it to his servant, who quickly prepared it. When the food was ready, Abraham took some yogurt and milk and the roasted meat, and he served it to the men. As they ate, Abraham waited on them in the shade of the trees.*

"Where is Sarah, your wife?" the visitors asked. "She's inside the tent," Abraham replied. Then one of them said, "I will return to you about this time next year, and your wife, Sarah, will have a son!" NLT

It was another year that getting on the AT was necessary escape from my driven lifestyle.[31] Fortunately, my neighbor and adult Girl Scout friend, Debra, felt the same need, and was eager

---

[31] 2010 Sept. Hiking Trip

for the relief and adventure as well. I was particularly blessed that Debra wanted to join my annual September AT trip because Smasher could not get away from her responsibilities at home. Sharing the straight-through drive time with Debra was a great way to begin. We arrived at our starting point, the Pennsylvania/Maryland border, only a few hours before dusk. We needed a shuttle service at the beginning of the Trail to allow our bodies time to adjust by day hiking a while before we started backpacking. Studying our *Trail Companion* resource book, we found exactly what we needed, "Bud's Shuttle Service". We called Bud and found that not only was he available for shuttle service the next few days, but he was quick to answer questions over the phone on the most immediate need we had, inexpensive lodging for that night.

That night, while we were still complete strangers, Bud and his wife invited us to their home. They had a small hiker's cabin that we could rent while we were day hiking in the area. We were completely exhausted from being on the road for 18. hours and Debra was not feeling well. It felt a little risky to trust strangers, but we needed immediate help with lodging for the night. Upon arrival, we were invited into their living room, they served a light meal to us and were totally tuned into our depleted physical state and immediate needs. I could feel the road miles flowing off my physical being as I relaxed into their hospitable presence.

Debra and I relished their hospitality for at least five nights using the backyard cabin and Bud's shuttle service. With Bud's help, we dropped our car at one end of the day's hike. He then drove us to the AT trailhead at a road crossing and dropped us off so we could hike back to our car. Bud educated us on the Civil War sights and other local historical sights and daily prepared us for the terrain of each day's Trail section that we would hike. To further the miracle of Grace we received, several evenings after returning to our cabin following a long day on the Trail, this hospitable couple invited us to their dinner table for a hot home cooked meal. By the time we left their hospitality, Bud and his wife had shared their family history and their faith journey with us. Of course, we shared our hearts with them as well, feeling like they were family to us.

On another AT trip, I had the host opportunity rather than the role of a guest.[32] We fell into a precious host role with the thru-hiker "T-bird". In Vermont, Smasher and I were on a series of day hikes. We wanted to accomplish big mileage days so my husband Tim would drop us off and pick us up at specific road crossings of the AT, just like the help from Bud. Tim always had a hot meal ready for us when we returned to the camper, a delightful treat at the end of a long mileage day. T-bird, a middle-aged New York woman, greeted us on the Trail and we stopped to rest and chat. By backpacking from Georgia northbound, she had already completed 1500 AT miles when we happened to meet her on the Trail. After many months on the Trail, T-bird was beginning to wane in motivation and energy to finish the entire AT. This is a common problem for the thru-hikers we had met over the years. She was lonely, bored and a bit homesick for her family. I invited her to take a break from her solitary pace and join us at the camper for an overnight stay and a hot meal too. T-bird jumped at the invitation. Her spirits were immediately lifted. Since she hiked much faster than us, we instructed her on how to find Tim at the next road crossing and to let him know of our invitation to her. When T-bird got to the road and flagged down Tim's truck with a Texas license plate, her quick sense of humor surprised Tim. T-bird said "Hi Tim, I am T-bird and I'm spending the night with you tonight!" My 67-year-old retired husband was quite excited! Tim, Smasher,

---

[32] 2014 Aug/Sept Hiking Trip

and I were thrilled to enjoy the role of hosts after so many years of being the guests receiving the hospitality of others.

Hospitality is in the DNA of the AT culture. The most common acts of hospitality by AT trekkers happen in the AT shelters. Picture this! It is raining hard and has been all day. You arrive at the long-awaited destination of the AT shelter, totally soaked and cold. You are welcomed by a crowd of fellow hikers who genuinely greet you by moving their belongings to make room on the shelter's wood floor for you. After eating something while you unpack and dry off, you climb into your dry sleeping bag thankful for the hospitality of these kindred spirits. Just as you are dozing off and listening to the rain and thunder in the forest, another hiker arrives at the shelter. The drenched human being eagerly awaits your hospitality along with the others. And as crowded as it is, hospitality happens again and again.

Hospitality is a highly under rated means of God's grace, not only in the past but also today. For instance, the scripture reading describes Abraham jumping at the chance to be a lavish host to strangers. Why? I suggest that Abraham's deep trust in God kindled expectations of God's blessings. And we read that God's angels came as strangers bringing a big blessing. Abraham was ready to be a blessing as a host in hopes of receiving a blessing. Sarah and Abraham were in their elder years and therefore no longer expecting to have children. Imagine their surprise at the glorious blessing they received announced by "strangers" who were their guests.

God's grace comes to both sides in a human relationship when hospitality is practiced. You see this evidenced in the previous descriptions of hospitality, especially in the AT shelters. Hospitality in everyday life of human relationships happens. The world would be a better place if we would reject rigid roles in all kinds of relationships and replace this with intentional acceptance and hospitality toward one another.

Prayer: God of Grace, Your faithfulness reminds me that I can always be a better friend or even an acquaintance. Your compassion and goodness are light in the darkness. Even my smile purposely given to a stranger holds Your Spirit's message. You have led me to understand that having alone time with You is the greatest hospitality I can experience. You knew me even before I was born. It is a mystery how Your Love is so personable to all, yet You are also the Divine Creator of all. Help me to share with others some measure of the acceptance and hospitality You have given me. And, when You knock at my door, sweet Jesus, teach me to know it is You and to let You into my heart and soul. Amen.

Questions to provoke spiritual journaling:
1. When did you miss an opportunity to be a host?
2. When did you receive hospitality at a time you least expected it?
3. Did you see this as God's hospitality?

Unexpected

A Step To Grace: God turns mourning into joyful dancing!

Psalm 30: 4-5 and 11-12 *Sing to the LORD, all you godly ones! Praise his holy name. For his anger lasts only a moment, but his favor lasts a lifetime! Weeping may last through the night, but joy comes with the morning. You have turned my mourning into joyful dancing. You have taken away my clothes of mourning and clothed me with joy, that I might sing praises to you and not be silent. O LORD my God, I will give you thanks forever!* LNT

The AT traverses the NC/TN border just north of the Smoky Mountain National Park. This is where I had solo backpacked for a week.[33] It is appropriate for you to challenge me about solo backpacking, but I want to share the rationale for taking this risk:

- Smasher was going through a bitter and messy divorce at the time. It was necessary for her to remain at home to address this battle constructively. Therefore, I had no trail buddy.
- I was experiencing a heavy load of pressure from my counseling business with clients bringing extraordinary levels of trauma into my office. I knew that time on the AT would totally renew me as it had in the past.
- This particular 70 mile Trail section was a part of the AT that Smasher had previously hiked but I had not. This seemed like the ideal time to get it done.

---

[33] 2007 September Section Hiking Trip

Beyond these rational arguments for embarking on a solo hike despite the increased risk of going it alone, I was experiencing God calling me to dedicated time together on the Trail. By now, I had learned that when I am overwhelmed with life, God will relentlessly hit my consciousness with friendly reminders that we need quality time together! Being attentive to that signal from my soul had become a part of the guidance and relationship with Jesus. I knew the risks that I was taking, but my backpacking experience from the previous years prepared me to face this solo challenge. I was certain that God's guidance would be with me.

The daytime walks through God's creation were a comforting balm that only sweet Jesus could bring. I finished many conversations with Him. Conversations that had been lingering over many months. Even with a fully loaded backpack, my footsteps on the trail were no longer a burden to carry but a solace that silently moved through the dense forest, with God's presence. This experience gave me renewed peace about my life direction.

I was surprised how difficult it was to get to sleep at night. As the sun set and dark came into the silent woods, I lay in my sleeping bag and began worrying and fretting about the news that Black bears were supposedly in the area. The Smoky Mountain National Park rangers were moving Black bears that had grown too friendly with people and eating their food. The Park Rangers were resettling the bears away from the Park into the national forest area of my trek. Laying there alone in the woods, I wrote in my journal and sang spiritual songs. By practicing my faith, the fretting dissipated, and sleep came to me.

On the last day of this solo hike, I awoke from a night of restless sleep, ate breakfast, and packed my gear while thinking of my husband Tim and our marriage. I got on the Trail with thoughts of deeply longing for my life partner. My heart yearned for our companionship, so I took those human needs to Jesus in a way that I had come to know as "prayer walking." I was surprised to find that Jesus had answers for me. Deep answers of joy that far surpassed my human solutions for missing Tim. Through my prayer walking, I found a deeper perspective on answered prayers that addressed years of worrying about the midlife transition's negative impact on our marriage. Jesus pointed out to me that Tim recently had left a business career to return to church ministry because of his faith-led life direction. Now in his first year of pastoral ministry, we were walking together with Jesus into a deeper journey than any of the previous 40 years of marriage. Each in our own way, we sought Christ in our lives and in our marriage, and particularly, both of us sought Jesus beyond the walls of the church.

Later that Sunday morning, I climbed to a mountain top where a cell phone signal was barely accessible, and I called Tim. By reaching out to him, I received that precious human tie that I cherish in our holy marriage. We reminded one another about why I had chosen this spiritual time and space to be on the AT and how blessed I was to have the opportunity to get away from life's difficulties and responsibilities. After the phone conversation, my enthusiasm for the Trail life was rekindled, and I took to the Trail climbing up the mountain with a renewed joy for life.

Just minutes after the blessing of catching Tim when he was available to talk, another blessing unexpectedly came my way. Out on a wilderness mountain top of the Trail, I came upon a ragged peacock who was just as bewildered to see me as I was to see him. I could almost hear the peacock say, "What are you doing here woman?" I laughed and laughed aloud as I said, "Now I know why I am here! Thank you, Lord Jesus for this unexpected joy and laughter that comes from you!" I opened myself to God's presence that morning and I found even more joy! God played with me and got me laughing with His joy!

Through his marvelous Grace, God transformed that time of loneliness into a time of joy and gave me the strength to enjoy the AT moments alone. Over the years I have learned from these experiences to transfer the lesson into my daily life. With God's Holy Spirit present to help me, I am able to witness to others God's power to transform our lives with joy, and to give us strength in His name.

Prayer: God of comfort and joy, loving Creator of all beauty and splendor in this world, I humbly praise Your ways and ask for Your continued deep guidance in my life. Thank You for giving to me the free will to find a purposeful life path which You will bless. I praise You for giving me the strength to continue when the trail is difficult. And, most of all, I praise You and glorify You for bringing unexpected joy and laughter in those challenging moments, reminding me of Your loving companionship. Amen

A question to provoke faith journaling: Have you ever tried prayer walking? If you try it, look for God's deep message of joy in the time together, and be sure to write about it for future reference.

Trail Angels

A Step To Grace: *Greatness comes from being a servant of Jesus*

Scripture: Mark 10: 43b-45 *"Instead, whoever wants to become great among you must be your servant, [44] and whoever wants to be first must be slave of all. [45] For even the Son of Man did not come to be served, but to serve, and to give his life as a ransom for many."* NIV

I am known by some as a Methodist pastor. But to many others, I am Beth's husband. Her remarkable adventure of hiking the AT over many years has been a privilege to watch. But it also became clear to us that we were only getting older and although we were physically well and strong, we could no longer take our health for granted. To complete the remaining 500 miles, a new plan was required. Three weeks a year wasn't going to do it. None of the AT is easy, but the section from the New Hampshire/Maine border to the Hudson River bridge at Bear Mountain State Park in New York was going to be tough.

We made a plan that following my retirement in June 2014, I would accompany Beth and Smasher, and be their support team as they completed this last leg of the AT. We decided to take on New Hampshire and Vermont in 2014, and the remainder in 2015.

My first task was to find accommodations. We had a truck, but we also needed a trailer that would work for two women and one male for weeks at a time. Biggest need was a bathroom with a door! Second need was to be able to have two sleeping areas without having to take apart the kitchen table every night. Good news is that we found one.

My job was to support the hikers. Find a place to set up a base camp. Get them on the trail every morning. Pick them up at the end of their hike at night and to have a hot meal ready for them when we got back to camp. It was a joy to see them coming off the day's hike and to watch them pour over the trail map to plot out the next day's section after our evening meal. When it was time to move forward to the next section, my day was spent breaking camp and relocating to the next RV park before picking up the team from their day's hike.

Hiking in Vermont and New Hampshire in August and September was a challenge. The first three weeks were cold and wet. We were in an area where cell phone coverage was spotty at best. The hikers were out of contact most of the day. I knew on the map where they needed to be picked up at night but finding 'a hole in the woods' on unmarked mountain roads was a challenge. My job was to be 'there' for them when they got 'there' and I didn't know where 'there' was.

It took about two weeks to get the rhythm of support life down. I came to embrace the opportunities of getting to know the people and the culture of the area where we were camping. Outside of Barrington, Vermont, the AT crossed a major highway. As I traveled from our campsite to town, I kept seeing small groups of hikers walking the 3 miles from that crossing into town. They were on a mission! There was a Taco Bell ahead. I then spent my days as a shuttle service between the Trail head and the Taco Bell.

As we moved north to Rutland, VT, I looked for things to do during the day while the hikers were on the trail. I was able to connect with a Methodist pastor and enjoyed taking her to lunch. I found out that this area was experiencing an unemployment rate of more than 30% and that addiction to opioids was devastating to the community. After that experience, I chose to learn more about the communities along the Trail.

My day was spent reading, getting groceries, doing laundry, and then trying to find where my weary but happy hikers would pop out of the woods. This was a challenge due to the fact that Hurricane Sandy had washed out many of the river crossings and our maps had not been updated to show those changes. All I could do was to drive back and forth looking for Spirit and Smasher to emerge from their green tunnel.

Flea markets, thrift stores, and Farmer's markets were welcome diversions and gave me a feel for the area where we were camping. There were towns like Woodstock, VT that catered to affluent tourists. They had the best Thrift stores. I was able to buy an LL Bean full length down coat for $20. There were also towns like Warren, NH that showed the results of significant economic challenges caused by their industries shutting down due to globalization. While the spirit of these communities remained strong, homes were is general disrepair and many needed roof replacements and upkeep. While my Texas drawl made communication a challenge, I enjoyed the interaction with the people in these communities that were far different from my previous experiences.

The hardest part of the trip was watching Spirit and Smasher head out from the top of Mt. Washington and into the cold, wet fog, to start a 4-day, 3-night trek above the tree line in New Hampshire. The State Park memorial plaque at the summit of this incredible mountain with the names of those who had died on that peak stayed in my mind as I drove back to the campsite. I knew the day that they would show up and the place that they would leave the Trail but didn't know when. I found the Trail head in early afternoon at Franconia Notch. I got a nice lunch and sat in a folding chair with a good book. I could see the trail steeply descending from the Mt Lafayette. I asked every hiker coming down from the north if they had seen two old ladies on the Trail?

They had! I was filled with joy when we reconnected after their 4-day, three-night trek.

One of the joys of this experience was when the AT went right through Hanover, NH, and Dartmouth University. The trail markers took you down Main Street. We were able to connect for lunch at a Chinese restaurant. This was a real treat for me.

Another joy was to watch the movie "A Walk in the Woods," based on Bill Bryson's book about the AT, at a small Massachusetts town near the AT in a theater that sat less than 50 people.

Finding an RV park was another challenge. We needed to find a place midway between the next section of our trek. Many were great! Others were closed or nearly deserted after the Labor Day weekend. Making friends at evening campfires in these parks help me to experience the somewhat nomadic life of those retirees who chose to live in their RV's moving from park to park.

Those who take on this support role are sometimes called "Trail Angels." I had it easy. For the most part, my hikers were off the trail every night. That is not the case for so many others who are there to support their thru-hiker. We met a lady from Texas at the RV park in Gorham, NH just inside the Maine state line. She was her husband's support team as he completed his thru-hike. With just under 300 miles to go, it had been a 6-month experience for them. Her task was to be his outfitter every 5 or 6 days to replenish supplies and to be a cheerleader as he completed the long walk from Springer Mountain Georgia to central Maine. We invited her to join us for dinner one night. She was concerned about her husband because he had told her that the trail just over the Maine border was so difficult that he found himself trying to remember if he had made his last life insurance payment.

I never felt like a angel, but I recalled the Lullaby in the children's opera *Hansel and Grettel*. The lyrics start with "When at night I go to sleep, 14 angels watch do keep." At times I wondered where the other 13 were hiding. I believe in angels. But my experience was not as a big-time angel like Michael or Gabriel, or even one of the Heavenly Host that startled a group of shepherds that first Christmas Eve. I was a 'gofer' angel. To be there when needed, but to stay out of the way the rest of the time. The words from Mark remind us that we are called "not to be served, but to serve." To keep the wicks of the lamp trimmed so that the Light of the Lord can be seen by those who seek a light for their life.

This role that I played in Spirit's and Smasher's journey was important, but it was to support, to be there when needed, and not to point to oneself.

Prayer: Almighty Lord, help us to celebrate all those who work tirelessly in the shadows to make things work. Forgive us Father, when we seek out the spotlight when we should be content to just stand aside and praise and encourage those who are doing Your work. We give thanks to You for Your Son, who in the midst of his teaching and leadership, always stopped to lift up those who were in need. We are blessed by the opportunities that You continue to put before us to serve You, our Creator and our Redeemer. AMEN

A question to provoke faith journaling: Who has served as your 'Trail Angel?' Did you thank them, or just take them for granted? What can you do today to serve others without seeking their approval or affirmation?

Beauty

A Step To Grace: Notice God's goodness in the beauty of God's Nature

Genesis 1: 1-4 *In the beginning God created the heavens and the earth. The earth was formless and empty, and darkness covered the deep waters. And the Spirit of God was hovering over the surface of the waters. Then God said, "Let there be light," and there was light. And God saw that the light was good. Then he separated the light from the darkness.* LNT

God's beauty in Nature led me to understand where I always feel at home. When I am vacationing in sprawling large cities, regardless of the activities taking place, I always feel like a visitor or a tourist. When I am vacationing in God's Nature, whether the setting is the AT or some other setting of outdoor activities, I always feel at home. The "at home" feeling includes a sensation of belonging or being at peace. I first discovered this clear comparison during the annual AT trips when occasionally I needed to stay in a motel instead of sleeping and eating outdoors in a tent or AT shelter. Eventually I dreaded any necessity to leave the Trail with its lifestyle immersion in God's Nature because I began to feel homesickness in a motel! God's Nature is good for us, just as this scripture states.

Nature settings provoke an inner sensation of instinctively longing for connection to our Creator. Then we feel "at home." We are in a place that we belong. Personally, I feel like a loved child of God whenever I am in Nature. God's beauty displayed in Nature reminds me of His goodness.

My mother was a prolific watercolor and acrylic artist during her childhood years and throughout her entire life. She was quite talented in landscape paintings, and I am sure that she was motivated to paint God's creation to capture some of the beauty that drew her closer to God's loving presence.

The beauty of God's Nature is a natural attraction for we human beings. Why does God want to attract us into the beauty of Nature? God is courting us to notice the intricacies and order of His creation. By turning our attention to His beautiful Creation, we have turned away from the human made things of this world that often confuse and disturb us. God wants us to be happy and noticing God's goodness in Nature's beauty is a loving invitation to happiness. This Genesis scripture conveys the message that we should receive from the Maker.[34]

I remember the 2006 AT Hiking Trip with Smasher and Cheri when Nature's beauty healed and soothed our souls. We knew that our spirits needed prolonged rekindling. We also knew the only place to find the spiritual rekindling was in God's beautiful Nature. My mother passed away four months prior to the trip, and I was relieved to have Nature's beauty healing my loss with a spiritual belonging. The previous year Smasher had undergone multiple surgeries. Backpacking the Trail was a celebration of new health and fitness for Smasher. She was one with Nature again. Cheri had only recently completed cancer treatments, but the future prognosis had not ruled out a return of cancer. Cheri had this concern and other concerns as well. At her young adult age of 24, she went to the Trail seeking the time and space to reflect about her future. Cheri settled into the beauty of the Trail by walking and absorbing "the Spirit of God hovering over its surface."

Near the end of this 2006 trip, we stayed overnight at Bears Den Hiking Hostel in northern Virginia. The AT meanders on a

---

[34] 2006 September Hiking Trip

ridge a short distance from the hostel, and we knew there would be a great rock outcropping for viewing the sunset that evening. The three of us hiked out to the rocky ledge and found three separate spots to relax and watch the beautiful display of colors changing with the sun setting. It was a last big drink of God's goodness before we left the Trail and Nature behind.

Home Sweet Home! Whenever I think of the AT green tunnel, I remember it as home. I feel a belonging to God's Nature in that space that God has made good for all. A home that is not mine, nor does it belong to people. A home that belongs to God. A place where we are all welcome – a beautiful green tunnel home!

Recently I was reminded of God's goodness seen in the fascinating intricate beauty of Nature when I went on a Nature stroll with my four-year-old grandson. Luke noticed an ant climbing a pebble, a bird singing nearby, a spider web glistening with morning dew, and a faint smell of smoke in the air. He loves to pick wild flowers and give them to his Mommy. Morning dew drops glistening in sunlight capture Luke's attention. Children humble us with their innate wisdom of God's Creation speaking to the soul within and declaring – 'God is good!'

This scripture tells us that the Spirit of God was present everywhere before we humans were around. And the scripture describes God's light and God's declaration of goodness that preceded human beings. Let us be honest, we humans did not make Nature good: God did! There is a loving home for everyone throughout God's Creation. Let us choose to dwell in its beauty and Love together.

PRAYER: Creator God, You have given me beauty on earth that I would instinctively know Your goodness. You are the Divine gift of Love freely given by Your Son Jesus Christ. I praise You. I am grateful for the mindfulness You instilled within me. The senses You wove into my body naturally attracting me to Your holiness and beauty. Give me homesickness when I wander too far from Your presence! I see Your Glory, Gracious God, and I am Yours. Amen.

Question to provoke faith journaling: What are some of the ways God's goodness is apparent to you through the beauty of Nature?

Fun and Recreation

A Step To Grace: God's grace is present in the good times too!

John 2: 2; 4-11. *Jesus and his disciples were also invited to the celebration. The wine supply ran out during the wedding festivities, so Jesus' mother spoke to him about the problem. "How does that concern you and me?" Jesus asked. "My time has not yet come." But his mother told the servants, "Do whatever he tells you." Six stone waterpots were standing there; and held 20 to 30 gallons each. Jesus told the servants, "Fill the jars with water. Dip some out and take it to the master of ceremonies." When the master of ceremonies tasted the water that was now wine, he called the bridegroom over. "Usually a host serves the best wine first, then, when everyone is full and doesn't care, he brings out the less expensive. But you have kept the best until now!" This miraculous sign at Cana in Galilee was Jesus' first display of his glory. And his disciples believed in him.* NLT

Have you ever thought that Christians are basically not fun people? This assumption about Christians is false, but it comes from erroneously expecting that Christians will always be seriously righteous; not people looking for fun and adventure. When I got the chance to participate in a party gathering of hikers, sometimes a fellow hiker would notice my cross necklace and correlate the cross to my Trail name "Spirit." When a hiker noticed, it reminded me that I am visibly carrying the name of Jesus Christ in the first impression that I convey to others. My Trail name "Spirit" took on a deeper meaning about the cross around my neck. With Jesus as my guide, I happily conveyed that this Christian woman is fun loving and carries an unexplainable peace and joy that is easy to see.

There are countless ways to have fun while hiking long distance. One way Smasher and I made the leisurely grind of day hiking fun was to fill our Trail time with story making conversations. Whenever we saw wildlife tracks or scat on the Trail, we stopped to examine it closely and enthusiastically rendered a story about what might have happened in the creature's life that crossed our path. Those stories filled hours of Trail time with made-up solutions for our curiosity.

Another way of quenching our thirst for fun and adventure was leaving Trail magic for other hikers, knowing we would create a fun surprise for them. We left silly notes or riddles in the AT shelter journals to tweak the curiosity of others. Leaving a smiley face in the Trail dirt was a fun and simple thing to do as we journeyed onward, knowing it would lift someone's spirits. A sure winner was hanging a Ziploc bag with a Snicker candy bar inside it. We placed the Ziploc bag with a goodie treat on a tree branch overhanging the Trail and scurried down the Trail giggling like Brownie Girl Scouts doing a good deed. Fun and laughter is a natural part of the AT culture. Most trekkers enjoy creating these moments just as we did.

In Monson, Maine, we lucked out one evening when the locals gathered at the general store for a Hootenanny.[35] We were staying at the infamous hiker hostel Shaw's Lodging. Arriving in town after backpacking through the 100 Mile Wilderness, we were walking the streets of Monson looking for fun. My Trail buddies Willow (Jana Jones is her real name), Smasher and I followed the sounds of live music by the town folk musicians gleefully entertaining a crowd squeezed into the small country store. The sing-along fun was so refreshing.

You may not know of the fun and entertainment that historically happens at the AT huts in the White Mountains of

---

[35] 2008 July Hiking Trip

New Hampshire. Unlike the open-air AT shelters, the huts are enclosed hiking hostels in this remote region where above tree line weather conditions can quickly become dangerous. The huts are managed by college students who simply love hosting and entertaining the audience of hikers with after dinner silly skits.[36] Enjoying this comfy lodging and fun entertainment on two hiking trips are precious memories for me.

I have a favorite Trail story that ultimately became a Trail legend but originated in the AT hiking community news stream in 2004.[37] The story was told to us by a young man, trail name, "Sweetfish." We met Sweetfish at the Dutch Haus in Montebello, Va. while we were sheltered there during Hurricane Frances. Several of his thru-hiker trail buddies were a day or two behind him when the Hurricane hit the area. Sweetfish shared with us the bizarre and silly story associated with his thru-hiker group. Sweetfish's Trail buddy, "Gnome Sherpa," was quite shy and had difficulty starting up conversations with women so he prepared for the long trek by carrying a conversation starter with him. In his backpack, Gnome Sherpa carried a concrete yard gnome. It also had a Trail name, "Nigel."

The yard gnome, Nigel, talked to women on behalf of the Gnome Sherpa, explaining his shyness and boldly flirting with women so Gnome Sherpa did not have to do it. Nigel even signed the Trail shelter journal entries. And, you know what? It worked! Nigel was the ultimate chick magnet! The women flocked to this group of fun loving thru-hikers as they headed southbound to the Georgia end of the AT. The Gnome Sherpa completed the AT carrying Nigel over the 2,000 miles of rough terrain. By the end of the Trail, Nigel was only a piece of himself.

---

[36] 2001 September and 2014 September Hiking Trips

[37] 2004 September Hiking Trip

Smasher and I enjoyed this fun-making ongoing saga which the Trail community made into a legend. We loved the fun so much that we added to the story line with our yard gnome, Natasha! Smasher placed Natasha in the Standing Indian shelter near her home in Franklin, NC. Natasha was placed in the AT shelter with a note on her for Nigel and the Gnome Sherpa. Natasha offered to be Nigel's romantic fling on the remainder of his AT adventure. Everybody along the AT network of hikers got into the fun!

This Bible scripture describes Jesus and his disciples enjoying the festivities of a wedding celebration in Cana. You would imagine that Mary and her son Jesus knew the wedding couple hosts, but not Jesus' disciples, who were strangers to the area. Jesus had only recently assembled his disciples who came from places outside Cana. They were a motley and diverse group of twelve, and many were stinky fisherman. Likewise, groups of long-distance hikers are known for being motley and stinky as well! But regardless of how the wedding guests received an invitation, we know that all the wedding guests were welcome. A wide variety of people contributed to a fun and celebratory party. That "party hardy" description also fits the campfire camaraderie climate at a Trail shelter gathering. As the wedding celebration continued, some were aware of the shortage of wine. But unknown to the guests, Jesus created a miracle by turning many gallons of water into a new wine. The servants knew what happened because they helped Jesus by serving the new wine. The disciples witnessed this early miracle in Jesus' ministry, which increased their early beliefs in Jesus the Messiah. But the wedding gathering did not notice the miracle because they accepted the assumption of the master of ceremonies. When the new and finest wine suddenly appeared, the master of ceremonies announced that the wedding host had a novel approach in saving the best wine for the last serving. And the party went on. A noted Biblical scholar once noted that the feast did not run out of wine until Jesus showed up with a bunch of sailors!

The fruit of the Spirit is experienced by all who were present, believers and non-believers alike. Jesus and everyone at the wedding celebration enjoyed the party, which happened to include the new wine that mysteriously appeared. Likewise, the fruit of the Spirit is experienced when hikers gather for good fellowship. Whatever the fun-filled setting might be, the fruit of the Spirit is joyfully shared. In other words, God's beneficence is for everyone, even though many will not see a formidable miracle of Grace happen. That is one of many attributes of God. As I continue knowing God, it is a comfort to me that God is like this – everywhere, all-knowing, infinite, and good. God is never stagnant and detached from us.

Our Heavenly Maker is the Creator, constantly re-creating within us and through us. That is why I love the definition of the word re-creation. By embracing recreation in our lives, we embrace God's very Nature into the fiber of our lifestyle. Noticing God's Grace brings transformation to the one who is a witness. Noticing the attributes of God's grace helps to build a trusting relationship with God. In whatever setting God's grace is witnessed, we might experience God speaking in that moment, saying "follow me!"

Let us enjoy the fun and re-creation that Jesus has for us in this scripture, Matthew 19:14-15. *"Jesus said, 'Let the children come to me. Do not stop them! For the Kingdom of Heaven belongs to such as these.' And he put his hands on their heads and blessed them."*

Prayer: Holy and Gracious God, Creator of Heaven and Earth. You are the Maker of all things good, and we are Your blessed children. You are mysterious in the way You show up unexpectedly. When we praise You and give thanks for Your presence in our lives, let us reflect on how Your presence happens, re-Creating our very existence. You come in the good times too, and we often forget to thank You and praise You for those blessings. Thank You for the natural surroundings of Your Creation in Nature which comforts us with the Truth that You are sovereign over all the universe. The beauty of Your creation is unfathomable. That You want us to seek You and to be our Savior and trusted Guide is hard to comprehend. Amen

Question to provoke faith journaling: How are you forfeiting the fun and re-creation of Jesus' children? You are a child of God!

Sanctuary

A Step To Grace: This is God's world. Be gracious to it.

Exodus 25:8 *Build me a sanctuary.* NLT

Hebrews 8:2 *There he ministers in the sacred tent, the true place of worship that was built by the Lord and not by human hands.* NLT

    These two scriptures, Exodus from the Old Testament, and Hebrews, from the New Testament, underline God's direction to his people to create a safe and dedicated space to worship and praise God. A sanctuary is a place where believers experience an amplified presence of God. A place where worship is easy. A sanctuary is also a solitary place within oneself where deep communion with God happens and resonates within the soul. Comparing the Old Testament and New Testament scriptures, I see that God wants us to cultivate both spheres of communion with Him. My AT hiking trips became a spiritual journey when I began witnessing the sanctuary I found in God's Nature and searching for Jesus Christ's presence as well.

    When I first met Smasher through phone conversations, we agreed to share our faith while we became acquainted in the wilderness setting. Through Smasher's spiritual companionship while hiking the Trail, I could talk about my life experiences and share how the Lord was working in my life. And Smasher understood my musings because she was on a similar faith journey. Smasher is one of God's greatest answers to my prayers.

    Hiking long distances together led us to sharing the *Upper Room* devotionals along the way. Reading these daily devotional messages while witnessing the Nature of God's presence around us, amplified our shared worship experience. Sometimes we read a devotional and prayed as we stopped for a break on the Trail. Other days we kept the *Upper Room* devotional pocket booklet handy, sharing it at lunch time as we viewed a beautiful panorama overlook of God's creation. Or we shared our devotional time at the end of the day after setting up camp. These times became a place of God's presence, a sanctuary. At times, fellow trekkers would join us in our short devotional times, even though they were strangers to us. [38]

I particularly remember sharing lunch and devotional time under the massive Keefer Oak in Central Virginia. This is the largest oak tree in the southern part of the Trail. Last measured, the girth was 18 feet, 3 inches; it is estimated to be 300 years old. The Texas sanctuary of God's Nature does not include trees this gigantic! Because of my AT experiences of trees and forests, my newfound word for Texas trees is "broccoli!"

From Georgia to Maine, there are areas where the forest canopies remind me of the lofty cathedral ceilings in a church's sanctuary. Smasher and I enjoyed singing hymn tunes as we walked the Trail especially in these locations. One of our favorite hymn tunes to sing was "This is my Father's World." As you read the lyrics, I hope you find the comfort of God's presence in Nature that I feel when singing in the cathedral of the forest.

> *This is my Father's world, and to my listening ears*
> *all nature sings and round me rings the music of the spheres.*
> *This is my Father's world: I rest me in the thought*
> *of rocks and trees, of skies and seas; his hand the wonders wrought.*
>
> *This is my Father's world, the birds their carols raise,*

---

[38] The Upper Room. Nashville, TN

the morning light, the lily white, declare their maker's praise.
This is my Father's world: he shines in all that's fair;
In the rustling grass I hear him pass; He speaks to me everywhere.

This is my Father's world. O let me ne'er forget
that though the wrong seems oft so strong, God is the ruler yet.
This is my Father's world: why should my heart be sad?
The Lord is King; let the heaven's ring! God reigns; let the earth be glad![39]

My cornerstone of spiritual experiences in God's Nature is praying aloud while I walk alone. I mention this faith practice in many of the reflection devotionals, and it must be mentioned here as a place of deep sanctuary. In addition to the Trail experience of prayer walking, I practiced this discipline during physical conditioning in preparation for the hiking trips. With annual September hiking trips, the primary weeks of physical conditioning were the hot Texas summer months. With a loaded backpack, I hiked the streets of my home neighborhood in the cool of the morning dawn, enamored by the star constellations as I prayer walked.

With my faith friend and trail buddy Smasher, we felt moved to visit local church worship services on some of our Zero Days. Townsfolk notice Trail hikers as they come into town for food resupply and to make use of the town's resources. But the worshippers were delightfully surprised when we arrived at their church sanctuary for Sunday worship. After worshipping together, the church folk enjoyed getting acquainted with us and hearing our opinions about their Appalachian Mountain region. We

---
[39] Maltbie D. Babcock (1901)

were interested in their community pride and their concerns. Sometimes we would learn of a minor conflict between the transient trekkers on the AT and the town folk. There are many country churches within view of the Trail path, which adds to the Trail's spiritual serenity. From North Carolina to Maine, we attended worship services at small town churches in the mountains, on six occasions or more. We always left the fellowship of believers feeling welcomed and uplifted by the fellowship of corporate worship. By worshipping in a local fellowship of believers, we felt spiritually connected to the communities through which we were hiking.

This devotional is an account of the variety of ways that God's presence happened, related to the AT journey in some way. Each of these experiences gave Smasher and I awareness of God's presence, a sanctuary. Please do not view our experiences as the only way God's presence happens. Know that if you seek God by establishing a space to be in His presence, our glorious Savior will appear to you in your sanctuary.

Prayer: O Holy God, Maker of creation. Your amazing Love is beyond our meager comprehension. I want to easily associate Your forests and mountains and all of creation with the majesty and beauty of You. When life seems so wrong, I will praise you, Merciful Ruler. Send forth Your Holy Spirit and move me into community and into fellowship that carries Your Love. Guide me deeper into the power of your Love, transforming me as a contributor to the Body of Christ. I yearn to grow the sanctuary of Your presence in my soul. Guide me to Your Holy presence, precious Savior, Jesus Christ. Amen.

A question to promote faith journaling: Are you creating time and space as a sanctuary with God?

Giving

A Step To Grace: Ask the Holy Spirit to amplify your giving.

John 6: 5–11 *Jesus soon saw a great crowd of people climbing the hill, looking for him. Turning to Philip, he asked, "Philip, where can we buy bread to feed all these people?" He was testing Philip, for he already knew what he was going to do. Philip replied, "It would take a small fortune to feed them!" Then Andrew, Simon Peter's brother, spoke up, "There's a young boy here with five barley loaves and two fish. But what good is that with this huge crowd?" "Tell everyone to sit down," Jesus ordered. So all of them – the men alone numbered five thousand – sat down on the grassy slopes. Then Jesus took the loaves, gave thanks to God, and passed them out to the people. Afterward he did the same with the fish. And they all ate until they were full.* LNT

This scripture describes people gathering to hear Jesus because they had heard of his healing powers. The miracle of the boy's loaves and fish that fed thousands of people captured their attention even before Jesus spoke to them. I believe Jesus knew the Holy Spirit was with Him, preparing the way for His words to be truly heard. Giving to others like the boy gave his food to the crowd is an example of the Holy Spirit moving among us. Giving helps us grow in ways that Jesus wants us to do. When we act with generosity, our souls resonate with our awareness of Jesus' love. When we graciously accept the generosity of others, we are also sharing in the celebration of God's love. Giving and receiving graciously is fruit of the Holy Spirit.

After a long day on the Trail, Smasher and I wearily arrived at the chosen destination, an AT shelter. Other backpackers were already there, settling into the shelter space, laying out their sleeping bags, and pulling food from backpacks preparing to cook. Other hikers were gathering kindling and wood. It was a cool evening so building a campfire for warmth as well as an optional cooking site was a great idea. As we came into the shelter clearing, congenial chatter filled the air, welcoming us into the fold. We laid down our backpacks and began our evening tasks while getting acquainted. Out of the seven hikers at the shelter, only Smasher and I knew each other.

A rustling in the nearby underbrush made everyone stop what they were doing. The sound announced that something was quickly approaching the shelter area. It sounded like a large creature rustling and struggling to climb the steep mountain which was thickly covered with underbrush and trees. This unusual sound came from a side of the shelter that was opposite the Trail access, so logic said it could not be a hiker. Breaking through the forest into the clearing came a middle-aged man with a cheerful grin on his face. He carried two heavy cast iron cooking pots in his arms and a backpack filled with groceries. The trailblazing man announced to the gathering at the shelter that he lived at the bottom of the mountain. He was eager to make his appearance before supper time, so he took the quickest route to the shelter by climbing straight up the mountain, bushwhacking his way through the woods. He declared that everyone was invited to partake in the meal he was about to prepare. The man proceeded to cook a luscious hot meal over the campfire. His gracious gift expanded the good fellowship that evening. That campfire evening experience rests among my warmest memories because we enjoyed shared food, laughter, and storytelling and his "giving" is what made it especially meaningful.

Hiking the AT in the autumn months has given me deep appreciation of God's ways at a time when Nature is becoming dormant. I enjoy watching the autumn leaves begin to take color, the wind scattering leaves everywhere and the leaves falling to the ground. I find meaning in defining the autumn season as more than Nature becoming dormant. I like to think of the autumn season as the beginning step toward new life. As leaves fall, the seeds also fall from the trees, and some of the seeds settle into the forest floor, taking root below the tree of origin. Some of the seeds are disbursed by the wind and fall on rocky ground. Other seeds journey far away from the parent tree. Maybe the seeds settle into fertile soil. Who knows where some seeds ultimately land? The seeds that drop directly under the tree are like those people who are under our immediate sphere of influence in life. We have a calling to cultivate the fertile soil for our immediate family and friendship circle. I believe that Jesus calls us to be His giving presence to loved ones nearby where we can frequently pass on God's love and grace to them. I dwelt on spiritual thoughts like this while I enjoyed my autumn walks in the woods.

My reflections about the autumn forests are like Jesus' parable of the farmer sowing seeds, Matthew 13: 3–24. To those who were ready to hear, the parable teaches that a bountiful harvest of new believers will come from believers who spread the Good News.

Giving is acting on the belief of the Holy Spirit dwelling within us. By believing that God's Holy Spirit will equip us to be "givers" and to also be gracious "receivers", we are allowing the Holy Spirit to empower us wherever we wander. As instruments of the Holy Spirit, wherever we are, we will be prepared to give (and receive) God's nourishing light.

There are occasions when we need to ask ourselves these questions. "What are our motives behind an occasion of giving? Does our giving serve us and our "needs" or serve God by serving the discipleship that we are doing in His Name?"

Let us be the magical moment. Let us be a giver and instantly be blessed. Let us be the magical moment for a loved one or a stranger. Let us be like the trailblazing stranger delivering a magical moment at the AT shelter. Let us be a giving vessel of the Holy Spirit, and God will guide that nourished seed that this person's future will be impacted.

Remember dear faith friends, God gave us His Son. Not because we were entitled to this gift or because we expected this gift. We never knew this gift was coming. We are still surprised by the fact that we need this gift, the Messiah, Our Savior. Jesus came to us a powerless baby born in a lowly manger to homeless parents. God came to us with this unexpected gift and yes, He had a motive. God's motive is pure and real. God's gift of His Son came to us so that we might believe in God's saving grace through His Love. The very gift of Jesus as a baby told us of THE GIFT of Love. God wants us to choose the self-understanding that we need His Love, His Gift. Let us pass it on by Giving and sharing the Light. [40] The hymn, *Pass It On,* captures this perfectly. *"That's how it is with God's love once you've experienced it; you spread his love to everyone: you want to pass it on. "*

Prayer: I give You all the Glory, oh Gracious God! Your generosity to me is immeasurable. Giving me Your Son Jesus Christ is the everlasting gift that saves me from despair. Your Grace and Love provides all that I need. I ask that You continue Your patient presence in my life so Your nourishment grows my belief in You. I want to be Your faithful follower and pass on Your light and love to all around me. Amen

Question to provoke faith journaling – How do your acts of giving integrate with your beliefs in God?

---

[40] *Pass It On*, copyright Kurt Kaiser, 1969

Moments of Belief

Spence Field Shelter, Great Smoky Mountains NP In 2005, Marine Helicopters donated their services for airlifting materials for shelter rehab; volunteers from the SMHC rebuilt the shelter.
Courtesy of Appalachian Trail Conservancy

Storms

A Step to Belief: During a storm, despite your fears, pray what you believe!

Matthew 8:23 - 27 *Then Jesus got into the boat and started across the lake with his disciples. Suddenly, a terrible storm came up, with waves breaking into the boat. But Jesus was sleeping. The disciples went to him and woke him up, shouting, "Lord, save us! We're going to drown!" And Jesus answered, "Why are you afraid? You have so little faith!" Then he stood up and rebuked the wind and waves, and suddenly all was calm. The disciples just sat there in awe. "Who is this? They asked themselves. "Even the wind and waves obey him!"* NLT

Isaiah 43:16 *I am the Lord, who opened a way through the waters, making a dry path through the sea.* NLT

Storms frequently happened during my twenty hiking trips to complete 2000 AT miles. Living in the outdoors and being alert to Nature's elements suddenly changing is a part of the precious journey that I chose. Here are three hiking trip stories that illustrate some of God's Nature and the growing faith that came when I prayed what I believed while the storm raged.

"Stand By Me"
When the storms of life are raging, stand by me.
When the storms of life are raging, stand by me.
When the world is tossing me, like a ship upon the sea,
Thou who rulest wind and sea, stand by me. [41]

---
[41] Charles Albert Tindley, 1905

It was the first day of a six-week planned backpacking trip through the Presidential mountain range of New Hampshire.[42] My hiking partner and I launched from Pinkham Notch (elevation 2,000 feet) with minimum weight in our backpacks. We headed southbound with hopes of climbing Mt. Washington, elevation 6,288 feet. The climb to Mt Washington is bouldering and not a traditional trail path through a forest. On the second day out, we left our Osgood campsite and climbed 3,000 feet in three miles! As we arrived at the peak of Mt Webster, exhausted, we happened to meet a park ranger on the Trail. The park ranger informed us that we must leave the mountain ridge area immediately. We were well above tree line, and totally exposed to the weather elements with a rapidly arriving thunderstorm. When he told us to descend below the tree line, we shared with him our plans to stay at the Lake of the Clouds Hut, a short distance beyond Mt Washington. The ranger informed us that we were wrong to expect the Hut to be open. The Hut had recently closed for the season. Again, the ranger emphatically stated that we must go, and he pointed to the Gulfside Trail as the blue blaze trail leading off the mountain. We were only three miles from Mt Washington! We swiftly moved downhill, our leg muscles enjoying the change from the morning's uphill workout. Within two hours we arrived at Valley Way tent site and set up camp in the thick woods. We had just enough daylight to prepare for the coming thunderstorm. I carried a lightweight tarp tent which we erected on a wooden tent platform. The tarp tent was open to the elements unlike the enclosed traditional tent.

Shortly after nightfall, the storm arrived and lasted throughout the night. In the minimal shelter of the tarp tent, we had protection and were grateful for it. The powerful storm was frightening, and I felt exposed and vulnerable. Throughout the night I

---

[42] 2001 September Hiking Trip

watched the lightning, some trees falling near us, and the heavy rainfall. The tarp tent was a true blessing because I included it at the last minute despite the extra pack weight, as a safety option. I do not know how we otherwise could have found shelter from the storm. Looking back on this day, I am grateful that the ranger gave us early warning and insisted that we descend the mountain immediately. The following morning, the forest was drenching wet, and broken tree limbs littered the forest floor. We packed up and continued to follow the blue blaze Gulfside Trail downhill to the trailhead at a road crossing. From there we were able to hitch hike into Gorham and make our way by bus to another side of Mt Washington for further backpacking days.

I first learned about hurricane season on the East Coast in 2003. [43]Smasher and I were backpacking through southwestern Virginia for several days when we noticed odd circumstances wherever the Trail intersected with major roadway thoroughfares, like Interstate 81. We saw electric utility repair trucks parked at every single motel, filling all the parking lots. When we asked a worker in a fast-food diner what was happening, she explained that Hurricane Isabel was expected to arrive in the area any day. The forecast for Hurricane Isabel was ominous, the worst hurricane in decades to hit the East Coast as well as inland areas. Hurricane Isabel lived up to that forecast. Knowing that our safety meant leaving the Trail quickly, Smasher and I started calling motels within a one-hour radius. There were no vacancies.

Our AT resource book listed hiking hostels in the area, but when we called them, it was the same outcome. We were feeling desperate to find immediate shelter and very little time to find a solution. We considered the option of stopping our backpacking trip. We considered going to Smasher's home which was hours away. With a final effort to quickly find shelter, we decided to

---

[43] 2003 September Hiking Trip

expand the search to places that were two hours further north on the Trail from our location. That did it! A hiking hostel in Montebello, Va. had room for us and welcomed us to come immediately. Driving our two cars north on Interstate 81, then navigating our way at night through the backwoods on mountain roads, we finally arrived at the Dutch Haus. Lois and Earl Arnold welcomed us with cheerful hospitality! Their warm welcome to we strangers felt like we had entered God's light!

After living in a dark and hopeless place due to the approaching storm and arduous search for a place of safety, we were on God's safe path. The next morning, looking out from our comfy shelter, we saw the surrounding forest trees bending from the force of the misty hurricane winds . The local weather forecast promised that Hurricane Isabel was approaching. By late afternoon, the hurricane force wind and rain would be upon us. The Arnold's understood our desire to accomplish any Trail miles that we could that day before the storm arrived. Earl Arnold drove us to an AT road crossing and dropped us off for an eight-mile day hike back to their hiking hostel. Knowing that we had safe shelter before Hurricane Isabel's arrival allowed us to embrace the wind and rain without fear, thereby enjoying the adventurous walk in the woods.

The next year, as the September 2004 hiking trip began, Smasher and I again found ourselves back in the trials of hurricane season in Virginia.[44] Hurricane Frances came first and weeks later Hurricane Ivan followed. The previous year's Hurricane Isabel had caused great devastation in Virginia. This experience caused people to be especially wary of the coming hurricanes. When Hurricane Frances was forecast, we immediately left the Trail and again sought refuge in Lois and Earl Arnold's cozy lodging.

It was this visit with the Arnolds that cemented our friendship for years to come. Earl Arnold gave us the nickname "Hurricane

---

[44] 2004 September Hiking Trip

Hussies!" We enjoyed a hurricane party atmosphere with other hikers gathered beside us, enjoying tasty food, and telling Trail stories in the candlelight of electrical outages. Though we were not confident of someday completing the 2,000 miles on the AT, Smasher and I leaned into Lois Arnold's belief in us, and her insistent invitation to celebrate completion of the final AT miles near their place. We knew a final celebration with them would surely be a great memorable experience for us.[45]

Weeks later, when Hurricane Ivan was forecasted, not long after our stay at the Dutch Haus, we were tent camping in Shenandoah National Park (SNP) using Loft Mountain as a base camp. Once again, to error on the side of caution, we left the outdoors and moved into a nearby Park cabin. AT thru-hikers were seeking last minute cheap shelter from this Hurricane. We helped those that we could. One hiker slept on our cabin floor. And another hiker slept in my truck bed with a camper cover. The next few Trail days were slow travel because of the numerous forest tree blowdowns obstructing the Trail. Hurricane Ivan had left its damaging mark.

I relate to the disciples' fear of being in the fishing boat during a storm. Fear is real, but faith is also real. Fear is informative, but only to a point. After that point, fear feeds on itself. As Jesus pointed out to the disciples, we believers must exercise faith, use our faith, especially in times of fear. When we do not go to our faith, despair, and fear creep in. When a problem needs to be addressed, faith in God is what gets us through the storm. I have found that one part of acting on faith is talking through fear in my prayer conversations. By doing so, Jesus brings God's calming presence into my soul. God makes a way forward, as stated in Isaiah 40:16:

---

[45] 2015 August/September Hiking Trip

'I am the Lord, who opened a way through the waters, making a dry path through the sea.'

My faith was nourished and I found new determination during the storms on the AT. With the assuring faithfulness of Jesus, I can remain calmer through the problem-solving process.

Ultimately, I am going to be okay, because of God's enduring faithfulness. I do not need to know the solution while the storm is raging. I am held in His arms. I do not need to be in total control while the storm is raging because God's got this. My faith friends, please remember the following verse from the song, "Blessings" by Laura Story, a beautiful praise song about storms:

'Cause what if Your blessings come through raindrops
What if Your healing comes through tears?
And what if a thousand sleepless nights
Are what it takes to know You're near?
And what if trials of this life
Are Your mercies in disguise?

Prayer – Precious Savior, Your presence in the boat with the disciples during that frightening storm comforts me. You are never far away, and You are always responding to my need for comforting reassurance. When I see a storm in my life coming, help me to first turn to You, my Refuge in the storm. You are my ever-faithful Guide, giving me safe harbor while the storm rages on. Holy Jesus, help me to face fear and turn to You, believing in and trusting Your way forward instead of relying on my limited understanding. Amen.

Question to provoke faith journaling – When you have storms in life, how do you recall God comforting your soul with His love and presence? What do you believe about God that helps you?

Diligence

A Step To Belief: With diligence, wear your blessings well.

Romans 12: 1–2 *And so, dear brothers and sisters, I plead with you to give your bodies to God because of all he has done for you. Let them be a living and holy sacrifice—the kind he will find acceptable. This is truly the way to worship him.¹ Don't copy the behavior and customs of this world, but let God transform you into a new person by changing the way you think. Then you will learn to know God's will for you, which is good and pleasing and perfect.* NLT

For many years, my lifestyle of annual AT hiking trips caused me to sometimes feel guilt and shame. Upon returning home from a hiking trip and telling others of my renewed soul and energy for living, I often worried that people saw me as a self-absorbed, privileged white woman who frivolously used time and money for adventure trips while dumping all family responsibilities. I felt others were jealous of my happiness. Eventually, to avoid the discomfort of my assumptions, I chose to give a quick trip report whenever someone voiced an interest in my latest hiking trip. I wanted to appear humble to others, hoping they would approve of me. By choosing a dismissive attitude and voice, I was discounting the value of my soul renewing trips and as well my faith journey. Letting the indifference of our worldly culture negatively impact me was not the best approach. Unfortunately, I gave up my victory voice by silencing my witness statements about the grace and love of Jesus.

A Texas pastor caught my attention when he said, "Wear your blessings well." This phrase fits well with the message of this scripture from Romans. This scripture tells us that conforming to the ways of the world opposes God's desire to transform us. Seeking acceptance from others in place of learning to be obedient to God's ways leaves us confused and eventually indifferent about life's purpose. Having a lifestyle permeated by Jesus' favor because we diligently choose to answer His call is living a joy filled life journey. This is the Good News!

When we share these countless blessings with others, it is a message of God's hope for their lives too, and not a statement of bragging and self-pride. Others will sometimes be jealous of our happiness sustained by faith, but that is not your responsibility or your fault. Let God be God! Wear your blessings joyfully. Tell others what grace is happening as you witness it. Your diligence of choosing Jesus' presence in all earthly happenings brings proof of the Living God to those who hear your irrefutable testimony. Take ownership of the joy you have from God because doing so declares His victory over life and death.

Reflecting over the many hiking trip years, I can see that I slowly claimed my walk with the Lord, and increasingly shared with others my victory in Him. There was a pivotal experience on the Trail where I quickly learned to not lose my witnessing voice to the forces of indifference as I left the Trail and returned to normal daily living. In 2003, as I shared a September in Virginia with Smasher and Millerman.[46] We were bringing the trip to a close on the banks of the James River, and we had finished an evening of tasty food and leisurely campfire chats about our numerous days of hiking. As the day ended, it was a good opportunity to call home, so I walked across the campground to the public pay phone and called my husband. Prior to the era of cell phones, this was the practice that Tim and I had where every two or three days, I would "come out of the woods" and check in.

---

[46] September 2003 Section Hiking Trip

Tim was anxiously waiting for my call with an urgent request that I drop everything and catch the next plane home to Texas. Our college age daughter, Adrianne, was hospitalized with an unexpected mental health crisis and she needed me at her side immediately. Hearing the need for my help, I was overwhelmed with feelings of guilt that I was not available at home for Adrianne and the family. Instead of being a responsible family member, I was on the Trail and living "the good life."

Thank you, Holy Jesus! The simplicity of Trail life made a diligent practice of daily prayer an easy habit to develop. Therefore, when my initial inner response to the unexpected crisis was so debilitating, even so I was tuned-in and focused on my faith. In the safe fellowship of Trail friends around our comforting campfire, I was able to unload my feelings of guilt and the self-blame burden. With fervent prayers for Adrianne's healing and my readiness to witness to her, I felt the Holy Spirit preparing me to depart the sanctuary of Nature and fellow believers. I received invaluable advice and help from them, quickly packed the necessary items, left the campground, caught a plane out of Virginia and returned home. My Trail friend, Millerman, gave four days of help to my family by driving my truck with his in tow carrying my backpacking gear to Texas. He then had a long drive back to his home in Alabama.

Lo and behold! I soon discovered that my well-honed spiritual practices and faith, acquired from uninterrupted time with Jesus, enabled me to be Jesus' witness and voice the healing medicine of hope that Adrianne and the family so desperately needed. Powered by the unfathomable love of Jesus, my presence brought divine light to our precious daughter in her time of darkness. Without the diligence of daily practicing of time with Jesus, I could not have victoriously claimed the favor of Jesus, and then shown Adrianne the blessings abounding all around her at that time. Faith, Hope and Love - the healing balm of Holy Jesus.

Adrianne and I both learned to correct a faulty belief about relating to God through this shared challenging time. You may know that common saying, "God helps those who help themselves." That saying is not biblical and it is not a belief that relates to God, in my opinion. Let's fix this faulty belief and make a better saying. "God helps those who need help and know that they need help: So they ask for help!"

Our Lord and Savior was healing and strengthening me while also caring for our daughter. As Adrianne and I studied the Bible and shared daily prayers, I saw the truth that secular based mental health measures do not make people appreciate you, nor does it win real battles in life. We both needed diligent trust in Jesus to find real happiness. Over time I increasingly let go of worldly discourse and progressed in trusting the Lord first. When I feel the impulse towards negative self-talk or the negative assumptions about others, I try to notice the impulse and reflect on its inaccuracy. The reflective thoughts inevitably drown out the negative thoughts and my soul fills up with precious conversations with Jesus. In this process, destructive self-talk and negative influences have less power over me, and the love and grace of Jesus meets my every need. As the scripture implies, there is a turn away from indifference when we turn toward our faith with diligence. As I practice this diligence, I embrace God's purpose in my life more completely. Joyfully, I am ready to be His obedient servant.

Prayer: Glorious God, Your constant presence at the door to my life gives me the necessary courage to step into daily living with You at my side. It is so hard to turn away from the alluring recognition and admiration of other people which feeds my ego. Help me overcome my indifference and diligently seek Your ways and glorify You in all that I do. Show me the way to share Your light and witness to Your Grace and Love. I long to sit at the table of Your victory and to celebrate with You. Amen

A question to promote faith journaling: Through the ebb and flow of apathy and diligence in your faith journey, what event of Grace in your life were your prepared to embrace? Write down this Grace moment that you noticed God transforming you by changing the way you think. Consider how your diligence to obey God's transformation of you would impact your walk with Jesus.

Pacing

A Step to Belief: Pause and praise. We cannot pray our way out of a silent season.

Jonah 4:1-5 *This change of plans greatly upset Jonah, and he became very angry. So he complained to the L*ORD *about it: "Didn't I say before I left home that you would do this, L*ORD*? That is why I ran away to Tarshish! I knew that you are a merciful and compassionate God, slow to get angry and filled with unfailing love. You are eager to turn back from destroying people. Just kill me now, L*ORD*! I'd rather be dead than alive if what I predicted will not happen."*

*The L*ORD *replied, "Is it right for you to be angry about this?" Then Jonah went out to the east side of the city and made a shelter to sit under as he waited to see what would happen to the city.* NLT

One of the most valuable trail lessons I learned was how to pace my journey. I define pacing as the approach to daily life that incorporates listening to what God has to say before choosing the priorities for the day. When I lose track of God's input, I try to stop, to listen more intently and thereby recalculate my approach to the day. My personality temperament enjoys following a plan to its completion while checking off to-do's along the way. I like to focus on getting to the completion of a plan as soon as possible. Praise God that I no longer easily fall for this foolishness of a blind tunnel vision that only focuses on the destination. Pacing life has taught me a counterbalance to my tendencies. I learned to focus on a quality process to the destination.

In the Old Testament Book of Jonah, God is showing compassion not only for the Jews but for all peoples and nations. God called Jonah to warn the people of Nineveh that they faced destruction if they refused to repent of their sins. But Jonah ran away from this calling because he disagreed with God. He wanted God to destroy the wicked city. While on the run, Jonah is swallowed by a great fish where he remains for three days and nights in its belly. Then Jonah accepts God's deliverance and redirects his obedience back to God. The great fish spits him out and Jonah continues to Nineveh to voice God's warning to the people. Jonah is angry that the outcome was not what he wanted for the people of Nineveh. After Jonah gave them the warning which God called him to do, the people repented of their sins and God showed them mercy. Notice how the scripture describes Jonah complaining to God and then he sits down to wait out how God's plan will further unfold. Jonah has begrudgingly remained amid challenges that God has called him to do.

As Jonah accepted the obedience of following God's will and plan, he experienced the wisdom of pacing. By pacing his journey to be in step with the Lord, Jonah learned a deeper faith lesson. Specifically, he learned about forgiving others rather than seeking revenge. Like Jonah, I too get frustrated and angry when God is calling me to more important revelations and actions than what my personal agenda for the day had in mind.

In my mind, there is one person who holds the grand title of quality pacing in all dimensions. In 1990, while thru-hiking the AT, Bill Irwin a blind man with his seeing-eye dog Orient, solo hiked the AT in nine months. In his book, *Blind Courage*, Irwin describes how the co-author, Dave McCasland, was his only trail companion. McCasland joined him for the last five weeks of the trek. At the age of 49, Bill chose to mark his third anniversary of sobriety by embarking on the AT thru-hike journey. Because of his blindness,

Bill could not see the AT trail markers, white paint stripes, two inches wide and six inches long. His dog Orient eventually learned to follow the AT trail markers to guide them. Orient also learned to take Bill to the trail signage so that he could read the signs by touching them.

Bill's laborious journey came to mind whenever I was facing an ordeal on the AT. Overwhelmed about how I would pass through the challenge, I would declare "How in the world did Bill Irwin survive this trail spot?" Certainly, Bill's perseverance over daily peril required great courage. However, Bill says that it was his faith in God's presence that gave him strength to continue.

To keep a hiking pace that eliminates wearing out before the completion of the day's hike, I take a ten-minute break every hour. My body needs that regular rest stop to manage all sorts of bodily functions like hot spots on a foot, potty time, and full orientation on my trail location. Pacing like this allows the most valuable tool I have to function at its best – my brain. The brain manages the emotions best when the body is self-regulating instead of being impulse driven. It required several years for me to form this habit and reap the benefits of a paced hiked.

Bill Irwin's trail accounts describe a struggle to find the pacing approach that worked for him. With Orient the dog his constant companion guiding him through pleasures and perils, Bill describes making time to stop and listen to God's guidance as well as the guidance of Orient.

Finding a pace that includes mind, body and soul is clearly a journey that we struggle to achieve. Jonah struggled with this, as well as Bill Irwin and me. The struggle is worth the reward because pacing is integral to building a relationship with God. Through a growing relationship with God, I personally know that all challenges in life are more easily addressed. Consciously choose to stop – complain – blame – pout - even run away – but eventually choose to finish the self-discipline steps of seeking God's guidance and companionship.

Prayer: Holy Jesus, sometimes I struggle to trust Your faithfulness to me. When I am headstrong and impulsive, I forfeit Your precious companionship. You are always ready to protect and to purify me if I will only set a pace inclusive to Your presence. Forgive me when I fail to do this. Help me to seek Your Grace and Love as integral to my pacing in life. Amen

A question to provoke faith journaling: Are you moving at a pace that leaves God out of companionship with you?

False Summits

A Step to Belief: True summits are moments of celebrating the shared vista with Jesus Our Savior

Mark 9: 2–9 *Six days later Jesus took Peter, James, and John to the top of a high mountain to be alone. As the men watched, Jesus' appearance was transformed, and his clothing became dazzling white, far whiter than any earthly bleach could ever make them. Then Elijah and Moses appeared and began talking with Jesus. Peter exclaimed. "Rabbi, this is wonderful for us to be here! "Let's make three shelters as memorials – one for you, one for Moses, and one for Elijah." He said this because he didn't really know what else to say, for they were all terrified. Then a cloud overshadowed them, and a voice from the cloud said, "This is my dearly loved Son. Listen to him." Suddenly when they looked around, and Moses and Elijah were gone, and they only saw Jesus with them. As they went back down the mountain, he told them not to tell anyone what they had seen until the Son of Man, had risen from the dead. So they kept it to themselves, but they often asked each other what he meant by "rising from the dead."* NLT

This scripture describes what has become known as "The Transfiguration of Jesus Christ," when three disciples witnessed but did not understand what they were seeing. They misinterpreted many aspects of this extraordinary moment of God's presence, and Jesus' Transfiguration as well as the appearance of the prophets Moses and Elijah who had died long ago. The disciples interpreted the moment as a sign pointing to the significant prophets in their Jewish faith which now included Jesus. One disciple witness, Peter, exclaimed the importance of building a shrine for each one of the prophets, identifying them as equal messengers from God. Then God pointed specifically to Jesus as His Son, and Jesus told the disciples that he is the Son of Man. Even so, the disciples remained confused. Jesus goes on to tell them more about his life to come as they depart from the mountain. Jesus tells the disciples of his pending death and resurrection. Jesus' prediction makes no sense to the disciples. Over the coming months, they continued to discuss its meaning as Jesus continued to tell them multiple times that his death and Resurrection was coming. In further readings from the Gospel of Mark, we learn that everyone, including those who witnessed Christ's death on the cross, were resigned to a closed door on their hope for an earthly King over Israel.

When we get hooked into our worldly view of a precious spiritual experience like this one conveyed through scripture, we tend to cling to our earthly viewpoint and succumb to natural disappointments. We do this because our expectations from the viewpoint our human condition are not realized. That is what happened to the disciples on that mountaintop with Jesus. I have come to think of these moments as false summits. From our limited vantage point of life's journey, we erroneously assume that we know it all; we think that we know the journey step by step as well as the destination. I totally relate with the disciples as they witnessed this unfathomable spiritual moment. There is no doubt that I would have been confused, just like the disciples, and tried to create my own limited explanation. My worldly viewpoint would have ignored this open doorway to learning more about God's Truth in my life. False summits also occur in mountainous terrain. A false peak that appears to be the pinnacle of the mountain, but upon reaching it, the true summit is higher or further away.

False peaks can have significant effects on a hiker's psychological state by inducing feelings of dashed hopes or even failure. When you realize that you are at a false summit and your hopes are dashed, it is hard to feel motivated about climbing further up the mountainside trail. It feels like you have been wronged by the world, by Nature, or maybe by God.

All my life I have been eager to set goals and to obtain them. As I became hooked on my AT hiking trips, my natural desire for attaining goals creeped into the enjoyment of this recreational time. For me, the enjoyment of planning and experiencing a hiking trip is an easy analogy to enjoyment of creating and attaining personal long-term life goals. Over time, I developed a personal goal setting methodology, first for my own usage, test driving the model on myself and eventually perfecting the model for female clients to use in my life coaching practice.

Eventually the model became a self-published 220-page workbook, *Life Maps Workbook, Lifestyle Goal Setting Journey for Women*. The workbook gives women a practical model on how to envision and implement a plan for a lifestyle goal journey. Many of the life skill examples in the workbook came from personal experiential lessons learned on the AT journey.

My Lifestyle Goal Statement, written in 1998, guided my Life Map journey throughout the following years. I still embrace it today. The following is found in my AT journal. My goal statement had not changed in those four years.

"June 30, 2012, I am enjoying the spiritual, relational and physical health of completing 2,000 miles on the Appalachian Trail. My retirement lifestyle is well grounded in maintaining these key components of well-being."

When planning for meaningful change in life, first you create a written goal statement briefly describing what your Lifestyle Goal attainment looks like when it is achieved in all the segments of your desired lifestyle. An example of that first step is the statement that I shared with you in the previous paragraph. After completing this critical first step, you then develop a step-by-step plan for reaching the goal. In this step of writing the plan for your desired future, you accurately define the major subgoals that comprise the integral parts of your Lifestyle Goal statement. Each subgoal is a portion of what gives you passion and purpose for daily living. The subgoals are not easily articulated in writing, but once accomplished, you then place the subgoals on the Life Map timeline that leads to your Lifestyle Goal statement.

False summits in personal goal setting will usually occur when attempting to reach a subgoal. By addressing this specific stumbling block in life's path, I hope to entice you to take your chosen plans for a life direction into a closer walk with Jesus.

False summits occur when I forget to include Jesus' counsel in the creating, the on-going implementation, and the evaluation of personal goals. Recognizing the cautionary signals of a pending false summit is critical to the development of a reliable life direction plan. If you do not recognize these signals and experience a false summit, your life direction becomes less comfortable and more chaotic. One cautionary signal is when I develop a bad attitude. When I stubbornly seek my plan, defending it without hesitancy, this is a cautionary signal that I am creating a false summit.

As you read other reflection devotionals describing early years of my faith journey and AT trips, you will notice an evolving process. Early on I focus on a personal goal of spiritual health and later, after discovering many false summits, I begin to open the door to Jesus in my life by taking leaps of faith in Him. As I learned to minimize the number of false summits by asking for counsel from Jesus before acting, the journey was no longer a solo thing. The welcomed presence of Jesus transformed my daily living into a living faith journey. Faith and trust in Jesus does not make your troubles go away. Trusting in Jesus makes the troubled times so much easier to handle. Reflecting on this lengthy evolution, I see how my personal goals continued to guide my life direction yet my relationship with Christ Jesus transformed the personal goals into a greater accomplishments than I could have ever imagined. [47]

In 2008, the long-anticipated challenge of summiting Mt. Katahdin, elevation 5,268 feet was upon us. I had 13 AT hiking trips of experience informing me that I was ready to tackle what Trail-talk denotes as the ultimate measuring stick on performance. Additionally, I had learned about the elusive false summits in life, on and off the Trail. I could trust myself to lean into Jesus in the good times and the tough times rather than fail by defaulting to stubborn humanistic independence.

In the previous years, Jesus walked with me through difficult times like Mom's passing away, my husband's occupational change, my business flourishing, both adult children taking on post-college careers, and more. My hiking buddy and Trail soulmate, Smasher, went through major surgeries as well as similar life transition issues during this time. Though we felt the timing was right to tackle Mt. Katahdin (before our knees got too old!) and the rugged desolate 281 trail miles of Maine, wisdom and faith kept our eyes on Jesus as we planned the four week-long trip. Just one month before the well-planned hiking trip was to launch, Smasher was diagnosed with Multiple Sclerosis (MS), which nearly caused us to cancel. But we prayerfully considered the options and chose to carry on with seasoned and managed expectations of what we could do once we hit the Trail. Never had we so fervently leaned into God's protection and presence as we embarked.

---

[47] 2008 July Hiking Trip

The day before climbing Mt Katahdin we rendezvoused at the Bangor, Maine airport, Smasher flying in from North Carolina, and I flew in from Texas. We put our loaded backpacks in the vehicle of the hired shuttle service driver, rode two hours to the state park where we had a tent campsite reserved, and set up our tents to establish our base camp. The base camp was located at the Trailhead leading to Mt Katahdin, where the AT ascends 4,198 feet in five miles to the Trail's end on the mountain summit. After setting up the basecamp, we went about cooking and eating dinner, and then relaxed under the starry night sky to talk. That evening Smasher and I established a holy space with our Maker's presence. We prayed about the next day's plan, about our worries, about our hopes and expectations. We praised God for all the blessings that brought us to this moment. We gave thanks for the opportunity to focus on an important step in our faith journey. As we asked God to be with us in so many ways, a calm and peace came over us and we felt ready for sleep.

We started out hiking in a beautiful dawn that illuminated the pine trees with delicate flickers of light in the forest. God was with us as we walked along a bubbling mountain stream flowing over large rocks; the sound soothing the soul. The morning sounds in the forest included birds singing but the Trail was otherwise quietly sleeping. Our spirits were hopeful and courageous as we started this challenging day.

Many hikers joined us soon after dawn, but they were decades younger than us, and more physically fit. We were quickly left in their Trail dust. Being out paced by younger legs was not a new experience. This day we were particularly resolved to keeping our steady reliable pace. Unlike us, most of the hikers on Mt. Katahdin were thru-hikers about to celebrate months of hiking 2,126 miles and finishing it on this day. People were in particularly good spirits for that reason.

As the Trail left the forest and continued to climb above the tree line, the Trail was no longer dirt, but became boulder climbing. Smasher and I were fearful when this challenge came so early in the day because we knew the Trail would remain like this all the way to the Trail terminus on the summit. Climbing Mt Katahdin, the northern end of the AT, is a day hike event for everyone. Because hikers go from point A to point B and then back to point A, this type of trail section is described as an "Out and Back". Our backup safety plan for this day hike was to leave basecamp at daybreak and be prepared for a hard stop and turnaround at 2 PM if necessary. This plan left time to descend the mountain before we were too dangerously fatigued and before nightfall.

Once the Trail turned from dirt surface to boulders, our pace was significantly slower. Following the AT markers on the boulders, I was exposed to the wind and sun elements and felt so vulnerable. Sometimes I was afraid of falling as I climbed. When I found a safe spot to rest, I relished in the sight of God's magnificent creation below, above, and all around me. It was breath taking to see. The wind gusted at times, reminding me that Nature has far more power than me. The granite rock boulders were unforgivingly rough and hard on the skin.

Smasher and I were old enough to be mothers to most of the young hikers on the Trail. People noticed and told us so! They were surprised to see us on the mountain climb. Some said we reminded them of their grandmothers! I felt unexpectedly validated that this day's challenge was my own and not to be compared to other hikers on the mountain.

There was no way to accurately measure how far from the summit we were. We relied on hikers descending to report their guess of how much farther the summit was. When we looked up the mountainside, the view was a constant false summit because the mountain has a slow curved bare rock top. The false summits gave a discouraging and frustrating constant viewpoint from the Trail. In preparation for this day, I had not anticipated viewing constant discouragement like this, but soon I realized the need to take this feeling to Jesus in prayer as I kept climbing. My body was losing stamina as we continued to climb and yet, I knew there were many hours left of this stark challenge.

Young hikers began noticing the fatigue in Smasher and me. Two young men, Trail names Barefoot and Ranger, offered their help to us. They assured our safety when boulders were too tall for us to climb by standing behind us and give us a boost.

During the lunchtime break, we evaluated the current situation of our bodies, minds, and spirits. In that conversation with Smasher, I privately realized that reaching the end of the AT on the summit of Mt. Katahdin was unlikely. We continued climbing after lunch. At 2 PM we stopped, talked to descending hikers, and assessed that there was one more mile of climbing to go. But we were exhausted. Continuing to climb would put us in danger physically and leave us without enough time to descend before dark.

Jesus was with us in that somber moment as we asked ourselves two questions. Why are we here? What would Jesus have us do? We decided to use our previously safety plan for this situation. We stopped climbing. On the descent, feeling very fatigued and weak, Barefoot and Ranger stayed with us and provided safety when we could not reach solid footing. Truthfully, it was humbling, but in a good way. We felt God's loving care through the assistance of these strangers who made our safety needs their priority.

Hikers that had summited Mt Katahdin were victoriously descending the mountain with great joy from their accomplishments. It was a victory that I could not claim, as hard as I had tried. I was only one mile short of claiming that personal goal.

As I descended Mt Katahdin, my thoughts and feelings were mixed but I knew there would never be another attempt to summit this mountain. Though I was disappointed, I was simultaneously relishing in Christ's presence comforting me in my loss. But His presence moved on to affirm all that I had accomplished on this first day of a four-week arduous backpacking trip. There I was, descending in human defeat yet experiencing a true summit with Jesus! I relished in God's Grace in many ways – feeling physically safe, supported, and protected by others, assured that Smasher was safe, and most of all, confident that my trust and faith in Jesus is my true stronghold. I descended that mountain eager to live the bigger picture of my life with Jesus always at my side. God never fails to provide all that I need.

Christ died for us when we were yet sinners. (Romans 5:8) We who believe in Him have a life direction filled with His resurrection forgiveness, power, provision, and Love. We have life direction filled with purpose that goes unfathomably beyond our personal goals.

Prayer: Holy Jesus, You are the Way Maker of my life's purpose and I praise Your trustworthy and love-filled companionship. When I stumble, Your mercy comforts me and reminds me that I do not have to measure up to earthly measuring sticks, including my own self-judgment. You are my Savior and Redeemer in the steps of daily living as well as the wholeness of my lifetime. Whenever I seek You, there You are with a "true summit" presence that inspires me to keep going. You give me hope that the long journey of my life will bear great fruit in Your holy name. Amen

A question to provokes faith journaling: Have you invited Jesus to share in the construction of your personal goals? Write a prayer asking Jesus to be with you to intertwine your goals with His purpose in you.

Grieving

A Step to Belief: When we grieve, whether individually or even nationally, God provides all that we need.

Proverbs 3: 5-6 Trust in the Lord with all your heart; do not depend on your own understanding. Seek his will in all you do, and he will show you which path to take. LNT

My faith journey was impacted by twenty years of being on the AT in God's Nature in the month of September, while the American people were memorializing and grieving the tragedy of September 11, 2001. I am called to address the connection of a national grief journey with my own personal grief journey. Both grief journeys are transitions in life where only God's all-knowing presence and provision can bring true healing and peace.

The lengthy experience of grieving is one of the most challenging transitions in life, as an individual, a family group or even in a community. Even a community as large as our nation. We are impacted by times of transition even though we often deny that impact. God understands our humanity. Proverbs speaks to us about trusting God to lead us on the path forward rather than trusting our own understanding. God is so good to us. Because God knows we tend towards denial of reality that we find uncomfortable, God offers up grieving as a life process countless times in our journey of life. In this way, we slowly open up to our need for God as the center of our lives, especially in times of transition.

As I reflect on my faith journey and the annual memorializing of 9/11 while on the Trail, my perspective of 20 years provides some deeper understanding of God's omnipresence. God is the center of Creation in the ongoing unfolding of all the complexities of humanity. In the early years of my counseling career, my understanding of grief was guided by the work of Elisabeth Kubler-Ross in her book, *Death and Dying*. The author describes the life transition of grieving as "The 5 Stages of Grief". The Stages of Grief are in a loose sequential order of Denial, Anger, Bargaining, Depression and Acceptance. I have found the work of Kubler-Ross to be validated in my life as well as the lives of others. I now understand that my professional knowledge was informed by my journey of faith. I see God's Hands holding onto our hands as individuals and the collective, walking us through these stages, if we will seek His will and His way.

After years of planning and preparation, I was closing my backpack and preparing my bags for boarding an airplane to New Hampshire to launch the first long-distance backpacking trip of my life on the morning of September 11, 2001.[48] Two women hiking companions were preparing to meet me on the Appalachian Trail's most challenging section, the White Mountains in New Hampshire. My packing was interrupted by a panicked phone call from our daughter notifying me that an airplane had crashed into the Twin Towers in New York City. Life stopped! When the nation's airports reopened four days later, I was on the first flight out of Austin, Texas headed for New Hampshire. One woman in my hiking group was re-routed to Nova Scotia for three days as her flight from London was stranded, unable to get her home to New Jersey. At the Austin airport, there were military armed guards protecting against the unknown. On my eastbound flight, the aircraft passed over the still smoking rubble of the Twin Towers. In the community of fellow airplane passengers, we saw reality. It was no longer deniable. We watched silently, in the depths of sorrow while we so clearly viewed the devastating tragedy on the ground. As I witnessed this chaos and terrorist destruction, worry

---

[48] 2001 September Hiking Trip

struck me that my college age son could be drafted. The plane flew onward towards the northern end of the Appalachian Trail.

I was determined to go on with The Hike. Regardless of the national collective shock and fear, and the pending warfare around me, I was determined to go on. Grieving about the Empty Nest lifestyle back home was blinding me with stubborn need for control. I was drowning in the Anger Stage of grieving. This was a challenging life transition time. On the national level, the nation was understandably stuck in the early Stages of Grief – Denial and Anger. The nation is still challenged with this transition, 20 years later.

Fifteen days into my AT trip, I awoke in the pre-dawn hours before the challenging climb up Mount Lafayette in New Hampshire. I was struggling with God about my stubborn plan to finish the AT section hike as planned. Even as the crippled nation was in shock, on the Trail I was driven to continue The Hike. I had trusted my hiking partners to understand my needs. I needed to hike slower and to have their companionship on the Trail. But because I trusted them without establishing appropriate personal boundaries, my well-being was suffering greatly. Reflecting on this time of suffering, I was slowly learning that only God is unconditionally worthy of my trust. After days of backpacking the difficult Trail, stumbling, and falling frequently, with a bruised and weak body, I was slowly addressing my blind drive and stubborn determination to keep going at a pace unsuitable for me. Through the spectacular fall foliage colors in the White mountains, God's Nature was speaking to me, responding to my prayerful cries for help. God's presence in Nature was preparing me to accept His beautiful Grace.

I recall thinking that God would not have time for me or my personal dilemma. The world was falling apart, and I was a low priority. As I wrote in my journal and silently talked to God, a better way began to materialize. I did not have to continue the hiking trip I planned with these two companions. God's presence was offering me help and all that I needed for safe decision making about my problems. Slowly I realized that God was present with me. And God did have all the time that I needed to find my trust in Him. Once I accepted my personal physical limitations as a hiker, and after letting go of my stubborn need for control, I heard God's support for my well-being. He was giving me encouragement to find a new immediate way forward. His love quickly supplied the protection and the provision I needed.

Later that same day, after climbing Mount Lafayette and arriving at the AT Greenleaf Hut, I privately told my hiking partners that I was leaving their company and departing from the Trail. They responded with disinterest. With God's love covering me, I calmly announced my plan to the large gathering of trekkers at the Hut's evening meal. I requested guidance off the mountain. Once again, God's help came quickly and in the form of a local hiker, Anita, offering hospitality. The following morning, Anita and I hiked off the mountain range and to the trailhead parking lot in the village of Franconia. Anita and her husband hosted me in their home overnight. Comforted by their hot tub and rested by a good night's sleep, I found transport to the airport the next day, and flew home to Texas.

In 2014, thirteen years later, I returned to the Greenleaf Hut where God's provision had moved me in 2001 from a debilitating Anger stage of grieving and transformed me with His Grace.[49] With Christ at my side, as I reflected on 2001, I sought the Hut's archived Trail Journals. I was searching for my hand written entry in the Hut's journals in 2001, as evidence of this pivotal life moment. I found it! Here is my entry from the Hut's journals.

---

[49] 2014 August/September Hiking Trip

---※---

September 26, 2001. After hiking SOBO for ten days, I'm unfortunately getting off the Trail. Fatigue has set in beyond any short-term recovery. But I'll revamp my planning and come this way again because I'm not going to give up my goal, the entire AT. Your mountains are just gorgeous. I'll spread the word back home of their beauty and the hospitality of the local folk. "Spirit" Beth Abel, Austin, Texas

---※---

Praise God's omnipresence in my life and in your life too!

I have embraced the healing that God provides through Nature and through my faith in His provision, particularly in regards to memorializing 9/11. I have learned to lean on God for wisdom and not blindly trust my own understanding like I did in September, 2001. I came to an Acceptance Stage of grief about my Empty Nest transition through my maturing faith in God. Over time, I grieved the loss of my Mom, my last living parent, in 2006. Thanks be to God's faithfulness, now when I grieve, I more readily move towards the Stage of Acceptance.

The 9/11 memorializing rituals continue and national grieving must continue because we, as a nation, must acknowledge that the transition time is still happening. How can we move on to the Stage of Acceptance? My opinion is that our nation must reaffirm our national motto "In God We Trust" if we are to transition towards a healthy Acceptance.

Prayer: My wise and patient Counselor, I worship Your presence in my life. Though I falter and stumble over my own feet because I want to be in control, You forgive my self-centeredness. Alleluia! I do not want this distance that I cause between us. Preserve my salvation in Jesus Christ. You are my Stronghold that mercifully guides me as the despair of grief derails me and derails my world.

Help me to reach out for Your guidance, oh Sovereign King, for this is Your Kingdom and I am yours. Amen

A question to provoke faith journaling: When has God offered help to you with grieving and loss but your need for control of the outcome gets in the way?

Hope

A Step to Belief: God is the hope of the world, whether you are a believer or not.

Romans 5: 2-5 *Through whom we have gained access by faith into this grace in which we now stand. And we boast in the hope of the glory of God. Not only so, but we also glory in our sufferings, because we know that suffering produces perseverance; perseverance, character; and character, hope. And hope does not put us to shame, because God's love has been poured out into our hearts through the Holy Spirit, who has been given to us.* (NRSV)

In this scripture, the apostle Paul, is reflecting on the journey of faith in Christ. Hope is described as essential in the initial stages of faith development. But experience informs me that we always need Hope throughout our journey of faith. The beginning of faith is like a mustard seed that needs the watering of Hope to grow into a tree. Hope comes from innumerable sources such as God's Nature, other people, and mysterious circumstances that are God's grace. This scripture reminds us that God also gives Hope to the believer in times of suffering.

When we see God's glorious presence amid our suffering, instead of dismissing God's presence with reliance on human luck, our perseverance with grow. A growing character can not prevail based on humanism. Our hope is based on God's grace and God's glory at work in our lives. The deeper our trust in faith develops and the more that we glorify God, Hope in God's presence prevails.

Reflecting over the 20 AT hiking trips I discovered the newfound Truth that in the first 12 hikes, I was seeking Hope as my motivation. By the 13th hiking trip, there was enough Hope accumulated in the form of endurance that I began living my faith. This accumulated Hope transformed into endurance that encompassed both physical and emotional stamina. The accumulated Hope encompassed an awareness of God's trustworthiness. I am sharing this self-understanding of Hope in God in relation to the long journey of faith because I believe you will more readily embrace God's grace when you foresee Hope as a first essential step in your faith journey. Hope always comes before a faith that endures. Know that Doubt is the natural sidekick to Hope. They travel together.

While planning the 13th hiking trip, I reluctantly accepted that my trail buddy Smasher could not join me on the Trail that year.[50] On the previous hiking trips, I had grown accustomed to eleven different hiking partners as well as one large group of Girl Scouts. Looking back on the previous hiking trips, I benefited from the Hope that hiking partners contributed to companionship and the Trail experience, especially Smasher. She revealed her decision months ahead of the traditional September AT trip time, so I used the early notice to think about my options. The previous hiking trips had prepared me with Hope and enough endurance such that I considered the option of backpacking alone. Before this situation arose, I had never considered solo backpacking on the Trail because I did not think it was safe. My husband Tim had the same opinion! But 2007 had been an exceedingly difficult year in my life and I felt a strong need for the refreshing getaway of the September hiking trip to replenish my spirit for everyday life. Weighing out the options, I chose to solo backpack on the AT north of the Smoky Mountain National Park.

In preparation for this solo experience, I wrestled with the ways that I could stretch and strengthen my faith and not just

---

[50] 2007 September Hiking Trip

Hope the trip experience would be good. When I prayed about the upcoming solo trip, my conversations with Jesus shifted from wanting more Hope to wanting a dedicated faith-centered time with Him.

By holding this focus in my prayers, I realized the need to prepare for structured time with Jesus, praying for His protection and praising Jesus for all the provision that I would need. With faith as my forethought, I compiled hours of praise and worship audio recordings for listening pleasure. Pre-planned faith journaling became a major part of nighttime leisure. Once on the Trail, the benefits were apparent immediately. Not only did I find sleep at night but my steps on the Trail carried an extraordinary lift of joy. I was calmed by walking and talking with Jesus as never before. Courage to backpack alone came from my faith in Jesus, not Hope alone. It is a good thing that I carried a courageous faith in Jesus on the Trail because I never saw a living soul.

On this solo trip, I memorized a hymn to keep me focused on God's presence, even setting a walking cadence to the tune. I've repetitively sung the hymn in difficult times, and when I could not get to sleep.

Our God our help in ages past, our Hope for years to come. Our shelter from the stormy blast, and our eternal home.[51]

There is another AT story of enduring Hope. I accepted God's grace and my Faith began to bloom.[52] The 2006 hiking trip on the AT took place north of Shenandoah National Park. Smasher and I invited my daughter's long-time Girl Scout friend to join us, and Cheri quickly accepted the invitation. At the age of 24, Cheri had

---

[51] Isaac Watts (1719)

[52] 2006 September Hiking Trip

already lived a lifetime of troubles. When her husband returned from the Iraq War with devastating mental illness, Cheri eventually separated from him and was contemplating divorce. In addition to marital distress, Cheri had cancer, went through surgery and chemotherapy, and then was told the cancer would return. Cheri took her private anguish onto the Trail and walked through it. Cheri was in search of Hope from God. I witnessed Cheri comforted by God's Nature. Seeing Smasher and I practicing our faith lifted Cheri's awareness of God's loving presence and gave her Hope. As I look back on Cheri's life unfolding in the years that followed our hiking trip, Cheri found a church home, married, and proudly led her daughters to learn about faith in Jesus.

Prayer: Holy Jesus, You are the Hope of the world! The Way Maker in my hopeless and doubtful times. Do not let me dismiss Your Grace and miracles with thoughts of how lucky I am. That rainbow at just the right moment, that friend from the past that reaches out when I need it desperately, that reflective moment telling me that You were present all along – these ways that You reach out are the daily food of my baby faith. You are touching every heart and healing all those who seek You as their Savior. Guide me to ways that grow that seed of Hope into a tree of faith with deep roots. Help me to share Your Light with those around me who are overcome by darkness. Amen.

Question to provoke faith journaling: Are you exploring your experiences of Hope looking for God's presence?

Joy

A Step to Belief: Look for Christ's joy in everyone

Matthew 11:2-11 *John the Baptist, who was now in prison, heard about all the things the Messiah was doing. So, he sent his disciples to ask Jesus, "Are you the Messiah we've been expecting, or should we keep looking for someone else?" Jesus told them, "Go back to John and tell him about what you have heard and seen. The blind see, the lame walk, those with leprosy are cured, the deaf hear, the dead are raised to life and the Good News is being preached to the poor. And he added, 'God blesses those who do not fall away because of me' ". As John's disciples were leaving, Jesus began talking about him to the crowds. "What kind of man did you go into the wilderness to see? Was he a weak reed, swayed by every breath of wind? Or were you expecting to see a man dressed in expensive clothes? No, people with expensive clothes live in palaces. Were you looking for a prophet? Yes, and he is more than a prophet. John is the man whom the Scriptures refer when they say, 'Look, I am sending my messenger ahead of you, and he will prepare your way before you.'* NLT

I first met my trail buddy "Millerman," on the AT near Blood Mountain, Georgia where he befriended my college age son and me. An Alabama man recently retired from a military career, Millerman came across as a fellow southerner and a self-confident natural outdoorsman. At first impression, Millerman is one who enjoys making new friends. A year later, when my next section hike was being planned, Millerman chose to join Smasher and me. We three became trail buddies through multiple September section hikes. [53]

It wasn't long after our friendship began that Millerman's newly acquired retirement lifestyle totally disintegrated due to a divorce that brought him painful grief and tremendous suffering. The energetic spirit of our dear friend and trail buddy dissolved into a lost soul, filled with doubts about himself and life's meaning and purpose.

Millerman resurfaced a few years later to join us on a section hike in Pennsylvania. He was a changed man. [54] Amazing Grace! He turned his life to center on his faith in Jesus Christ and his life changed! Through faith in Christ, he was led to an obscure new vocation that became his enthusiastic life purpose. Millerman transformed his persona and became the joy of Christmas for everyone - Santa Claus! It helped that his wilderness outdoorsmen appearance of a great white beard already made him look the part! On days that we left the Pennsylvania AT to resupply at Walmart or a grocery store, before leaving the parked car, Millerman put on his Santa hat. A purposeful jolly demeanor came over him. Suddenly, strangers did not see an AT hiker, these strangers saw the joy and love of Christmas in the face of Santa Claus walking into a local grocery store. People of all ages would constantly stop us because they needed to exchange hugs with Santa and talk about the coming Christmas, just around the corner. To this day, each November and December, Millerman continues to become Santa, and takes the Good News to places all around the world as a professional Santa Claus. When I visit with my trail buddy Millerman, the conversation centers on his Santa Claus experiences of sharing God's Love with children.

---

[53] 2003 May Hiking Trip

[54] 2013 September Hiking Trip

Sometimes, children sitting on Santa's lap are having a first experience with a stranger. But the stranger, Santa Millerman, shows them God's love, and joy abounds.

Lives change for the better because people seek the saving Grace and Joy of Jesus Christ. Christ transformed Millerman's life just as my life and yours changed when we chose to look for the Messiah. When we know and trust the indwelling of Christ in our souls, we will then recognize Christ's presence in others, even when that person is unaware of God's grace. Do not worry about the times of doubting your faith. Doubts are something we all carry. Doubting your faith is a part of everyone's faith journey. Just keep letting in the Good News. Keep sharing with others the Joy and the Forgiveness and the Love that is ours because of Jesus Christ, who came to us as a baby in a humble manger. Keep looking for Christ in those you meet, even if it is a small glimpse. Be sure to tell that person what it is that you are witnessing, using a language that the individual will embrace. Christ is the Way, the Truth, and the Life. (John 14:6.)

Prayer: Precious Messiah, You come to me as a vulnerable newborn baby filled with God's Love. Help me to especially recognize You in the joyful and loving gestures of other people, even strangers. Teach me to joyfully witness aloud to the gifts of Grace that You have given to me, not just in those joyful times of the Christmas season. Fortify me against the cultural influence to appear strongly independent of You, never needing the tender love You have for me. Encourage me to live with Christmas Joy every day! Help me to be a Santa Claus that worships You, the baby Jesus! Amen.

A question to provoke faith journaling: Notice how being grateful leads to experiencing joy. Over seven days, write down ten different things that you are grateful for in your life. It can be people, objects, or experiences. Re-read your journal notes upon completion and you will find joy.

Shelter

A Step to Belief: Find your shelter in the rock of Jesus.

Matthew 7: 24–27 *"Anyone who listens to my teaching and follows is wise, like a person who builds a house on solid rock. Though the rain comes in torrents and the floodwaters rise and the winds beat against that house, it won't collapse, because it is built on bedrock. But anyone who hears my teaching and doesn't obey it is foolish, like a person who builds a house on sand. When the rains and floods come and the winds beat against that house, it will collapse with a mighty crash."* NLT

Shelter is extremely important for humans to withstand a lengthy experience outdoors. Without shelter, it is difficult to endure weather conditions over time. Over the millennia of humans traveling great distances, tents have been the portable shelter choice for survival. Whenever I face a new day on the Trail, my first thoughts go to the basic concerns of safety and comfort. The most important item to address is food and water, but shelter is the next priority.

My deep interest in backpacking brought a lasting fondness for tent shopping over the years. I even tried sewing my own lightweight tent – not a good idea. I do appreciate lightweight durable shelter. When my son and I backpacked on the AT in his teenage years, an unexpected thunderstorm overnight left us drenched. We wanted to enjoy the dark starry night sky, so we wrongly chose to remove the tent's rainfly to enjoy a breeze and to sleep under the stars. With all our gear and belongings wet, we loaded our backpacks, left the Trail and hitch hiked into a nearby mountain town for lodging where our gear could dry out.

Being without shelter is often a public disgrace. I will always remember my humiliation when we were hitch hiking in a town near the Trail, and strangers passed us with an assuming look that we were a homeless mother and son. Let us all remember the non-profit organization, Habitat for Humanity, and give them our aid.

Because of the three-sided shelters alongside the Trail's expanse, the AT's 2,000 trail miles are particularly accommodating for long distance backpackers. Trekkers see the AT shelters as the community centers of the Trail. Every ten or twelve miles, a three-sided shelter stands in a remote wilderness setting. The shelters are maintained by AT volunteers. They are First-come, first-serve, and they are Free! Hikers depend on the sleeping space which averages ten people on the wood flooring with reliable metal roofing overhead. AT shelters are a true luxury even though the one open side exposes the weary occupants to the weather. AT maps and data resource books indicate the shelter locations so you can set the trail mileage plans for every night in a shelter, if you so choose. Tent sites, campfire circles, outhouses and a convenient water stream usually accompany the AT shelter footprint. After a long day on the Trail, seeing a shelter appear in the depths of a forest brings a sigh of relief. It feels like you have arrived home.

One of my favorite AT shelters is the Partnership Shelter in the Highlands of southern Virginia. [55]It is particularly luxurious with a solar heated shower and a location near a ranger station and road. Before cell phones were born, access to a pay phone outside the ranger station made ordering a pizza delivery an incredibly special treat! Smasher and I enjoyed hot showers while waiting on the pizza delivery and then pigged out on pizza with the whole shelter all to ourselves.

---

[55] 2002 September Hiking Trip

501 Shelter in Pennsylvania is unusual because it is an enclosed cabin with a large sunlight in the ceiling and the amenity of several bunkbeds.[56] Hikers with cars use a parking lot off highway 501, walking distance from the cabin. Driving from out-of-state as we did, this AT Shelter became a convenient base camp for us while we hiked through Trail miles of Pennsylvania. We visited the Pennsylvania Dutch community in nearby Lancaster and frequently drove to local cafes to eat out, a real luxury. There were other hikers staying at the shelter during that September hiking trip. One evening just before dark, an elderly couple arrived carrying full backpacks. They were small in stature and gave the first impression of being rugged individuals. This couple certainly were true to their appearance. They were celebrating their 50th wedding anniversary by thru-hiking the AT for the second time. The first thru-hike for this cheerful couple was their honeymoon. It was a lovely evening chat with this inspiring couple as we sat inside the comfortable accommodations of 501 Shelter

Port Clinton, Pennsylvania welcomes AT hikers by providing free use of a municipal park with a large open-air pavilion. [57]What a blessing this shelter became during a fierce thunderstorm that lasted several days and flooded the streams and the valleys. We spent three nights erecting our tents in the pavilion and watching the nearby streams flood the park. But we were able to keep hiking and looked forward to ending the day at the pavilion shelter, dry and safe.

All along the AT there are family-owned cottage businesses that operate as a small shelter near the Trail. There were times that I found inexpensive shelter in these personable settings which were advertised in the *AT Thru-Hiker Companion*, a resource book

---

[56] 2011 September Hiking Trip

[57] 2012 September Hiking Trip

updated each year. The shelter might be a garage floor or an outbuilding behind the home. One such place of shelter became our "home away from home" when they opened their doors to us as Hurricane Isabel arrived in 2003. The Dutch Haus was a bed and breakfast lodging with an additional bunkhouse for AT backpackers. The owners, Lois and Earl Arnold, became close friends over the years as we rendezvoused at their Montebello, Virginia BnB; Smasher coming in from North Carolina and I drove in from Texas. From the Arnold's establishment, for years we caravanned north to hike another AT section each September. We chose this "home away from home" to be our destination for completion of the AT 2,000 miles in 2015.

Let us be grateful for the shelter we have that protects us from the harshness of weather. Let us never take any level of shelter for granted. Psalm 61:4 says *Let me live forever in your sanctuary, safe beneath the shelter of your wings!* NLT

If there is any one thing I have learned about faith from annual submersion in the wilderness where finding shelter is difficult, I have learned to question the secular world on everything, including the definition of shelter. As a Christian, I try to hold a worldview that keeps Jesus as the cornerstone of my shelter, the rock foundation on which I build my shelter.

When I began searching for a deeper trust in Jesus as I embarked on the AT trips, my trust and faith in Jesus was like the house on shifting sand in this scripture. If you actively seek a stronger trust and faith in Jesus, my witness to you is that Jesus, the solid foundation, is waiting for you to let Him in. Jesus is our Rock!

In today's troubled times, we live in a culture dominated by secularism and humanism. Any trace of Christian faith is highly criticized. We are living in a culture of shifting sand where people without a faith become paralyzed with fear and anxiety because their lives include storms that destroy their flimsy shelter. Choose the company of faith friends and together build your houses on the Rock. And go on to share your faith and lead the younger generations to Jesus, the Rock, for our culture is desperately needing the discernment that comes from faith in Jesus and his teachings.

Prayer: Almighty God, wherever I wander, You are with me, providing the resting place and the shelter I need. You are my everlasting and nurturing Mother and Father comforting me through all my problems. Your teachings guide the building blocks of my life where Jesus Christ my Savior and my rock. I give You all the praise and glory for Your strong arms protecting me from all that I fear. I stand tall because You are my fortress and my protector. Amen

A question to provoke spiritual journaling: How could you increase use of the teachings of Jesus to be more sheltered in this world?

Soul Food

A Step to Belief: Be grateful for Jesus Christ, *The Bread of Life!*

Exodus 16: 15–18 *And Moses told them, "It is the food the Lord has given you to eat. These are the Lord's instructions: Each household should gather as much as it needs. Pick up two quarts for each person in your tent." So, the people of Israel did as they were told. – some gathered a lot, some only a little. But when they measured it out, everyone had just enough. Those who gathered a lot had nothing left over, and those who gathered only a little had enough. Each family had just what it needed.* NLT

A month after fleeing Egypt, the Israelites wandered in the wilderness led by Moses and Aaron. The people could not find food in the desert, and they complained to their leaders about their hunger. Though they were slaves in Egypt, the Israelites argued that they were better off in Egypt because there was plenty to eat. Moses and Aaron called a meeting of the people and reminded them that it was the Lord God that brought them out of the land of Egypt. And they promised the people that the Lord's presence would be evident in the morning. God told the leaders that He would provide food for all the Israelites. Over the next 40 years in their search for the Promise Land, God kept his promise to the people by providing Manna each morning. After the morning dew disappeared, thin white flakes tasting like honey cakes covered the ground. This was God's provision of food.

In this passage, Moses instructs the people that God's word commands them to take only the Manna they need. But some of the people were disobedient and felt entitled. They gathered all the Manna they wanted. Regardless of their behavior, God changed their collected portion to result in each family receiving only what they needed. The scripture goes on describing how the people continued to test the limits of God's instruction and provisions. When they did not get the food quantity they wanted, the people asked Moses to explain. Moses instructed the people about the ways of God including a day of rest, the Sabbath. After many years in the desert relying on God's ways for their survival, the Israelite people came to worship God and rely on His commandments.

Food is bodily fuel to the AT hiker, but it is also the source of comfort, much like it is in everyday living.[58] When a backpacker decides that the pack weight is too burdensome and evaluates where he has splurged to enjoy comfort on the Trail, packing too much food is often the culprit. Food is a common topic amongst hikers as we chat around the evening campfire or hike together. We are motivated to keep on trekking despite the weather conditions or Trail challenges when there are salivating dreams of the next town's food sources. Smasher and I went to the same Dairy Queen several hiking days in a row to stay motivated in the never-ending Brushy Mountains of Virginia. Looking back on my conversations with trekker companions, we AT hikers are the original "Foodies!"

I have experienced many blessings directly from Jesus pertaining to food and that is why I think of these blessings as Soul Food. Sometimes that blessing comes in a non-edible form that still relieves the body of hunger pains. I have struggled with climbing a mountainside trail at the end of the day and experienced fatigue and preoccupation with hunger rumbles in my tummy. Suddenly, I am distracted by a rare mushroom species or a meandering porcupine that captures my attention. That stop to

---

[58] 2002 September Hiking Trip

enjoy God's blessing through Nature turned off the hunger pain. It was Soul Food to me.

All along the AT, Jesus provides Trail Angels that surprise the hikers with all sorts of Soul Food. A Trail Angel is someone who enjoys depositing free food on the Trail for the passing hikers to be unexpectedly blessed.

Smasher and I fondly remember a Trail Angel family leaving an ice chest filled with food bags in a remote location. The family attached a note indicating that the free food bags were a gift to hikers commemorating their recently deceased son. He had hiked the entire AT. That was a touching Soul Food experience.

Trail Angels often choose to remain anonymous. Every single hiking trip over the years included a surprising gift of food from some local Trail Angel. Knowing that I could anticipate this experience became a 'Soul Food' craving.

My first experience with Soul Food from Trail Angels was a group of twenty or more volunteers in a bird watching group that prepared and served an outdoor hot meal at a wilderness clearing next to the AT. Smasher and I exited the forest canopy and found welcoming strangers that encouraged us to receive their hot meal sharing a fellowship in Nature. When we stopped to visit and eat lunch, we discovered one of the volunteers was a daughter of Grandma Gatewood! Read the devotional "Outcast" to learn about the first woman to hike the entire AT.

"It's a small world after all...," just as the song says. We can celebrate that truth when we stay alert to God's blessing through Nature, through people, and also through food. When we break bread together in a special setting of people on the AT with vast differences of age, race, social class and whatever, a soul food moment is born. The Israelites eventually quit complaining and feeling entitled and embraced survival through God's gift of Manna, Soul Food.

Prayer: Holy God, You are the bread of life. Moses did not give his people bread from heaven when they were desperate for food. You provided! Governments cannot provide the sustenance of bread from heaven. The sacrifice of Your son, Jesus Christ, is the bread of life. You will never abandon me wherever I wander and Your provision for me will always be sufficient. Comfort me with this truth, for You are my strong deliverer. Turn me away from temptations and lead me to You, for I am grateful for Your abundant blessings to me. Amen.

A question to provoke faith journaling: Have you conversed with Jesus about your needs by first separating your wants from the list of needs?

Strength

A Step to Belief: Our Strength first comes from the Lord, when we choose to lean into Him

Luke 4: 4-12 *Jesus said to him, "It is written, 'Man is not to live by bread alone.'" The devil took Jesus up on a high mountain. He had Jesus look at all the nations of the world at one time. The devil said to Jesus, "I will give You all this power and greatness. It has been given to me. I can give it to anyone I want to. If You will worship me, all this will be Yours." Jesus said to the devil, "Get behind Me, Satan! For it is written, 'You must worship the Lord your God. You must obey Him only.'" Then the devil took Jesus up to Jerusalem. He had Jesus stand on the highest part of the house of God. The devil said to Jesus, "If You are the Son of God, throw Yourself down from here. For it is written, 'He has told His angels to care for You and to keep You. In their hands they will hold You up. Then Your foot will not hit against a stone.'" Jesus said to the devil, "It is written, 'You must not tempt the Lord your God.' NLT*

When I started annual AT hikes, I was a typical 47-year-old woman with marriage and family responsibilities. But I was also a woman very much aware of a hollowness in my life, something I could not fix by being a responsible adult. I was searching for the purpose and meaning of my life. I wanted to prove to myself that I was not a helpless female, that I was strong in every way. I also wanted to model womanly strength and self-confidence to my daughter, to many teenage Girl Scouts in my volunteer life, and to the many women clients in my counseling and life coaching business practice. I was seeking a strong woman self-image to

Natural Fibers in the Weaving of a Faith Journey

fill that hole in my life due to the empty nest life stage coming on the horizon.

On the first AT hiking trip I had some surprises and frightening challenges as a novice backpacker.[59] Two female friends and I hiked the AT southbound from Damascus, Virginia along the NC/TN border. Just a few days down the trail, it was at Bear Tree Gap that I first encountered fear of being on my own in the wilderness. I ended up in a scary situation because both hiking partners unexpectedly had to leave the campsite to seek medical help for one who had developed a stomach flu. I chose the job of remaining in the woods alone to watch over the campsite and our gear. When they left the campsite, the gloom of night in the dark forest came, and I was frightened. I tried to find the strength from within me to overcome my imagination and fears. But my fear prevailed until deep into the night.

Women are not innately helpless when facing threatening and powerful forces. However, it is also true that the strength and power of a woman does not ultimately come from her own abilities. Nor does her strength come from having a man or any other person covering up for her indecision and indifference.

I started singing hymns as I sat alone inside my tent that night. My faith, small as it was, brought the comforting presence of Jesus and his strength to protect me. Eventually, tired from singing, I did get some sleep. The next morning, as I reflected on the experience of moving from fear of the unknown to faith in the protection of Jesus, I was surprised to realize just how much my faith in God's presence gave me a calm courage to face my fears. At the time, my self-awareness barely allowed me to briefly admit to myself that I needed the protection of Jesus Christ.

Luke's scripture about the Devil tempting Jesus to use his strength and power to dominate humanity and the world reminds

---

[59] 1997 June Hiking Trip.

me of the temptations that I poorly faced that night at Bear Tree Gap. I was poorly equipped to handle the fears that I imagined, because my image of strength rested on my self-image alone. Jesus' strength comes from the sacrificial love of God, directly counter to the Devil's strength of worldly temptations of power and authority. Jesus, Our Savior, is present with believers ready to guide and protect us through the life experience of being human. Jesus gives me grace and love even when my self-image is warped and confused. Over time, my faith journey with God's help molded my image of self into being a strong woman. Please read about two strong and spiritually wise women in the Bible: Ruth and Abigail.[60]

I backpacked and hiked the AT from age 47 to 65. Inevitably people asked me throughout that span of time "Wasn't it scary to be out there on your own or without a man to protect you?" As the years on the AT progressed after this first voyage, I realized that the only true answer to this question was a faith-based answer. At Bear Tree Gap my trust in the Lord was out of desperation that God would actually show up! Mine was not a mature faith at that time. For me, Bear Tree Gap campsite was the starting place for a trust building relationship with the Lord that developed over time. This was why I chose the AT adventure in the first place! I wanted to be in a place that I was helpless without my growing faith in God. At that campsite, I learned that strength comes for God, and from choosing to lean on Him.

Prayer: Precious Lord and Savior, help me find the patience to cultivate my trust in You, and to remember my trust in You when I need strength. Help me to practice leaps of faith in You until I have gained a reflex of first leaning on Your strength. There is

---

[60] Ruth 1–4, The story of Ruth is an inspiring journey of faith.
 1 Samuel 25: 2-35, Abigail: a woman guided by her faith in the One True God

no one like You in all my relationships, and yet I expect instantaneous relationship with You. Send Your Holy Spirit to remind me that strength comes from You and not from myself. Teach me to accept the everlasting peace and joy that comes when I let You be God and accept that I am not. You are my loving God, and I am Your beloved child. Amen

A question to provoke faith journaling: Does your image of self allow you to embrace a relationship with God where God is God, and you are His child?

Asking

A Step to Belief: Ask our Savior for help. God is ever present and loves you.

Matthew 7:7 -12 *Keep on asking, and you will be given what you ask for. Keep on looking, and you will find. Keep on knocking, and the door will be opened. For everyone who asks, receives. Everyone who seeks, finds. And the door is opened to everyone who knocks. You parents – if your children ask for a loaf of bread, do you give them a stone instead? Or, if they ask for a fish, do you give them a snake? Of course not! If sinful people know how to give good gifts to their children, how much more will your heavenly Father give good gifts to those who ask him.* NLV

On the second hiking trip with Smasher,[61] we quickly became emboldened with confidence on the Trail because we had met many challenges the previous year and successfully solved those problems. We knew the rhythm of one another on the Trail and we had developed many team habits that worked well for us. Briefly stated, we were sassy and sure of ourselves! Fortunately, as we developed our friendship, we also began praying together each day.

One Sunday late afternoon, we were ending four days of backpacking the AT. Due to a lack of roads that crossed the Trail in the area near Blacksburg, Virginia, there was no way to day hike between our two parked cars. Backpacking this section of the Trail was the only option, so we lived day and night on the Trail to complete the mileage. Despite our weary bodies, our confident spirits soared! Our dream of enjoying a large ice cream sundae

---
[61] 2003 September Hiking Trip

at the local air-conditioned Dairy Queen was all that we could talk about.

Our complex plan was good, but the plan's execution turned out to be problematic. We parked my truck at the backpacking destination, which was a remote and small parking spot off a rural dirt road. After the strategic parking of my truck, we then drove together in Smasher's car to a parking lot adjacent to the AT trailhead, or starting point, where we began backpacking through a remote and beautiful area of southwest Virginia. Four days later, as we were coming to the end of our lengthy immersion in Nature, with just a couple of trail miles remaining to arrive at my parked truck, I began thinking about where I had stored the truck keys in my backpack. With a jolt of realization that stopped me in my tracks on the Trail, I envisioned the truck keys' location. Sadly, I realized the keys were not in my backpack, but instead, I had left the truck keys in my purse, which was hidden inside Smasher's car. In panic mode, I turned to Smasher and told her the bad news. Our boastful attitudes disappeared as we stood still on the Trail, lost in private thoughts of hopelessness. The infrequent foot traffic on this remote Trail section had depleted entirely as the Sunday afternoon came and went. We knew that the tiny parking spot where the truck was located only held a total of three cars. Therefore, the chances of local hikers choosing this Trail section for a short hike were quickly fading as the sun was setting.

Even though the opportunity to ask someone to help us was dismal, it made no sense to turn around and backpack four days to Smasher's car. Our backpacks were empty of food and limited water sources were behind us. Though we remembered a stream where we could acquire drinking water near the truck's parking lot, there was nothing else at the parking lot to help us with the immediate dilemma. With great resignation, we eventually chose to keep walking onward to the truck because it was only two miles away.

We started praying and asking for God's help. In our silent private prayers, we asked God to help us get off the Trail soon, since our food supply was gone. We asked God to help us return to Smasher's car to retrieve the truck keys, and then to drive back to the truck and be able to continue our hiking trip plans.

Minutes later, on the Trail ahead of us a dog came running. The friendly dog greeted us and we joyfully pet the dog knowing this was a very good sign. Sure enough, a minute later, from around a bend in the Trail, the dog's owner appeared, leisurely enjoying a Sunday evening hike with his dog. As we engaged with the man's friendly demeanor, we knew that he was God's answer to our fervent prayers. A miracle! After hearing our plight, the family man and local business owner drove us 30 minutes out of his way to drop us off at Smasher's parked car. This man knew the miracle of the moment and was happy to be of help to us!

Asking for help is not built into the basic tendencies of a human being. In fact, it is one of the hardest things to learn in life, and Smasher and I are no different from other people. Our sassy attitudes were promptly humbled when the great plan was foiled by simple mistakes.

How does our Loving God answer calls for help from those who seek Him? The problem is not God answering our calls, for there are countless ways that God answers our calls for help. The problem is the human challenge of being ready to receive God's answer in whatever shape or form it comes. As the scripture indicates, our human condition requires a repetition of asking God to help us. Like a child, we need to repeat our words of asking because it is difficult for us to accept God's unique omnipresence with us in those critical moments of need. This relationship building with God is truly necessary whether we are new in our faith or a long-time believer. Additionally, it is humbling to wait on God's answer, even though His love-filled solutions are far better than we could foresee. God responds to our requests for help with transformative outcomes. The example of God's miracle on the Trail is easier for people to see because the context is so uncluttered with the complexities of normal living.

When we ask God for help, then we expect His response in any form, then we accept the Truth of His presence, then we witness to others that Grace happened, then ultimately, we will place our trust and faith in Him. Asking for help eventually transforms times of distress into precious times with our Savior Jesus Christ. Be specific about your requests for help from God, in part, because this forethought will cause you to think through your needs accurately. When you think through your needs in detail, it is easier to overcome fear in the moment. You will be more equipped to help yourself when you ask God to help you. Now you are looking up with hope, and you will surely overcome the dilemma. With God beside you!

Jennifer Pharr Davis, author of *Becoming Odyssa, Adventures on the Appalachian Trail,* shares many Trail moments where she asks for God's help. During her first thru-hike at the age of 21, Jennifer prayed whenever she felt the need to do so. One particular night in a Connecticut AT Shelter alone, Jen was overcome with isolation and fear despite her advanced experience of thru-hiking. In her book, she graciously shares a tender talk with God, asking for help.

———————❊———————

I looked up toward the rafters and started talking to God. "'God,' I said, sniffling, 'I'm scared. I don't know why I'm out here. When I started, I was so strong and healthy and confident.

But now I feel weak, I feel broken, There is so much hurt and heartache out here. I don't know why I wanted to do this alone. That was stupid.'

At one point I felt like You wanted me here, like You were calling me on the trail, but why would You make me go through all this'…. There is never any doubt in my mind that God hears my prayers….lying in the darkness, I never felt comforted. I continued to feel scared and alone, and I slept in fits of fear. But in the morning, things were different. … I felt like God had designed this moment just for me. He was communicating to me through the sunrise. He was talking – no, He was singing to me with colors. I was like being woken up with a lullaby. The pink said, "I am here." The orange said, "I am going with you." And the gold, the bright gold, said "Trust in me."[62]

Most thru-hikes require about five and a half months to complete the entire AT. In 2011, on her third AT thru-hike, Jen achieved the fastest thru-hiker record – 46 days, 11 hours, 20 minutes. As of that date, it was the non-gender specific record.

Prayer: Holy Jesus, when I'm in a panic, it's even harder than usual for me to remember to turn to You promptly. I get so easily side-tracked by my own and others' knee-jerk solutions to problems that I forget to focus on what is lacking, what I need. Help me to accept, not deny, my child-like needs for Your Love and Wisdom as the obedient believer that I want to be. I yearn to voice these needs in prayer with You, my patient Guide. Thank you for the Good News in Your Word that encourages me to never consider myself as unworthy of Your Love. Keep prompting me with Your Grace so that my well-lit path is a witness to those who seek You. Amen

---

[62] Jennifer Pharr Davis, *Becoming Odyssa*. Page 224.

A question to provoke faith journaling: Write down the specifics of how you are asking God to help you. What if you prayed aloud these written words frequently? What might happen?

Chosen

A Step to Belief: Choose to follow Christ and the path with Him will appear.

James 1:12-18 *God blesses the people who patiently endure testing. Afterward they will receive the crown of life that God has promised to those who love him. And remember, no one who wants to do wrong should ever say, "God is tempting me." God is never tempted to do wrong, and he never tempts anyone else either. Temptation comes from the lure of our own evil desires. These evil desires lead to evil actions, and evil actions lead to death. So don't be misled my brothers and sisters. Whatever is good and perfect comes to us from God above, who created all heaven's lights. Unlike them, he never changes or casts shifting shadows. In his goodness he chose to make us his own children by giving us his true word. And we, out of all creation, became his choice possessions.* NLT

Our world is filled with attractions and distractions both positive and negative. We can easily lose our way and roam without direction. We need landmarks to help us stay on our chosen life path. In the Gospel of John 14:6, Jesus said, *"I am the way, the truth and the life."* Christians choose to follow Jesus because He first chose us! Through faith in God's love, we are His chosen ones. Yet Christ gives us freedom of choice along the way.

Choosing a clearly marked trail was an important part of selecting the best long-distance trail for me to enjoy backpacking trips. The clear and frequent Trail markings on the AT appealed to me compared to the random trail markings of the Pacific Crest Trail or the Continental Divide Trail. I could depend on the

Natural Fibers in the Weaving of a Faith Journey

predictable white blazes on the AT. They are found on tree trunks, on fence posts and on other objects along the AT. This fact reassured me of a clear path in the wilderness regardless of the confusing side trails. Trail cairns (a large pile of rocks beside the trail path) are particularly consoling landmarks on the bald mountain top settings above the tree line. [63]

In 2002, after a difficult ending to the previous year's hiking trip where I cut away from unpleasant hiking partners, I left the Trail early and found an early plane ride home. That experience made me learn to take a more cautious approach to my choices. I needed to find a New Way!

I knew that Jesus would guide me in finding a new hiking partner if I only asked Him to help me along the decision-making process. Many times, I prayed over a written list of attributes in a hiking partner. A hiking partner's Christian faith was at the top of the list. Little did I know how my choices were miniscule compared to the all-encompassing nature of God's impact. Looking back, I see how God was steering His chosen ones together to bind us in His name.

Through our early phone conversations, I learned of Marcia Roland's vast backpacking experience. However, the crucial point of value was Marcia's readiness to address and to express her current life issues and faith struggles. Smasher, Marcia's Trail name, started an AT thru-hike in March 2000 along with her older brother, but he eventually left the Trail with knee problems. Smasher continued the AT quest, on a solo journey. After several weeks and miles of solo backpacking, Smasher felt an absence of trail companionship and chose to go home. She laughingly called herself the "Forest Gump of the AT" because she could walk forever.

When Smasher, an experienced backpacker, chose me, one step above a novice – as a trail companion, I really could not

---

[63] 2002 September Hiking Trip

grasp what was in it for her. Additionally preposterous to me was Smasher's promise to re-hike 578 miles because I had not hiked those AT miles yet.

We further cemented the mutually chosen partnership by allowing time to evaluate our compatibility with a seven day backpacking trip together which included times of spiritual reflection. I now see how the choice to regularly leave room for God's input in private prayer time allowed a faith-based new friendship to bloom. God chose Smasher and Spirit to be AT trail buddies but most of all, to have an ongoing shared spiritual pilgrimage. Becoming sisters in Christ happened because initially, we openly chose to trust God throughout the process of getting acquainted. I speak for both of us when I say that 13 years of 2,000 Trail miles together would not have been possible without our faith-based sisterhood.

Unlike the simple task of following AT trail markers to remain on the correct path, living a Christian life is comparatively not easy. Every day we face choices to either build our Christian identity, or to choose to wander off our path. Suffering and failures are just part of life as well as the walk with Christ. Believers do not get a break from the ways of this world. But leaning into Christ's love and final victory will give us encouragement and hope that builds our endurance for the journey. We are lost at times, despite our efforts to let Christ be our Guide. Remember that we are Christ's chosen possession, and He is always seeking us and guiding us home to his forgiveness and love. We are chosen, but we must also choose the trail with Him.

Prayer: Dear Holy Redeemer and Guide, help me to daily remember the power of Your love. You are an everlasting presence, waiting for me to seek You. As the scripture says, You are never tempting or misleading, but instead You are always guiding me into Your everlasting love. Thank You for the sacrificial gift of Your Son, Jesus Christ. Because Jesus suffered for me, I can accept that You understand my sufferings, my needs, and my human condition. Even so, You respect me with the additional gift of free will. Though You are all powerful and mighty, You do not command the details of my life path as if I am a child. It is by my choice that I come to You and seek Your guidance on my life path.

Awaken me every morning precious Jesus with reminders of Your loving presence and that You have chosen me to be Your witness. My path with You brings all the joy, hope and love that I need. Amen.

A question to provoke spiritual journaling: When has your path forward been unclear? Reflect on how you included God to choose a way forward.

Trusting

A Step to Belief: Trusting God leads to leaps of faith

Matthew 14:24-33 *Meanwhile, the disciples were in trouble far away from land, for a strong wind had risen, and they were fighting heavy waves. About three o'clock in the morning Jesus came to them, walking on the water. When the disciples saw him, they screamed in terror, thinking he was a ghost. But Jesus spoke to them at once. "It's all right," he said. "I am here! Don't be afraid." Then Peter called to him, "Lord, if it's really you, tell me to come to you by walking on water." "All right, come," Jesus said. So Peter went over the side of the boat and walked on the water toward Jesus. But when he looked around at the high waves, he was terrified and began to sink. "Save me, Lord!" he shouted. Instantly Jesus reached out his hand and grabbed him. "You don't have much faith," Jesus said. "Why did you doubt me?" And when they climbed back into the boat, the wind stopped. Then the disciples worshipped him. "You really are the Son of God!" they exclaimed. NLT*

What does it mean to take a leap of faith? I think of a leap of faith as a process where I've already taken several small steps forward using tiny amounts of trust. But the next step forward requires something much bigger built on the previous sequence of small trustworthy steps. These small steps forward eventually lead to the big step - a leap of faith.

I kept hiking the Trail each year because to do so was fueling the trustworthy relationship that I wanted with Jesus Christ. Of course, I was the problem in building such a relationship, not Jesus. Jesus is Our Savior and totally worthy of trust. But as a human, I had to discover this Truth about Jesus for myself. By stepping outside my safety and comfort zone, I learned that I could trust that Jesus would always be there.

Trusting is best illustrated in the team building activity called the Trust Fall. Team members pair up and one person stands in front of his partner, with his hands placed across his chest and a blindfold placed over his eyes. With the partner behind him, outstretching his arms to catch, the blindfolded person falls backward. Imagine the blindfolded person trusting that his partner will catch him before he hits the ground. This group activity creates robust discussions of trust issues in the team relationships.

Back to my doubts and trusting issues with God on the AT, where I was often outside my comfort zone. I needed small steps to experience trusting God and to overcome doubts about myself, as well as doubts about God. Somehow, I knew that finding a deeper trust in God was important to my life.

I used to think of trusting God as having the same risk factors for me as occur in trusting human relationships. Now I know that my assumption was wrong. God is perfect and unconditionally worthy of our trust. Humans, including me, are not instantly worthy of trust. Our human condition is imperfect and requires demonstrative acts to earn the trust of another human being.

Here is a trail story that exemplifies how different the trust dynamic is in a human relationship compared to a relationship with God. The origin of this fourth hiking trip began with a classified ad in the *AT Journey* magazine in 2000. [64] I placed the ad searching for women hiking partners for prospective annual September hikes on the AT. As a newbie backpacker, I chose two hiking partners from the thirty email responses selecting them because of their advanced level of AT backpacking experience. The three of us had never met, so we chose to become acquainted

---

[64] 2001 May and September Hiking Trips

on the AT by hiking one week together in North Carolina. While on the AT together in North Carolina, in addition to becoming acquainted, we jointly planned a September 2001 four-week trip. Before I could realize their insensitivity to my beginner skill level which was so different from their advanced level, I found that I was being left out of planning. Despite my input and because I blindly trusted them, they insisted on the four-week trip location in the most difficult section, the White Mountains of New Hampshire.

Fast forward to the week of September 11, 2001, the planned date to rendezvous in New Hampshire, with one coming from Florida, one from New Jersey, and me from Texas. After the epoch national tragedy of 9/11 postponing the rendezvous date a few days, we began the four-week hiking trip southbound on the AT from Pinkham Notch Lodge. About ten days down the Trail, I was physically and emotionally exhausted. These women had little compassion for me as they continually left me behind on the Trail. Slowly I came to grips with self-doubt and my distrust of them. Trust that I blindly gave to them. Trust they had not earned. Backpacking the Trail with only my troubled thoughts for company, I dwelled on what to do when I was so incredibly isolated in the wilderness.

My leap of faith came to me in a dream as I slept in the AT shelter on Mt. Garfield, glad to be protected from a fierce storm on the mountain. I woke from a troubling dream where God and I were addressing my immediate crisis of physical and emotional fatigue. Rather than focusing on the things I could not change, such as hiking partners I couldn't trust, God helped me focus on our trustworthy relationship. While lying in my sleeping bag watching the pouring rain and aware of hikers asleep around me, God guided my introspective thoughts through the previous ten days on the Trail. God was present during my experiences in God's creation of Nature. As I reflected on those affirming experiences of God, all my doubts began to evaporate and my faith in God's presence was magnified. This was God's Grace. Some of those Trail experiences were:

- Enduring physical challenges of mountain climbing without the support of friends.
- Consuming beautiful autumn colors of the Trail's massive forests and mountain vistas.
- At dusk, sitting on the ground in front of my tent awestruck by a moose sauntering through the mountain wilderness campsite just a few feet from me.
- Absorbing the beauty and sound of the expansive waterfalls near Zealand Falls Hut.
- Witnessing the grandeur of God's universe by gazing at the starry night sky from a mountain top.
- Finally, I accepted the Truth that could not trust my hiking partners.

But I could build on these recent signs of God's trustworthy presence. Because of that trustworthy assurance in my relationship with God, I knew that I would find a safe way forward through this crisis. [65]

When we have doubts and fears that cloud our trust in God, let us think of Peter's leap of faith. Peter's trust in Jesus caused a leap of faith, and Peter found himself suddenly walking on water to be with Jesus. Peter soon realized that he needed to reach out to Jesus for help! Let us focus on our growing faith journey that requires reflecting on our recent experiences of Grace, and our small steps of trusting in God. Yes, Peter needed Jesus to

---

[65] Read the Reflection Devotional *Grieving* to finish this story of God with me, finding a safe way off the AT and back to Texas.

rescue him when his faith weakened. But Peter also learned that Jesus was there when He was needed! Remember, Jesus is always worthy of our trust and faith in Him.

Prayer: Holy Gracious God, Your faithfulness goes before me, around me and is everywhere in my journey of trusting You. Before I am aware of doubts, You are there to comfort and protect me. I praise Your presence through Nature, magnifying for me the universal Nature of Your beauty and goodness. You are my trustworthy Guide, and I am Yours. Amen.

Question to provoke faith journaling: Have you reflected on the trusting steps that led to a leap of faith in your life?

Living Water

A Step to Belief: Renewal comes by focusing on your need for living water

John 4:10-11, 13-14 *Jesus replied, "If you only knew the gift God has for you and who I am, you would ask me, and I would give you living water." "But sir, you don't have a rope or a bucket", she said, "and this is a very deep well. Where would you get living water?" Jesus replied, "People soon become thirsty again after drinking this water. But the water I give them takes away the thirst altogether. It becomes a perpetual spring within them, giving them eternal life."* LNT

In this passage from John, Jesus speaks to my soul as well as acknowledges my human need for a drink of water after a long walk. The disciples left Jesus to rest after their long walk while they went into a village to buy food. As Jesus rested beside a well, a Samaritan woman comes to draw water from the well and Jesus, a Jew, asks her for a drink of water. This request from Jesus surprises the Samaritan woman because Jews and Samaritans did not speak to each other. After Jesus teaches her about the meaning of the living water, Jesus goes on to reveal how much he, a stranger to her land, knows her personally. When Jesus reveals he knows her troubles, five husbands in the past and a man living with her who is not her husband, the Samaritan woman is awestruck and calls Jesus a prophet. When Jesus continues to share who he is, she realizes that he is the Messiah. As I have come to know Jesus, I believe that he is ever reaching out to me with living water quenching the thirst of all my needs. Jesus is always present, whether I am striving to serve Him or am like the Samaritan woman, needing him to reach out to me.

We need water more than we need food to survive. In general, people can survive without water for about three days. I will never forget my first experiences along the TN/NC border and Virginia where mountain underground springs are spilling forth from the rocks, the cool water ready to capture, and later purify for drinking water. These mountain underground springs are along the AT throughout the 2,000 miles. The frequent water source availability on the AT was a primary feature that appealed to me when I chose a long-distance trail to traverse. Coming from the Hill Country of Texas, we rely on manmade lake reservoirs for most of our water supply. Drought conditions are common. The abundant springs among the Appalachian mountains are a refreshing change in Nature for me.

Through the experience of backpacking, I have learned to notice that every backpacker has a pronounced need, like an obsession. That need is manifested in the item that receives a dominant weight and/or space in the backpack. The distribution of weight in the backpack often reflects what the backpacker's priorities of needs are. Many backpackers pack too much food that requires excess weight to be carried. Others pack more clothing than is necessary. My greatest fear is running out of drinking water. Since my childhood chronic illness and subsequent restorative surgery, a physical health limitation remains. I am vulnerable to quick dehydration in comparison to the average person. Physical exertion, like backpacking, causes me to dehydrate even quicker. I had to learn through the first years of backpacking experiences just how much water would be "enough" for me. I have found that my 25 to 30 lbs. loaded backpack needs to allow approximately 75 ounces of water (approximately 5 lbs. weight) for an average Trail mileage day (10 miles).

When living on the Trail, purifying our drinking water is a daily necessity. We backpackers design a long-distance trip with two priorities in the plan – water sources and campsites. Through bad experiences, I have learned the importance of paying special attention to water sources as much as the Trail mileage for each day. The resources at AT shelters will usually include a nearby reliable water source such as a stream or underground spring. When I settle into a chosen campsite, after taking off my backpack, the first task I do is scout the area to find the water source that was noted in my Trail resource booklet. When I go in search of that water source, I bring a bandana, water filtration pump, my hydration bag, and a water storage container. If it's a shallow stream, I cover the filtration bud with the bandana to keep silt from clogging it. I need 75 ounces of drinking water for the next day's hike, and I need 45 ounces in the water storage bag for the evening meal and breakfast.

Once the water source is located, I find a comfortable spot to sit beside the stream while I purify the water that I am collecting. Using the water purification pump requires 20 minutes of sitting still by the stream. After hours of backpacking on the Trail, this setting is a unique meditative time in Nature. I listen to the gurgling stream, enjoying the tranquil sound and relaxing with the awareness of this basic human need being met: Drinking water. As I reflect on the relaxing occasions that I sat by a stream to gather my water, I can relate to the Samaritan woman who labored daily to gather her drinking water. It is true that our modern lifestyle allows us to take for granted how we obtain our basic human need of safe drinking water.

On the 2000 hiking trip, my second AT trip, I became dehydrated after choosing a wrong backpacking pace for the day. Becoming over exerted and was not stopping to rest and drink water, was not good for me. Through this unpleasant experience my untested beliefs about my needs for water became grounded in bodily reality. My body holds a memory maker which has created a clear signal to my self-care beliefs. I will never forget this belief. Dehydration is hard on the body. It took days for me to recover enough stamina to return to the Trail. [66]

On my first hiking trip with Smasher, we dealt with drought conditions.[67] We placed gallon jugs of water in hidden locations near AT road crossings. This was the only solution for backpacking through the region in southern Virginia. The reliable water sources were unusually dry. The AT community constantly shared updates on current water sources, which kept hikers safe. When we met hikers on the Trail that were low on their water supply, whenever possible, Smasher and I helped others by sharing our water with them. One AT through-hiker that we met reported his strategy to deal with the water shortage. Whenever he found a dry water source, he descended the ridge line and the Trail and found water sources in the valleys.

To enjoy life, it is imperative that we address the sobering fact that "needs" are starkly different from "wants." As in the story of my dehydration experience, when we know what we need, that experience becomes a lesson, or a belief, and that belief guides us to meet our "needs" in the future. In the spur of the moment, we can set priorities for action when the difference between needs and wants is clear to us.

Likewise, a resilient faith journey requires a self-understanding of our needs in contrast to our wants. God is ever-present and tuned into my needs, but my wants are a different matter. We learn to trust God when we take our needs to Him and discover His faithfulness and His provision. This is the living

---

[66] 2000 July Hiking Trip

[67] 2002 September Hiking Trip

water that Jesus offered to the Samaritan woman. When I am in prayerful conversation with Jesus, the relationship is not like my human relationships. Maybe that statement sounds irrelevant to you, but my professional counselor experience informs me of a relevant unexamined belief error that people hold. God does not have needs or wants. That fact alone makes for a relationship dynamic like no other relationship. God is always merciful and giving unconditional love. He does not expect us to be God-like. Do you and I accept that God's ways need to be accepted, respected, and glorified? I fall into "wanting" my way quite often!

Prayer: Your water quenches all thirst that I have. I humbly ask You to keep quenching my thirst with the living water, especially in those times that I do not realize how spiritually weak I am. Holy Jesus, my stubborn tendency to set a fast pace on the Trail and never stop for a drink of water is too strong. In these times, make me stop and turn to You. Make You my focus because living waters that flow from You will always satisfy my soul and give me peace. Amen

Question to provoke faith journaling – What untested beliefs about your needs do you hold? If you were to discover the depths of your need for the living water, how would it change your life?

Moments of Faith

When Nature Calls

A Step To Faith: Embrace the mystery of Jesus Christ: human and divine

John 1: 12–15: *But to all who believed him and accepted him, he gave the right to become children of God. They are reborn! This is not a physical birth resulting from human passion or plan – this rebirth comes from God. So the Word became human and lived here on earth among us. He was full of unfailing love and faithfulness. And we have seen his glory, the glory of the only Son of the Father.* NLT

God sent His Son to you and me in the flesh and blood of a human body, just like our bodies. Jesus came to us in the helpless form of a newborn infant, just as we did. In this scripture, "the Word" refers to the Bible. When "the Word became human" tells us that God's prophets foretold the Messiah's coming centuries before his birth. Many prophets told God's words to His people, which are recorded in the Old Testament of the Bible. This scripture concerning God's ways matches my personal experience. God wants us to comprehend that He understands our existence of being human. We are God's children whom He Loves.

This reflection devotional title was chosen because it captures the great mystery of Jesus Christ as both human and divine. Accepting this Truth into my beliefs and then my faith journey was a difficult step. I am convinced that other believers may be like me in the struggle with this leap of faith about the gift of Our Messiah. In my early years of faith, I believed in God alone. God's love for the world and for me was real but I had great doubts about Jesus the Messiah, both human and divine.

When Nature calls is a colloquialism used to address the disposal of human waste from our bodies. I am using this common phrase to remind us that Jesus also had bodily needs because God sent Jesus His Son to live in a human body just like you and me. Jesus was human and divine, a great mystery to me, until I needed Jesus Christ to be my Savior! In this devotional, I share my story of being reborn, the event in my faith journey when I accepted the newborn King as Jesus Christ Our Savior.

In the five years prior to the AT hiking trips, I privately felt trapped with burdens and responsibilities that seemed to grow with intensity. It was a time in life that I outwardly exhibited strength and responsibility but inwardly, hopelessness was winning out. My leadership roles of a minister's wife, a mother and a professional counselor were rewarding, yet the longer I let these roles define my life, the more my human needs declared their limitations.

The pivotal event was when my brother, Barry, committed suicide. Two years older than me, Barry died at age 44. Our family suffered with Barry through years of his depression and chemical dependency. When I failed in my family leadership role as a mental health professional who would save Barry, my view of the world and my part in it came crashing down. I could not do it! I could not save my brother and my entire extended family from despair using my professional talents. When I turned to my faith in God, my faith left me hopeless. Looking back on this pivotal time, my faith in God was shallow and unexplored. My faith was more of a social activity than a personal relationship with my Maker.

How did I get out of the despair that often ruins the lives of family members when a loved one commits suicide? How did I successfully continue in my professional counselor career rather than totally burnout? Where did I get the enthusiasm and energy that I gave to my precious loved ones? How did I find the motivation to start hiking the AT five years later? And how did I find perseverance to complete the Trail miles several years later?

I was saved from the Sin of relying on myself and others and turning away from Jesus. When I turned to Jesus and asked Him to come into my heart and soul, and to be my Savior. I was reborn.

Three months after Barry's death, our church sponsored my attendance at a weekend faith renewal retreat for women, The Walk to Emmaus. God placed a woman in my discussion group who had recently lost a loved one to suicide. The retreat setting gave me the holy space to deeply explore my beliefs about Jesus Christ. My doubts about the human suffering of Christ on the cross were countered by the new awareness of God's Love demonstrated by Christ on the cross. As I embraced God's profound message of Love that He would suffer the worst of being human so that I could grasp His trustworthy and divine presence, amazing Grace flooded my body and my soul. My faith grew by accepting the Truth that the divine Christ chose to live in a human body and suffer all the hate people could muster. Why? So that we would believe in God's Love for us, and therefore choose to trust God. I now try to turn to Jesus first in daily living, and this is why.

Privies, or outhouses, have been a luxury for outdoor living over the course of civilization. "When Nature calls" on the AT, there are two options to answer "the call." One, dig a cathole in the dirt or two, wait until you find a privy. I appreciate the AT shelter footprint because each shelter is accompanied by a unique privy. A privy is a deep hole in the ground covered by a small shack with an entry door. The interior is big enough to sit down on a platform with a toilet hole and to relieve your body of human waste. The AT privies usually have one hole for one person at a time. My favorite AT privy is the one at Partnership

Shelter because of the amenities attached to the privy in the overall design.[68]

Women are particularly uneasy about answering Nature's call in the outdoor setting. For this reason, I had years of difficulty finding a female hiking partner. On one occasion, while on the Trail with a female hiking partner, she shared that she was becoming dehydrated because she did not want to urinate in the woods. The following day the woman became sick and had to leave the Trail. There is an entertaining coffee-table book that humorously addresses "the call" of Nature in the outdoors. The book is entitled *How To Shit In The Woods* which was published years ago. Today there are female products designed to assist us in avoiding the accident of urinating on our legs. Look it up! When I train elementary age Girl Scouts on outdoor skills, they are usually uninhibited about this. The girls see it as an adventure, and they have fun learning this outdoor skill "when Nature calls."

There is a funny AT privy legend of a hiker enjoying Nature's call at a privy near the Georgia/North Carolina border. The AT in this area has historically been known for its proximity to a US Ranger training station. The privy is poised on a ridge overlooking a view into the valley. To enjoy "the call of Nature," while viewing Nature, the Trail volunteers built the privy with three walls and left the viewing side open to the scenic panorama. According to the Trail legend, a hiker had just settled into a leisurely pose on the privy hole while enjoying the sunset, when he heard a mechanical sound from nowhere. Climbing up from the valley below, a Ranger military helicopter rose to eye level contact with the hiker sitting there. I heard that the hiker and the helicopter pilot remained in a paralyzed gaze with each other for quite some time!

---

[68] Note the AT privy photo by Sara Jones Decker, an AT thru-hiker and professional photographer found in 2010 September Hiking Trip. Sarah has created a collage of AT privies as a poster. Check out her website.

When we come to grips with the limits of our human condition, we discover that fixing life's problems is not always possible. Sometimes we realize God's presence is in this moment. As we accept these moments of Grace, we accept the love-filled mystery of Jesus the Messiah. We have a possible moment to gain Belief about the Nature of Our Holy God, who chose to send His Son to us. A Belief examination moment will foster a faith journey into territory such as

- Logic no longer explains and settles everything.
- Efforts at harmonious relations will not prevail and resolve everything.

When a faith journey addresses these human concerns, mystery and doubt are less relevant and Faith fills the empty space. When we choose a continued faith journey, acceptance of our brokenness emerges, and we believe in Christ's redeeming Love.

Ephesians 2:10. *We are God's handiwork, created in Christ Jesus to do good works. Which God prepared in advance for us to do.* NIV. This scripture reminds us to admire God's masterpiece, creation, unique to each person.

We are wonderfully made and remade by our faithful Creator. This journey in life is a mystery that cannot be explained outside of faith in Jesus Christ Our Savior. The humanity of Jesus Christ is real, just as your human body is real. When Nature calls you next time, let that be a grace-filled reminder that Jesus Loves You!

Prayer: Glory be to the newborn King on high! Alleluia, I sing with the angels on the eve of Jesus' birth, "Peace on earth!" Jesus Christ, through Your love and mercy to me, I am reconciled and redeemed. Lift me to Your heavenly presence and guide me to choose You each day. With You by my side, every day is a new day, a new beginning. Amen

Question to provoke faith journaling – When the human limits of science cannot explain, how do your beliefs and faith inform you of the mystery?

Closeness To Christ

A Step To Faith: On a spiritual pilgrimage, moments of closeness to Christ are like Trail markers

Hebrews 5:11-14 *There is much more we would like to say about this, but it is difficult to explain, especially since you are spiritually dull and don't seem to listen. You have been believers so long now that you ought to be teaching others. Instead, you need someone to teach you again the basic things about God's word.[a] You are like babies who need milk and cannot eat solid food. For someone who lives on milk is still an infant and doesn't know how to do what is right. Solid food is for those who are mature, who through training have the skill to recognize the difference between right and wrong.* LNT

In Maine, the AT crosses a formidable mountain ledge that proved to be a significant challenge. Neither the guidebook, nor any other AT resource adequately informs you of the ledge on Chairback Mountain. Smasher and I were shocked when we emerged from a forested trail and saw a 45-degree angle slick rock ledge. We saw the AT blazes on the gigantic rocks, and there was no question that the Trail led straight across the difficult rock ledge. [69]

My faith had developed and matured over the years of annual hiking and backpacking trips. In my baby faith years, I was easily misled by others, unsure of my personal worth and quick to first lean on everything earthly to overcome fears and anxieties. Trusting my life experiences were the beginning and the end of how I coped with life's trials, not my faith.

---

[69] 2008 July Hiking Trip

This scripture describes a Christian's faith as a growth journey. Five years before my first AT hiking trip, I accepted Jesus as my Savior, I was born again. Before that time, I kept God in a Creator role because I did not understand that I needed the Savior Jesus Christ. When I asked Christ to come into my heart, I began participation in a women's prayer group for self-accountability to Christ. To this day, I continue to meet with this group of women, a Walk to Emmaus Reunion Group. One step in the structured self-accountability format for the group is to reflect on the previous week's experience where one felt "Closeness to Christ." Through these small steps of weekly reflection on specific moments where Christ's presence was so real that it was almost visible, my faith in Him has grown. Hearing my sisters in Christ witness to their "Closeness to Christ" experiences has further validated my trust in God's presence. Throughout the years of AT hiking trips, my faith sisters have witnessed with me the mystery of God's loving ways. For me, that growing faith journey has been both on and off the Trail.

We should expect a mature faith to no longer rely on the milk that a baby Christian truly needs. My baby Christian needs slowly transformed and matured when I sought prayerful guidance for daily life. Studying scripture also guided me beyond the early years of faith as I learned to first look for God's message on what is right and wrong. Slowly I came to embrace life's trials as opportunities to grow and to mature in my faith. I came to trust God as I experienced life's difficulties.

Back to that rock ledge! Once we saw this unexpected challenge, Smasher and I trembled with fear that we would fall off the slick rock ledge into the wilderness below and die. We took off our backpacks, rested and then prayed together. We prayed for the peace of Jesus Christ's presence and guidance to remain focused and calm. Then standing up and reloading our backpacks, we carefully moved on to the rock ledge. With very few hand-hold spots and wearing full backpacks, we were old lady cliff hangers inching our way across the rock ledge and eventually pulling ourselves to the dirt Trail once again. Minutes later, we did it! Thank you God!

Christ expects us to witness about our maturing faith. We are called to teach others what we have learned. We are called to go out into this broken world in His name. Christ is counting on us! Even though there was an end to the 2,000 miles of the AT journey, my faith journey has not ended. Faith in Jesus is what gets me through life each day! Just as I once shared the Good News on the Trail with strangers, my maturing faith now emboldens me to make note of my "Closeness to Christ" experiences and declare the "Closeness to Christ" experiences of others. Even when people describe the moment as "just lucky." Christ's love and forgiveness is ever present and ready for our asking. Where is Christ asking you to act in His name today?

Prayer: O precious Guide and Redeemer, help me to quickly notice how You are ever present, even before I am aware of my need for Your help. Whether I am afraid or am downtrodden with indecision, teach me, Holy Jesus, the discipline of being in Your precious companionship. Help me to rejoice daily in the benefits of solid food, such as experiencing the joy of Your Grace working through me, so that I can be Your light in this world.

Do not let me go backwards to only milk for baby Christians, such as only praying when I need something. Lead me to trust You as I practice self-accountability to You, so that my trust and faith in You matures. Let Your peace that is often a mystery and surpasses my understanding become my aide, like a hiking stick, as I walk the spiritual pilgrimage. Amen

A question to provokes faith journaling: In what ways can you choose to be more accountable in maturing your faith in Christ?

Freedom

A Step To Faith: Freedom to love oneself comes from God's love

Mark 12: 29–32 *Jesus replied, "The most important commandment is this: 'Listen, O Israel! The LORD our God is the one and only LORD. [30] And you must love the LORD your God with all your heart, all your soul, all your mind, and all your strength.'[1] The second is equally important: 'Love your neighbor as yourself.' No other commandment is greater than these.* NLT

Only God is the Creator of human beings and of all creation. Like no other living creature in God's world, God created us with the gift of free will. Webster's dictionary defines "free will" as "the freedom of humans to make choices that are not determined by prior causes or by divine intervention". In this scripture, Mark quotes Jesus describing the perimeters of our freedoms to use free will. First, God's Love reigns with sovereign authority over every aspect of the commandment. The commandment from Jesus says that "We are to love one another." And last, Jesus commands that we also "love oneself. "

An individual's freedom is explicitly defined in the scripture. One of those freedoms is the focus of this reflection devotional, the freedom to love oneself as God loves. This scripture is frequently used to declare how Jesus wants us to love others, but that is not the focus here.

When God created us, our human nature included free will. We human beings were created with an attribute unlike any other creature, the free will to make choices without God's intervention. Our freedoms are nowhere more evident than in the freedom to love God or not. The freedom to accept or reject the gift of God's sacrificial love. In the dynamics of an individual's relationship with God, this scripture gives two directives – 1) work at building a personal relationship with God, and 2) to love oneself, a loved child of God. This scripture is so grounding in the true origin of all freedoms and that free will is a gift. Free will is God's precious gift that has one string attached, one paramount commandment – Love God!

These words from Jesus clearly describe how to grow in true self-esteem. True self-esteem begins with accepting that God loves you personally and unconditionally. Individuals gain further self-esteem when our decision making becomes grounded in the learning journey of how God wants us to meet our human needs. By choosing to seek a personal relationship with Jesus Christ the Savior, our natural impulsivities and the hardships of life become conscious building blocks for our Christian character to grow and mature.

Our nation, the USA, was founded on this belief, that we have inalienable rights and freedoms that come from God. The first Amendment in the Bill of Rights is the freedom of religion, "both to an establishment as well as the free exercise thereof." This quotation from the first Amendment means freedom of worshipping God as an individual or as a group of believers. The US Constitution is not a secular governance structure, and it is not a mono-theistic governance structure either. The personal freedoms given by the governance structure come from God to the citizen directly, in other words, they are God-given freedoms, and are not to be denied by the government. Due to our human condition, there are tendencies in our human constructed systems and especially governmental systems to organically limit freedoms for the citizen, and sometimes create unhealthy human dependency on the governing system.

These beautiful freedoms from God encourage a person's free will to mature and to build all forms of healthy self-determination. Under the auspices of the US Constitution, we are a mass of citizens on a tumultuous journey to find God in our lives or choose not to acknowledge the divine. Our nation was built on the principle "In God We Trust." God's commandments are a cornerstone in the US Constitution where the founders honored specific citizen freedoms to be protected by a balance of powers, so that the government would fear "we the people," and the people need not fear the government. This unique governance structure that acknowledges the importance of God freely gifting love and freedom to the individual citizen is why the USA is called "the Great Experiment."

For thirty years, I have been blessed to be an adult volunteer in Girl Scouting. Throughout my mental health professional career and the whole of life, I have felt God's call to serve teenage girls in their human developmental stage of addressing needs for independence vs. dependence. It is my informed opinion that true self-esteem is well rooted when a teenage girl exercises free will to know God's personal love for her, as only the surroundings of God's Nature can convey.

With the help of other adult Girl Scout volunteers, I led twelve backpackers on a two-week older Girl Scout trip to the Great Smoky Mountain National Park section of the AT. [70] The seventy-five miles of Trail within the Park is among the most magnificent Trail sections because of the numerous extraordinary mountain vistas. The group of Central Texas Girl Scouts prepared and physically conditioned for months prior to our departure. Each teenage girl participant came from a separate Girl Scout troop using her individual "free will" to participate in this trip because backpacking was of personal interest to her. The Girl Scouts

---

[70] 2008 June Hiking Trip

quickly bonded by a shared interest in this outdoor adventure. New friendships were easily made. In the diverse group of teens, there were Girl Scouts with advanced backpacking experience, and there were also novices. There were Girl Scouts who hiked at a fast pace and there were girls who hiked a pace like mine, slower than a turtle. While everyone committed to teamwork on the backpacking trip, the girls experienced the importance of making an individual choice and then living with consequences of that choice. For instance, when you chose to carry too much pack weight, you face natural consequences of that choice, instead of expecting someone to fix your problem.

On the fourth trail day, we experienced God's Love in Nature when we happened upon a mama bear and her cubs. The mama bear was separated from the young cubs who had wandered off and climbed a tall tree deep in the canopy of the forest. As we arrived on the scene following the Trail, we spotted the cubs first, to the right side of the Trail path. Minutes later, while admiring the cubs in the treetop, the mama bear appeared on the left side of the Trail, which put us in the middle of the bear family crisis. Very quickly we moved on and later we discussed the unexpected bear encounter. The conclusion of our discussion was that we were in Nature's world, and we needed to honor and respect our place in it. In other words, we humans are a part of Nature's system, but we are not at the center or in control.

On another day, when we arrived at a famous AT location, Charlie's Bunion, our eclectic and diverse group of females exuded so much estrogen energy it was palpable to the witnessing spectator trekkers on the trail. Our group photo taken on that rock outcropping carries the evidence of that energy to this day.

When I watched a 75-pound Girl Scout carrying a 20-pound backpack down the mountainous Trail ahead of me looking like a backpack on legs, I envisioned the girl's spirit speaking to my soul proclaiming her oneness with God. On another occasion, I witnessed a teen Girl Scout standing on the Trail posed with great confidence as Nature sprinkled neon pink rhododendron blooms all around her. What a soulful smile she had!

A teenage girl exploring the nature of her identity in relationship to God and the world around her is the epitome of this devotional message of "loving oneself comes from God." Faith-based self-esteem develops as she chooses to spread her wings in the surroundings of God's great equalizer, the world of Nature. As she encounters the experiences of Nature, she is on a journey of individuation from her family, the ever more influential peer group, and her community home. Through being in Nature, she is full of God's personal relationship with her, but only if she chooses to accept it. When she discovers her personal limitations and human frailties in those adventures, her choice to notice and accept God's tender merciful presence will be abundantly clear through a sense of harmony with the surroundings of Nature.

The first line of the Girl Scout promise is "On my honor I will serve God and my country." When as a group we recite the Girl Scout promise and the US pledge of allegiance, my private thoughts go to a prayer for the girls in that moment. I pray that the teenage girls will personally see God's loving presence for them. I also pray that they will grow and mature as US citizens that acknowledge the inalienable rights, responsibilities, and freedoms of our nation. [71]

Prayer: Holy Jesus, it is an ongoing struggle for me to understand how to be a woman of God and additionally believe that You want me to love myself. Sometimes these thoughts contradict each other. When You allow me to struggle with my free will, too often

---

[71] If you enjoy reading true stories about Girl Scouts backpacking on the AT, read the book *The Appalachian Trail* in Bits and Pieces, by Mary Sands

I fail to keep You in the center of my world and remember Your sacrificial love for me. Too often, I am stuck in self-imposed chains, seeing myself as the victor or the victim. Help me to become more obedient and eager to turn naturally to Your redeeming Grace. Help me to celebrate the freedoms that You alone can give! Help me to drop those chains and witness to Your loving freedoms. Amen.

A question to provoke faith journaling: How are you proclaiming love of self because our Divine God loved you first and unconditionally?

Healing

A Step To Faith: Ask God for healing and expect help to come

James 1:2–6. *Dear brothers and sisters, when troubles of any kind come your way, consider it an opportunity for great joy. For you know that when your faith is tested, your endurance has a chance to grow. So let it grow, for when your endurance is fully developed, you will be perfect and complete, needing nothing. If you need wisdom, ask our generous God, and he will give it to you. He will not rebuke you for asking. But when you ask him, be sure that your faith is in God alone. Do not waver, for a person with divided loyalty is as unsettled as a wave of the sea that is blown and tossed by the wind.* NLT

Nine years into the annual AT hikes a well-disciplined approach to accomplishing a long-distance hiking pace had developed and thank God, a spiritual discipline had developed as well.[72] That was the year when Mother passed away in the Spring, a few months before the traditional September hiking trip. After Mother's death, only twelve weeks remained for hours of physical conditioning each week. Father died several years prior to Mother's death, so there were additional responsibilities in closing the family estate, selling a family home of fifty years, and dealing with the will and probate court. I also had the ordinary responsibilities to address of the counseling business and family affairs before leaving for weeks on the Trail. Therefore, I was not looking forward to the trip. Leaving for a hiking trip was difficult, and enjoying the trip seemed impossible.

---

[72] 2006 September Hiking Trip

Because of Mother's love for me and her ability to see my faith bloom, she was a big inspiration to me about life. For weeks after her death, I was totally depleted of energy and motivation and filled with grief. As I went about the daily pre-dawn physical conditioning routines, I tried to find Jesus to talk with as I walked in the dark. But grief overwhelmed every thought and word in my prayers. How could I look forward to the annual hiking trip without the anticipated joy of Mother's encouraging words whenever we had phone conversations from the Trail? It felt impossible to face the prospect of the coming annual hike without Mom's earthly support. With significant discipline, I began to take my needs to the Lord in prayer during early morning preparatory hikes. Spending regular time with Jesus in that private space brought my soul more clarity and I felt less burdened with loss. I fervently prayed aloud, pouring out my despair, in the dark, as I hiked the neighborhood with my loaded backpack. I asked Jesus to bring me healing from grief and to bring joy back into my life.

Over a period of weeks, answers came from Jesus with compassion and loving comfort for my soul. Jesus promised me that healing and peace would come soon. Because I believed in Jesus' promises, a spiritual discipline began to form within me, and with this strength a newfound endurance through faith emerged. Day after day, I specifically asked Jesus to heal the grief and loss of Mom. I expected an answer from those prayers, and Jesus Christ "gladly" delivered. Before the hiking trip departure, healing had begun, and I was able to conduct life's responsibilities with more enthusiasm. Once I got on the Trail, life transformed into a beautiful healing experience because of the concentrated time spent with Jesus and the beauty of God's Nature around me. I was dreading a trip that would be nothing more than an obligatory ordeal so that my hiking buddy wasn't disappointed. Instead, the Trail brought me healing, comfort, and joy as I hiked. Because I had invited Jesus to help me prepare for the hiking trip, it became a sacred respite from the grief laden daily life.

Here is one example of how Jesus guided me towards a healing journey. Before leaving on the hiking trip, I turned to an elderly faith friend and explained my needs to her for spiritual encouragement. We arranged a phone conversation while I was on the Trail path. Whenever I felt the pain of my mother's absence, I called my faith friend. It worked! When I came to Black Rock Cliffs, Maryland, there was just enough elevation and cell signal to connect with my Texas faith friend. I had to stand on a boulder and stretch tall to find phone call reception. Listening to Pat's elderly comforting voice soothed my longing for Mom. The hole in my heart was filled with God's loving presence in Jesus Christ. Focused on joyfully knowing that Mom was in heaven, I could enjoy His everlasting love all around her. I was grasping God's comfort through Nature all around me.

Ask for Jesus' help with grief and loss and expect him to be responsive and answer your needs. That is the wonderful message of this scripture. Rest assured that life wisdom will come to you and strengthen your life purpose in God's ways, ways that are far better than you ever anticipated.

Prayer: Jesus, our Healer and companion in grief. I need Your persistent presence, and I ask You to help me find You each day. You are the trustworthy Guide on my life's path. You will not abandon me in the wilderness. You will be the One who pulls me up over a rock ledge and the One who cushions my falls. Amen

A question to provoke faith journaling: Have you tried conversing with Jesus aloud? Take your needs to him and be ready to lay it all out there. Also be ready to listen with expectation. Make a note of these conversations for future reference.

Holy Matrimony

A Step To Faith: Walk humbly with the Lord

1 Corinthians 13: 1, 4-5, 11-13 *If I had all other gifts from heaven but I did not have love of others, I would have nothing. Love is patient, kind, not jealous or boastful, not demanding its own way, rejoices in truth, has faith and hope. When I was a child in my faith, I saw things dimly. But when I grew in faith, I have perfect clarity. What I know is still incomplete, but God knows me completely. There are three things that will endure – faith, hope, and love – and the greatest of these is love.* NLT

Colossians 3:12–13 *God chose you to be holy people whom he loves, you must clothe yourselves with tenderhearted mercy, kindness, humility, gentleness, and patience. You must make allowance for each other's faults and forgive those who offend you. Remember, the Lord forgave you so you must forgive others.* NLT

Six years into the annual hiking trips, it was time to celebrate our 25th wedding anniversary. Our children had embraced their own college lifestyles, my husband was enjoying a challenging career and I had overcome much of the empty-nest anxieties by finding my deep groove on the AT. For our 25th wedding anniversary celebration, I was expecting Tim to suggest a typical celebration like a cruise ship vacation when unexpectedly, he proposed a backpacking trip on the AT! His suggestion was shocking because we had established rigid marital patterns about the AT trips. I deeply loved the hiking trips and craved the annual refreshing time to myself. Tim enjoyed his alone time each September while I hiked the AT. He could binge watch TV football games and other leisure activities that he liked. For months, I refused to take his idea seriously, even though he persisted with the proposal. Quite honestly, I did not want to dampen our 25th wedding anniversary celebration with an obligatory sour experience that we would both regret.

Over months of conversation about how to celebrate the 25th wedding anniversary, we reflected on our shared Christian faith that bound us together from the very beginning. In our conversations we celebrated the growth of our marriage. We had learned to love each other beyond the initial rigid roles of our marriage in its earlier stages.[73] In our reflective talks, we dusted off the cornerstone of our twenty-five years and examined the foundation of our marriage. We realized that the cornerstone was not about us as two individuals. The cornerstone of our marriage relied on our shared faith in Jesus Christ. Because of Christ's guiding presence as we managed challenges and sufferings, our marriage relationship continued to grow. And we could see God's hand at work in our mid-life stage of marriage as our children launched into adulthood.

After multiple reflective conversations about the status of our marriage, I accepted Tim's proposal as a legitimate next step forward for us as a couple. We could break the old mold of individual leisure time and address a deeper sharing of our individual interests. Tim's life-long proficiency in camping and hiking made him well prepared for this trip. And this change was a natural progression in our commitment to trust Christ as our holy matrimony cornerstone.

The Appalachian Trail runs through the center of Shenandoah National Park, and after studying the options, we chose this Trail section as the perfect romantic location for our anniversary trip!

---

[73] 2002 May Hiking Trip

Over five days in May, we backpacked through the beauty of Nature in the spring season. Lady slipper wildflowers brightened the landscape and a family of grouse birds surprised us along the Trail. We found a spring fed waterfall and used our water purification pump to resupply the water bags in our backpacks. Sharing with Tim this essential task in the lifestyle of long-distance backpacking was fun. One day on the Trail, we met a solo female thru-hiker. A retired navy officer, she was northbound from the Everglades Trail and intended to hike all the way to Mt Katahdin, Maine. How inspirational she was to both of us.

A surprise May snowfall arrived just before we checked into the Big Meadows Lodge. Our new found acquaintance also had checked into the Lodge to get out of the bad weather. Over evening dinner at the lodge, we enjoyed the company of our new friend from the Trail. We learned of her AT adventures and shared ours as well. This woman backpacker convinced me to embrace lightweight backpacking. She introduced us to the value of inexpensive outerwear called Frogg Toggs.

After backpacking through the SNP, Tim and I added two days of luxury by staying at a Bed and Breakfast in Front Royal, Virginia. Front Royal is the town on the north edge of SNP, a town that Park tourists find convenient and luxurious accommodations after living in the outdoors.

Prayer: God grant me the serenity to accept the things I cannot change. The courage to change the things I can. And the wisdom to know the difference. Amen.

A question to provoke faith journaling: Using the scriptures cited here to help you, how is Jesus guiding your personal growth within marriage or a close relationship?

Lost

A Step To Faith: Through faith in God, we are never lost.

Psalm 23 *The LORD is my shepherd; I shall not want. He maketh me to lie down in green pastures: he leadeth me beside the still waters. He restoreth my soul: he leadeth me in the paths of righteousness for his name's sake. Yea, though I walk through the valley of the shadow of death, I will fear no evil: for thou art with me; thy rod and thy staff they comfort me. Thou preparest a table before me in the presence of mine enemies: thou anointest my head with oil; my cup runneth over. Surely goodness and mercy shall follow me all the days of my life: and I will dwell in the house of the LORD forever.* KJV

Isaiah 40:31 *But those who wait on the Lord will find new strength. They will fly high on wings like eagles. They will run and not grow weary. They will walk and not faint.* NLT

Does the author of the 23rd Psalm express the feelings associated with being lost? If you were lost, would you say these things? When someone is lost, a myriad of feelings take over the conscious mind. Some of those mixed feelings are panic, paralyzing fear, untethered impulsivity, hopelessness, rage, helplessness and more. I have been lost and wrestled with all of those feelings.

When I have every reason to be overwhelmed with feelings because I'm lost in the woods, lost in my own confusion, or basically disoriented with the world around me, I try to remember where "Home" is.

When I know where home is located, it is much easier to manage the feelings and the experience of being lost. Life has taught me that the author of the 23rd Psalm is correct about the location of home. This Truth is especially clear when I am lost.

Home is being in the comforting and protective presence of Jesus my Savior. Therefore, I am never away from home because God resides within me, ready for me to access, regardless of what location my earthly being is in. A phrase that captures this Truth for me is: *We are spiritual beings having a human experience, not human beings having a spiritual experience.*

Wilderness backpacking and hiking capture my deepest interests. It is the epitome of earthly living in God's presence through the setting of His creation, Nature. As we walk an individual spiritual path through life, we eventually discover that the path to heaven is never a straight path. The spiritual path is a crooked meandering trail in which we most often ask for God's presence only when we have run out of solutions, and now we are in panic mode. We, in our human condition, exercise free will first when making decisions, and we are more comfortable with independent choice, even if doing so contributes to being lost.

I have a personal story of blindly walking through life towards the destination of being lost. It occurred on the southern AT.[74] I knew that my hiking partners were strangers that didn't care about my best interests, but I didn't want to see this Truth. One day I ended up hiking alone because they didn't want to accompany me at the slower pace that I needed. I didn't object to being left behind because I didn't want to appear weaker than them. I wanted to prove to myself that I could successfully hike solo. After hiking all day long and I still hadn't arrived at the group campsite, I began to panic. Was I lost? It was after dusk, and I became worried that I had passed the side trail intersection leading to an AT shelter where we were to meet. Did I really know my whereabouts? Completely worn out and hungry, I sat down on the side

---

[74] 2001 May Hiking Trip

of the Trail, and leaning against my backpack. I asked God to help me. Soon I heard their voices which led me onward to the shelter. You would think that this experience of being lost taught me a few lessons. But no. I wanted to "freely fly by the seat of my pants!" I didn't listen to friends who pointed out my limitations and advised me against further hiking trips with hikers unwilling to accommodate my pace. I didn't ask God for wisdom to guide the choices I was making. I avoided deeper insight and remained partially blind to my needs and limitations, and the proper hiking partners for me. Four months later, I went on to participate in a disastrous AT hiking trip with the same women.

There are more tragic outcomes than mine that come from being lost as happened on a section of the AT in central Maine. *When You Find My Body*, by Denis Dauphinee, is the account of Gerry Largay, a solo thru-hiker who became lost on the AT in July, 2013 and died. This book is based on selections from Gerry's journal as well as interviews with hikers she met on the trail.

The author was a part of the search team that looked for her for months without success. All members of this search and rescue team were deeply affected by their experiences of this fruitless endeavor.

Her body was found two years later on October 14, 2015 in her campsite. Like me, she was fulfilling a dream of hiking the entire Trail in the latter years of her life. Also like me, Gerry deemed herself trained and prepared for the quest of her lifetime. Through the well-documented biography, I read the known facts about her preparation, as well as her trail practices once she got on the AT. The author also respectfully shared a great deal about Gerry as a warm and cheerful person who was well-liked in the Trail community.

In 2008, my hiking partner, Smasher, and I decided to skip over some Trail sections near the place where Gerry became lost because the torrential rains had destroyed the Trail. It was too dangerous to attempt. The entire AT section in the state of Maine is very rugged and desolate, so every choice one makes has potentially dire consequences. Though mature decision making is important in such crucial circumstances, of equal importance is living a trusting faith in God.

You might ask, why did Gerry, a woman of faith, not survive being lost on the AT through the Grace of God, and yet I did? That is an understandable question that no one can fully answer. But I should point out that Gerry made some bad choices as a long-distance backpacker:

- She chose to continue the solo thru-hike when her hiking partner had to go home.
- She chose to leave behind SPOT, a personal GPS locator device, and did not have the right orientation skills or equipment.
- When Gerry became lost, she did not stay put. During the first two days of being lost, she panicked and frantically roamed about and thus wandered further away from the Trail.

For every bad choice that Gerry made, there is an easily overlooked life context of God's Grace at work that surely bares punctuation. I believe the nature of God is constantly acting within us and around us for our own good.

- Gerry had a hiking partner who cautioned her to not continue alone. There were two female backpackers on the AT the night before she became lost who cautioned her to not solo hike. Isn't that God working through those informed people around her?

- Her supportive husband, who acted as a shuttle car driver for her, didn't want her to go without the locator device, especially because she wasn't skilled in map and compass orientation. Wasn't God working through the love of her husband's reasonable objections?
- Anybody can lose their critical thinking skills once the reality of being lost sets in. All that I can contribute on this point is my absolute belief that God's Grace came to Gerry in the form of merciful compassion amid her fears. **John 14:27**, *Jesus said "I am leaving you with a gift – peace of mind and heart. And the peace I give isn't like the peace the world gives. So don't be troubled or afraid."* NLV

Each of us have to walk our solo path of life. Yet God never abandons us. God did not have a horrific plan for the end of Gerry's life. It is so difficult for us to remember that the reality of life includes "being lost." "Being lost" cannot be avoided, regardless of how much we prepare ourselves for life's misfortunes, or how deeply we believe in Christ Jesus. We desperately need a trust relationship with Christ to lean on when these times occur.

Fortunately, despite the tragedy of becoming lost, Gerry was ultimately not lost at all! Scripture helps us remember that our relationship with the Almighty God is the most important part of preparing for and being on the journey of life. In the face of being lost and knowing that she had done all that she knew to do about how to be found, she then turned into her faith to guide her remaining days. Gerry found the comfort and peace that she needed to face her devastating reality. Her family publicly shared a few of Gerry's journal entries after her body and campsite were found. There were many troubled rescuers who grieved because they couldn't find her. These rescuers needed the comfort of knowing that Gerry's faith brought her merciful peace when they could not. God was with Gerry – God's arms were wrapped around her with everlasting love. God never abandoned Gerry and God never abandons us. In this outdoor sanctuary, Gerry prayed her rosary and she leaned into His trustworthy arms throughout the last three weeks of her life. Gerry knew that she was going home.

Prayer: Oh Lord and Savior, I praise You that Your creation includes the free will that You have given me to make my own decisions. You gave me the inalienable right to learn and to grow on my own life path. Your precious counsel and guidance is always available to me, in fact You are eager to be my companion. Thank you, Holy Jesus, for sending people into my life when I really needed it, like when I'm panicked and filled with fear, became lost.

Teach me to overcome shocking realities by finding You in the middle of it all. Help me to seek You first as my Rock, my Cornerstone. Guide me to Your light in the chaos of darkness. Send Your Holy Spirit to comfort me so that I can see Your Way, Your Truth and Your Life. You are my one True compass and I will always safely arrive at home with You. In Your holy name, I pray. Amen.

A question to provoke faith journaling: Think of a time in your life when you were lost. Once you have captured this experience fully, write about the ways that God's Grace was present, including the gift attempts of Grace that you did not recognize at the time.

Outcast

Trail Life Link – *Faith followers are never outcasts to God.*

Ruth 1: 15–18. *"See" Naomi said to her, "your sister-in-law has gone back to her people and to her gods. You should do the same." But Ruth replied, "Don't ask me to leave you and turn back. I will go wherever you go and live wherever you live. Your people will be my people, and your God will be my God. I will die where you die and will be buried there. May the Lord punish me severely if I allow anything but death to separate us!" So when Naomi saw that Ruth had made up her mind to go with her, she stopped urging her.*

When we choose to live by faith, many people around us will not understand what is happening. In fact, many people are afraid to understand the mystery of what they are witnessing. They will turn away in fear of the unknown. In these moments, it is easy to feel like an outsider. God understands.

Ruth's story in the Old Testament illustrates her decision to follow Yahweh[75], rather than what her culture deemed appropriate for a widow from another faith. She chose to be a stranger in a foreign land. Ruth knowingly became an outcast with all the tribulations that accompanied that chosen life direction. But more important, Ruth chose to listen to the Lord who gave her the strength and courage to follow Him.

Emma Gatewood was another woman who chose to be a mystery to the public and stay away from many prying eyes. She became the first woman to hike the entire AT. In 1956, Grandma Gatewood (her trail name) at age 67, quietly began her sojourn

---

[75] Yahweh is the name of God used by the Israelites in ancient times

northbound on the AT carrying a gunny sack of supplies and wearing Keds tennis shoes. She did not seek notoriety from her journey even after the national news media hunted her down in Virginia, and continually pestered her to reveal her back story. A popular TV show of the time, the Gary Moore show, interviewed her on live TV. Gatewood did not stop after this amazing feat of 2,168 miles hiked in a few months despite her advanced age. She did it two more times! Grandma Gatewood became the first person to hike the AT three times. When the public became aware of Grandma Gatewood, the US Congress noticed the important value of the AT as a national treasure in 1956.

In 1996, when I became enamored with the AT, I read profusely about it. Grandma Gatewood immediately became my role model. I had to be satisfied with only knowing the statistics about her age and her accomplishments. Gatewood never let the public focus on her personal story and her family respected that decision long after her death in 1973. 41 years later, in 2014, her family chose the author, Ben Montgomery, to tell Emma's story because they trusted his ability to capture the complex truth. The book is titled *Grandma Gatewood's Walk*. Despite a marriage to a physically abusive man and an impoverished lifestyle on a mountain farm in Ohio, Emma Gatewood raised eleven children. Through her faith, she endured much suffering, and she rejoiced in her blessings as well. The book reveals that Emma began the AT walk about fifteen years after getting a divorce, raising several children as a single parent, working to support herself, and then helped with the care of grandchildren. Emma's adult children shared the very private truth that their mother's primary coping skill to handle her husband's physical abuse was to escape into the woods for solace and wait for him to cool down.

I am so glad that my role model, Grandma Gatewood, kept her life story private rather than allow the media to hijack her story and using it as "click bait" while she was hiking the AT. Her decision forced me to look inward to my own life direction rather than focus on her back story. Our Savior wants us to search for him in this way, even when the path includes times alone or times of being a social outcast.

Grandma Gatewood kept a journal while she traversed the AT, and she frequently authored poems about her experiences. Her poem, *The Reward of Nature*, captures her journey of faith.

"The Reward of Nature"

*If you'll go with me to the mountains
And sleep on the leaf carpeted floors
And enjoy the bigness of nature
And the beauty of all out-of-doors,
You'll find your troubles all fading
And feel the Creator was not man
That made lovely mountains and forests
Which only a Supreme Power can.*

*When we trust in the Power above
And with the realm of nature hold fast,
We will have a jewel of great price
To brighten our lives till the last.
For the love of nature is healing,
If we will only give it a try
And our reward will be forthcoming,
If we go deeper than what meets the eye.*[76]

---

[76] Used with permission from the author, Ben Montgomery

Let us remember that our faith journey is primarily a solo hike with God. There will be many occasions that other people will not understand that private journey of faith. There will be times that you cannot articulate to a curious listener the depths of your experiences with God who loves you. Of course, this Truth applies both on and off a hiking trail. Capture the resounding love of Jesus in these moments, much like Emma did in her poetry. Hold onto these inner Truths like they are mileposts on the trail of life. By doing so, your faith will grow in strength and endurance.

Prayer: Holy Jesus, You are all-knowing. Nothing is hidden from You. When I feel misunderstood, yet my private thoughts are too painful to share with anyone, You are there. When my future is a scary mystery to me, give me the loving comfort of Your presence in my daily walk of life. Reassure me that my life story is in Your trustworthy hands. All praise and glory be Yours, my Gracious Redeemer and Guide. Amen

A question to provoke faith journaling: Are you carrying a life story too burdensome to share with others? Write a love letter to Jesus about your story. Pray the love letter aloud to him. Destroy the written work if necessary.

Suffering

A Step To Faith: In your sufferings, praise God's merciful understanding

Genesis 29:25-27, 31-35 *But when Jacob woke up in the morning – it was Leah! "What sort of trick is this?" Jacob raged at Laban. "I worked seven years for Rachel. What do you mean by this trickery?" It's not our custom to marry off a younger daughter ahead of the firstborn," Laban replied. "Wait until the bridal week is over, and you can have Rachel too – that is, if you promise to work another seven years for me." But because Leah was unloved, the Lord let her have a child, while Rachel was childless. So, Leah became pregnant and had a son. She named him Reuben, for she said, "The Lord has noticed my misery, and now my husband will love me." She soon became pregnant again and had another son. She named him Simeon, for she said, "The Lord heard that I was unloved and has given me another son." Again, she became pregnant and had a son. She named him Levi, for she said, "Surely now my husband will feel affection for me, since I have given him three sons!" Once again, she became pregnant and had a son. She named him Judah, for she said, "Now I will praise the Lord!" And then she stopped having children.* NLT

Now that I have experienced a few years of celebrating my completion of the AT, I reflect on the many years dedicated to completing this goal. Sometimes I reflect on the particulars of the suffering that was endured to accomplish this goal. I chose to strive for a goal that many people around me did not understand. And some people that I love disapproved of my actions to go on annual backpacking trips instead of remaining at home. Because

I was going against the grain of the expectations of some loved ones and the culture as a whole, I reflect on this chosen path as more than a personal challenge. It was suffering to me. Why didn't I choose a less contentious path for midlife change and simply relax in the comforts of my daily lifestyle? One would think that it would have been easier to grow my faith in God using a more traditional method, like a focus on attending church activities with my husband, family, and faith friends.

Certainly, loads of fun times happened due to the AT goal, and I do not want to minimize that fact. But I also suffered each year as I underwent months of physical conditioning, severe weather exposure, trail fatigue, homesickness, and the fact that I caused inconveniences to loved ones due to my absence in the customary lifestyle patterns.

Yes, I made the choice to suffer. I came to accept these sufferings, some chosen and some not chosen, because I ultimately realized that the sufferings were a part of my unique faith journey with God. I look back over the last 25 years and see that I needed this private pathway to fully trust that God truly was beside me and that God understood my every step along the way. To this day, I trust and depend on God's merciful understanding of me.

In Genesis the story of Leah, daughter in-law of Isaac and wife of Jacob, is one of the earliest descriptions of a woman believer turning to God in prayer. In a family filled with deceit and manipulation toward each other, God was actively working in their lives. Long before Jesus Christ, and even before the Old Testament was compiled, Leah turned to the One True God to profess her suffering due to a dysfunctional family. Families of this time accepted a cultural practice of polygamy and condoned marriages arranged solely for a financial transaction. Leah's father Laban tricked Jacob into marrying Leah instead of her sister, Rachel, whom Jacob loved. Jacob had labored for years to pay for Rachel's hand in marriage. Her father Laban convinced Leah to participate in this marriage trickery for his own financial gain. Leah feared that no one would love her and want to marry her because she was less attractive than her sister, so she participated in her father's plan of tricking Jacob in marriage to her.

Instead of worshipping the cultural household idol of the day, the scorned young Leah repetitively and courageously asked God to address her needs for love and mercy. Leah had no role model on how to relate to God. The scripturally documented faith journey of Leah occurs over many years as she addresses culturally demeaning norms and customs towards women. The cultural mores expected her to function as the submissive property of her father, and then, after marriage, to live as the property of her husband Jacob who does not love her. Because Leah's marriage had no foundation of mutual love, she pleaded with God to make Jacob love her. As the years of miserable humiliation and jealousy continue, Leah increasingly relies on God's comforting presence. Through the blessing of many children, Leah is transformed by each childbirth as the Lord God is at her side, The Holy and trustworthy companion. Through a deepening trust in God, Leah could realistically manage her expectations of the dysfunctional family members as well as manage expectations of herself. To Trust God to help her grow through her suffering, to worship God, rather than her husband or her family cultural traditions.

Leah's faith journey demonstrates how suffering will always be a part of life. Yet, when the believer trusts in God's mercy and comfort to prevail, strength to continue transcends the misery of this world. God does not choose for us to suffer. God is present in these challenging times seeking deeper relationship with us. During painful times, we do not always understand how beneficial outcomes might occur. That is part of God being God, and we are not. We are blessed to be His loved children. A faith journey is never a step-by-step path, instead it is a series of transcending life experiences where we choose to let God help us, especially in tough times.

Reflecting on the many years of Appalachian Trail hiking trips and my middle age years in general, how to incorporate suffering into the meaning of everyday life was a dominant challenge for me. I come from a culture quite different from the culture of Leah's time. My cultural roots are in the Baby Boomer generation, and I am one of the pioneers of the women's liberation movement. Women of my culture and generation tend to expect life to give us freedom and independence, including in a marriage relationship. However, faith has given me the wisdom to manage the illusions and limitations in those cultural norms. Leah experienced a similar journey of faith in God because she let go of her identity wrapped in the cultural norms' definition of a happy woman. Instead, Leah's faith in God gave her purpose in life beyond the culture's limited definition for her time.

Take the time to be with God and relish His trustworthiness, His grace, His mercies, and His love that is there for you, whenever you ask for Him to come into your life. Take all your needs for courage as well as peace and comfort to Him. Ask to be released from guilt, shame, and blame of that which burdens you. This is a journey that takes time, but your efforts to be in relationship with Jesus Our Lord and Savior will be rewarded tenfold. You will become kinder and gentler towards yourself, and likewise in the significant relationships of your life. Suffering cannot be avoided, but with God's help, it will strengthen you. By cultivating a Go-To-God-First response, with time your perseverance builds, and you will joyously praise Him for walking beside you.

Prayer: Oh God, Holy Comforter, Your mercies and understanding of my needs are limitless. I have no other relationship like You in life because You alone are God. And You are the Promise Keeper. Precious Savior, help me to want You, the Healer, more than the healing from the suffering. I praise Your merciful love and Your understanding of my human condition. Make Your encouragement to seek You evident to me. Teach me to accept Your help in carrying my burdens and sufferings. You alone are there to comfort me. With the Holy Spirit, guide me to seek Your daily companionship. Amen

A question to provoke faith journaling: What challenges are you carrying without requesting God's help to carry the burden?

Transitions

A Step To Faith: When you don't know what to do, seek the Waymaker

Acts 1: 6 – 11. *When the apostles were with Jesus, they kept asking him, "Lord, are you going to free Israel now and restore our kingdom? "The Father sets those dates," he replied, "and they are not for you to know. But when the Holy Spirit has come upon you, you will receive power and will tell people about me everywhere – in Jerusalem, throughout Judea, in Samaria, and to the ends of the earth." It was not long after he said this that he was taken up into the sky while they were watching, and he disappeared into a cloud. As they were straining their eyes to see him, two white-robed men suddenly stood there among them. They said, "Men of Galilee, why are you standing here staring at the sky? Jesus has been taken away from you into heaven. And someday, just as you saw him go, he will return!"* NLT

When I walked across the Bear Mountain Bridge over the Hudson river to the Bear Mountain State Park riverbank, I had just finished 2,000 miles on the AT.[77] Earlier that day, Smasher and I had enjoyed a beautiful day-hike through the Graymoor Franciscan Monastery grounds before making the steep mountain descent to the Hudson River. The monastery grounds have a majestic viewpoint along a cliff edge overlooking the Hudson River. Walking the Trail through these holy grounds laden with faith-filled symbols, traditions and memorials were precious last steps on my spiritual pilgrimage. My soul was uplifted. As I hiked these last steps, my thoughts and emotions were reflecting on

---
[77] 2015 September Hiking Trip

so many memories that informed this pivotal moment in my life. The Monastery had once provided a hiking hostel as an outreach to AT trekkers. I remember my anticipation of being an overnight guest in that monastery someday. But that era had passed and the monks no longer provided that unique hospitality.

I felt conflicted about the meaning of the big day. During the early months of 2015, as I had prepared for the final AT trip, I felt rumblings of being unsettled and bored with life. This feeling of ambivalence strengthened as the final hiking trip came to fruition and the finite ending of 2,000 miles came closer. What was happening to me?

Upon reflection, what was happening to me is similar to the experience Jesus' disciples were having as they were straining their eyes to see Jesus as he ascended into heaven. I will come back to this point and expand on it.

In my early years of annual hikes, returning home felt like the aftermath of a vacation. Like all vacationers, I looked forward to the luxury of getting away from my busy life. On the way home from those trips, the duties and responsibilities of normal life quickly filled my mind, and my trail experiences evaporated into the past.

Five years into the annual hikes, that vacation concept of the Trail hikes ended. These annual Trail hikes began to take on the form of Faith Journeys.[78] The Faith Journeys transformed my life into a spiritual pilgrimage. Year round I yearned for the annual hikes not so much as a vacation but as a deepening time with God. Living in the wilderness along the Trail became a sacred space. A sanctuary where my soul and spirit were fully renewed. As I returned home, I experienced an unexpected culture shock because I was moving from one world to another. I slowly came

---

[78] Read *Living a Spiritual Pilgrimage*

to realize that the normal world could not understand how I had changed on the inside.

Upon reflection, this period of annual hiking trips established a cornerstone for my new life. Consistently finding more self-worth through my relationship with Jesus as my Savior deeply fueled my life. Within a few years of annual concentrated time in God's wilderness sanctuary, I began returning home fully energized and equipped to "carry the Light." The Holy Spirit was spilling out of me, and impacting those around me. I exuded faith-based positive energy in all spheres of influence. Trail Life was beginning to stay with me, rather than evaporate as it had in the past. The energy I put into services for life coaching clientele easily tripled. Family members experienced me as "Beth on steroids." I saw myself as God's disciple in His kingdom. When I returned home, being God's servant was what mattered to me the most.

I realized that God had even more in mind for me. God was not done with me. My deepening trust in God informed me that being an agent of God's plan was the right path for me. I realized how easily I fell into actions that were my plan, not God's plan. I didn't want my life purpose to be centered on me but on God. Duh! My devoted actions needed to clearly point to God's plan, daily unfolding both in the me and in the world around me. God does not need me to be in-charge of what is happening in my life or the lives of others; God does not have needs. On the Trail, I could quickly grasp this Truth, as I watched the ebb and flow of Nature. I could grasp God's creation operating through those around me that tuned into this natural rhythm of God Almighty. Whenever I was blessed to be emerged in faith, whether on the Trail or not, I could see this Truth. But faith moments occurred infrequently at first, and required the ongoing practice to trust in Jesus, to live in this Truth. Somewhere in the last five years of the 20 AT hiking trips, I realized that because of God's help, I was going to complete the 2000 miles of the AT.

Re-entry to daily life is often a challenging life transition for hikers who traverse the 2000 miles in one long trip, a thru-hike. Some AT trekkers finish the thru-hike and easily re-start normal life. But many hikers feel lost due to a lack of purpose when their hiking goal completed. Trail friendships are in the rear-view mirror. Daily life back in normal land has not changed. The hiker has been changed, but the world has not.

The faith of some believers burns out, whether they are hiking enthusiasts or not. My faith almost did. Our human condition includes the need for a Savior and the fact that life transitions happen confirms this Truth.

The disciples were in a transition moment as Jesus shockingly ascended into heaven right before their eyes. Likewise, I was in a transition at both the beginning and the ending of my AT hiking. I did not grasp what I needed as I began the hikes, but I did seek Him and that is how I came out of both transition times with a life purpose that rested on my walk with Jesus.

There is a saying that goes something like this. "When Life closes a door, God opens a door. But it is hell in the hallway!" We do not like being confused, lost without a role or purpose. We do not like to feel left without a leader to save us and make the world perfect. We like being in safe spaces or rooms of comfort, not wandering around in the hallway waiting for a direction. I have learned that the saying needs one more closing sentence – God is with you in the hallway too, just ask for Him!

Prayer: Faithful God, only You are the Waymaker in my life, especially in those confusing times of transition and change. Help me to trust Your guidance especially when my pathway is foggy and ominous. When I am lost, communicate Your loving presence with signs that I cannot overlook. Assure me that Your righteous arm is steadying me when I stumble over my own feet. Holy Jesus, Your saving grace and love keeps me striving to be Your servant. I love You Jesus. Amen.

Question to provoke faith journaling: Are you telling others how Jesus led you through life transitions?

Truth

A Step To Faith: With curiosity, seek the Truth of God's ways

John 14: 6-7 *Jesus told him, "I am the way, the truth, and the life. No one can come to the Father except through me. If you had known who I am, then you would have known who my Father is."* NLT

Ephesians 4:14-15 *Then we will no longer be like children, forever changing our minds about what we believe because someone has told us something different or because someone has cleverly lied to us and made the lie sound like the truth. Instead, we will hold to the truth in love, becoming more and more in every way like Christ.* NLT

When I visited my elderly father two months before he passed away, I was 47 years old and had just returned from my first trip on the Appalachian Trail. Though Dad was not feeling well, he wanted to connect with me as we always did, conversing about the deeper questions of life. Beginning in my childhood years, our conversations often addressed my questions about this world. Dad knew of my deep love for outdoor recreation, but he was curious about my new quest. Why was I so interested in long distance backpacking as a personal feat? Addressing Dad's curiosity, I proudly shared the fun and adventures of being on the Trail, such as how I unexpectedly spent the night alone in the wilderness and overcame my fears. Beyond that news, my answers about the "whys" were superficial. At that time, I could not express why I yearned for these experiences on the Trail, not even to myself. I just knew of deep unanswered questions that left me unsettled and I had to find Truth. Being in God's Nature felt like the best environment for answers to come from within me and surface in my awareness. If I did not find Truth, my future would be lost.[79]

Reflecting on my last conversation with Dad, I hear one of the unanswered questions. The question concerned my brother's suicide five years earlier. Where was God coming from about my brother's death after he suffered years of mental illness? And was God disappointed in me because I did not fix my family and my brother using my professional counselor abilities? At that time, I could not initiate a conversation about these questions, and neither could Dad. Most importantly, I was blindly searching to understand God's ways on big questions so I could live in His peace.

Answers came to me about God's ways over time. As I backpacked on the Trail hour after hour and day after day, repetitively getting into "the zone," I listened more attentively and heard God answering me. Accepting that the ways of God are different from the ways of humanity was a crucial step in understanding who God is and my relationship with God. Watching Nature unfold in its order and balance spoke to me with a message of God's sovereign reign and peace.

Over years of annual AT hiking trips, the Truth about why I was seeking the wilderness each September began to emerge. Through uninterrupted conversations with God as my companion in these long walks in His creation, my earlier confusion about life's meaning and purpose waned. I began to understand God's ways, and the peace that surpasses all understanding was filling my soul.

God's Nature revealed basic Truths about God in my earliest Trail experiences. What Nature revealed to me matched God's attributes that I had discovered in my normal life patterns off the Trail. Here is a list of God's attributes that became apparent to

---

[79] 1997 June Hiking Trip

me early on. You may well experience a different order to getting acquainted with God. I came to know these attributes as some of God's ways, or as God's Truth:

- God is Creator of the universe. Everything came from God.
- God is Faithful and keeps His promises.
- God is Accessible and near and desires relationship with humans.
- God is Good and blesses us with His goodness personally.
- God's Glory is the total of all His attributes. His glory is in the beauty of Nature and creation. His glory is in His power, mercy, grace, and Love.
- Our Savior Jesus Christ reveals God's Love and Glory.

I enjoyed Bible readings attached to short daily devotionals during these years of AT trips, but I did not allow time for in depth Bible study until I finished the Trail. Once I began Bible study, I recognized that my experience of God's attributes was like the experiences of people in the Bible. I understood the pattern of God's ways over the centuries and how the Truth resonated with me in my relationship with God. The Bible is God's autobiography, it is the Word.

John's gospel is one of my favorites because it clearly describes Jesus' view of himself, of the Father, and who I am in relationship to Him.

The letter to the Ephesians reminds us that finding Truth is a lifelong effort. This scripture is challenging us, as a part of our human journey, to sort out what Truth is, and what are human manipulations and bold-faced lies. The apostle Paul's words to the Ephesians reminds us that our growth path as Christians requires us to search for Truth and Love in Christ. This scripture challenges everyone to look around us and to also look within ourselves for the Truth. The Truth be told, I am broken and need Jesus, my Savior, to forgive me and make me whole.

By spending dedicated time on the Trail searching for Truth in God's ways, I repeatedly found rest for my soul but also found more spiritual energy to transform the whole of life as I returned to a world filled with distractions from God's path. With God as my guide, I could focus on the best path at the crossroads not only on the Appalachian Trail, but more importantly, I could focus on the best path for the current life issues and decisions that I was facing.

Through God's redemptive power, my burdens were lifted from me. Burdens of undue responsibility and guilt associated with my brother's suicide were lifted off of me through God's grace. The burden of responsibility for my family's pain was lifted as well. Jesus, my Savior, bore my burdens and set me free. Alleluia![80]

I am blessed that my earthly father loved me. But the greatest blessing that Dad gave me was the permission to be curious about who God is and find God's Truth. Dad knew God's redeeming love and shared the Truth with me that "God loves me."

Prayer: God Almighty, You are the wonderful Counselor, revealing Truth in all Your ways. You lift burdens from my shoulders and carry those burdens, Jesus Christ Our Savior. I am free! Alleluia! With my freedom to seek Truth, I want to understand more of Your ways, Oh Holy One. I am not God; You are God, and I am Your child. I need Your grace and mercy. Your faithful presence assures me of Your Love. Be with me and pursue me so that I have the courage to seek Truth in You. Amen.

Question to provoke faith journaling: How do you want to better know God and the Truth of His ways?

---

[80] Matthew 11:30 "For my yoke is easy, and my burden is light."

Faithfulness

Trail Life Link – God's faithfulness empowers your Christian living.

1 John 1:9 *But if we confess our sins to him, he is faithful and just to forgive and to cleanse us from every wrong.* NLT

When I seek to understand this scripture, my first reflection is that God fulfills His words in 1 John. Repeatedly, God is offering me a new day, each and every day. When I look away from the world, and turn to God, I own my human condition and my need for Him as my Savior. A Savior whose faithfulness is immeasurable. When I allow this to happen, a new day dawns! I am renewed, forgiven, and cleansed. Our Redeemer and Friend has never turned away from me. God is everlastingly faithful. God shows mercy, never condemnation. God shows Love and favor, always providing what I truly need. Great is God's faithfulness!

In our journey of daily life, we tend to get sidetracked concerning our understanding of faithfulness. We think that it is a human trait instead of a divine attribute of God's Nature. Though we seek to be faithful, we inevitably fall short in our relationships as well as in the promises we make to Our Savior. When we fall short and turn to God for forgiveness, our Savior's cleansing presence renews a right spirit within us. I believe that obedience is as close to God's attribute of faithfulness as we believers can get. Our obedience to Christ eventually becomes a joyful response to God's faithfulness as we repeatedly receive His Love over time.

When we need it the most, God's faithfulness is revealed through His Grace. Whether we notice or not, God's Grace is constantly raining down on us. In September of 2001, God's faithfulness answered my desperate prayer for protection and provision.

God's provision came to me through a stranger's actions, even though we never shared a faith conversation. God is in control, and therefore God's faithfulness moves at God's command, both in heaven and in all the earth. [81]

God's faithfulness came to me through a stranger, Anita, rescuing me from the perils of pending injuries on the AT near Mt. Lafayette. When I realized that I was in danger of injury if I continued the backpacking trip with the my hiking partners, I turned away from their influence over me, and I turned to God. In my desperate prayers, I asked for God's protection and guidance out of the dangerous situation. I was astounded by God's response when I placed my trust in God. A new resolve for my personal safety came from within me. That was the first step of my spiritual transformation. Then I experienced ownership of a newly assertive voice. This new voice spoke to the hiking partners with an ultimatum about our continued companionship.

As the day of climbing Mt Lafayette proceeded, the hiking partners continued to ignore my requests for their cooperation. God's faithful presence swelled within me, giving me strength and resolve to finish the climb at my own safe but slow pace. Through God's unfailing presence up and over that mountain, I detached from the hiking partners and even felt blessed to soon be without them. With this second step of spiritual transformation, God's faithfulness became my protective shield, and I finished the arduous day walking into Greenleaf Hut alone. I then experienced my new assertive voice speaking to other hikers with a quiet and calm authority concerning my self-care. That evening, at the Greenleaf Hut's dinner table of hikers, I stood up and announced my need for help to leave the AT and the mountain range the next day. After dinner, God delivered a rescuer to me. Anita approached me and offered the help that I needed. God

---

[81] September 2001 Hiking Trip

provided Anita, a hiker from the local area, to guide me out of the mountains and to host me overnight in her home. I left Anita's home in Franconia Notch the next day, and I never saw her again. I never saw the hiking partners again either! I flew home to Texas newly aware of the great faithfulness of God.

The Mt Lafayette experience of God's provision and faithfulness was a pivotal spiritual transformation. My faith growth from this experience guided me to God in the following years on the Trail. I embraced Trail experiences of my human needs and limitations, and in that predicament, I looked to God to be present, faithful, and bringing me all that I needed. Going to God through His Creation, His Nature, was a necessity because my normal lifestyle had a built-in comfort that created a natural distance from God. We have crafted civilization to minimize the reality of our human limitations. To build a deeper relationship with God and lean into His faithfulness, I realized that I had work to do. I could not expect God to do all the work of finding me. Accepting God's faithfulness meant accepting a transformation from my well-honed self-reliance. I am stubborn! As I grew closer to God, learning His ways through being with Him in my life experiences, it was God's faithfulness that made me cherish and seek His Love. Psalm 46:10 applies in describing this ongoing moment of a faith journey, *"Be silent and know that I am God."*

As I grew in understanding God's faithfulness, I also sought the comfort of His Truth. I became aware that other believers also know God in this way. My experience of God's faithfulness was validated through studying the Bible and discussing these studies in a group of believers. Stories of people in the Bible relating to God reinforced my journey of relating to God. God has offered His omnipotent faithfulness to His people from the dawn of creation and to all generations of believers.

As my faith in God has deepened, God's faithfulness to me has become more evident. Once again, the setting of God's Nature on the AT was the best place to find that evidence; a setting where my observations were not over stimulated by multiple distractions, which often happens in my regular urban lifestyle. Meeting a random stranger in the setting of God's Nature helps my observations be focused on what my soul perceives. [82]

In New Hampshire, 2014, I encountered a believer on the AT that my soul instantly connected with as someone who knew God's faithfulness. The stranger was living out God's faithfulness in such an obvious way that could not be dismissed or denied. Joe patrolled the road crossings of the AT in his truck with a camper shell and his trusty dog. When Smasher and I initially met him, Jo was cheerfully greeting northbound hikers coming off Mt Washington and the difficult Presidential Mountain range. When we approached a Trailhead leading to a parking lot, we noticed Joe's demeanor of a spiritual eagerness for authentic connection with others. Watching him approach tired hikers leaving the Trail, there was no doubt that this middle-aged man was a Trail Angel. After retiring from the military, Joe went on to thru-hike the AT. Since he knew the Trail like the back of his hand, Joe was ready to encourage and assist hikers at the most challenging places along the AT. He offered the help of driving hikers into town for resupplies or lodging. Joe offered a variety of ways to be a servant to others. His help was not for the money or any other earthly reward. Joe was a servant to fellow hikers because of his resounding life experiences of God's faithfulness to him. Joe simply could not contain his joyful relationship with God and so he passed it on to others.

As we stood on the Trail getting acquainted, Joe shared with us how God's Nature through the Trail experience has saved him

---

[82] 2014 Hiking Trip

from the despair he experienced during his military career. When I gave him the balsawood dove and held his hand saying, "Peace be with you," the Holy Spirit ignited our encounter of faith fellowship. Smasher and I could have stood on the trailhead for hours getting to know Joe, a congenial servant of the Lord. Later that evening, I reflected on the blessed encounter with Joe. I realized that he was a healthy and stable man who chose this transient lifestyle to be a faithful servant of God by helping hikers in the AT wilderness. Joe could have chosen other lifestyles less burdened with servanthood.

Joe always had good trail stories to share but he was also ready to listen to your stories too. In addition to his good storytelling, I was particularly impressed by Joe's craft of balsawood replicas of the AT shelters. This was a hobby of his. On the following day, we happened to encounter Joe again at the same trailhead, and he had a gift for me. I was so blessed to receive one of his AT shelter replicas made of balsawood! Joe and I had shared the joy of God's faithfulness. I will never forget this brother in Christ.

PRAYER: Gracious God, You are patient in Your faithfulness to me. Despite my stubborn self-reliance, You never leave my side. You are the One True Savior and Redeemer. I used to think that You were too busy to be with me, but that is not true. The more I acknowledge Your faithfulness, I am humbled by the favor You give to me. Help me Holy Friend, to count on You more because the more I am bound to You, my joyful obedience will prevail! All Glory be Yours, everlasting God on high. Amen

Question to provoke spiritual journaling: Are you seeking a relationship with God where you lean on His faithfulness?

Forgiveness

A Step To Faith: Before judging someone, walk a mile in their shoes.

Galatians 6: 7–8: *Don't be misled. Remember that you can't ignore God and get away with it. You will always reap what you sow! Those who live only to satisfy their own sinful desires will harvest the consequences of decay and death. But those who live to please the Spirit will harvest everlasting life from the Spirit.* NLT

It was 4 AM when I suddenly woke up from a night of exhausted sleep.[83] I was snuggled in my sleeping bag inside the three-sided lean-to, Osgood Shelter, on the New Hampshire Presidential Mountain Range. The previous day, a torrential rainfall had turned the alpine area trails into swift streams and waterfalls making the backpacking trip the toughest ordeal that I had ever experienced. The weather conditions had been difficult, but the overall ordeal was magnified by more critical factors. I was a newbie hiker attempting to traverse one of the most difficult parts of the AT. I woke up to a personal reality check that my women hiking partners with advanced skill and experience were more interested in the sport of the adventure than my safety as a beginner. My wake-up awareness included how I feared their condemnation of my weaker physical stamina and inability to keep up with them. I feared their judgment of me. I was thoroughly frustrated with myself, given my depleting strength, and failing stamina.

Then I realized that the early wake-up prompt was the result of a dream where I was intensely angry with God for putting me in this situation where I was going to fail and probably get injured.

---

[83] 2001 September Hiking Trip

Within minutes of awakening from the dream, I began prayer journaling while the cold rain fell, and other hikers continued to sleep around me. As I wrote, the Lord Jesus guided me and transformed my brokenness into a spirit-filled plan of action. Christ pointed out my faulty blind trust in hiking partners that I had only recently met through a magazine ad. That wasn't very smart! After accepting that truth, I centered on Christ's love for me, and I began to look for a solution to the bad situation that I had created. The next day, I left the hiking partners and was blessed with help to leave the Trail. Ultimately, I was able to catch a flight home to Texas 48 hours later.

Looking back on this life changing moment, God was leading me on a journey of forgiveness that would ultimately help me to become more forgiving of others.

For years after this pivotal moment occurred, I forgot how angry I was with these women whom I called the "Hiking Partners from Hell." God's saving grace took the memory of this event and packaged my take-away as "God loves me, and God does not care about the Hiking Partners from Hell." I used this emotional energy as self-talk fuel to prove these women wrong! The negative fuel energized me towards greater physical fitness and endurance. I also elevated myself in the story, thinking of myself as a better person than these women. My very human tendencies kept me from forgiving these women. I could not even forgive them because I used the women as negative fuel to feed my self-perception. [84]

I would like to say that I grasped the message from Galatians one year later on the 2002 hiking trip. But I did not! Only recently have I realized that the story I am about to share is an illustration of God's work in me over years, bringing me to the place where I am capable of forgiving those who are my adversaries.

---

[84] 2002 September Hiking

Smasher and I arrived at the Pearisburg, Va. hiking hostel delighted to have it as a base camp and launching pad for day-hikes. The Holy Family Church hostel was a large cabin that could sleep 25 hikers and included bathroom and kitchen facilities. A caretaker checked on the church's outreach building but no one lived on site. We settled in as the only hiker guests, making ourselves at home. Just before dusk, a man arrived introducing himself by his Trail name, "Medicare Charlie." Though he arrived in his car, he announced plans for a multi-day backpacking trip. Medicare Charlie was an arrogant and grumpy man in his early 70s, and he promptly announced that women did not belong on the AT. He further alienated me by inferring that Girl Scouts did not have outdoor skills. He knew this to be true because he had been a Boy Scoutmaster. I decided to keep my distance from Medicare Charlie and to mind my own business.

The next morning, Medicare Charlie loaded his backpack, and as he departed, he stated a change in his backpacking plans. Medicare Charlie angrily complained that his male hiking buddies stood him up on the original plan for a group backpacking trip. He went on to say that those lazy old "couch potatoes" would not stop him from going out on the Trail by himself. After he left, Smasher and I briefly worried about his plan and moved on with our hiking plans for the day.

A day or two later, we were day hiking a mountain ridgeline on the AT headed back to the Holy Family Church hostel. As we were enjoying the glorious fall weather day, we noticed in the distance a body slumped on the ground and leaning against a tree beside the Trail. It was Medicare Charlie with his backpack, and he didn't look well. We stopped and asked if he needed our help. He angrily declared that he was resting and certainly did not need our help. Medicare Charlie's appearance clearly showed signs of dehydration and sunstroke. His agitation and incoherence were also signs of his poor condition, so we decided to help him despite his refusal to accept our help. I stayed with Medicare Charlie and coaxed him to drink water while Smasher hiked into town and guided EMS down the Trail to the spot where Medicare Charlie and I had continued to rest. Medicare Charlie spent the night in the hospital where he received necessary medical attention. Smasher and I were just glad that we came along and found him in time to get help.

The next morning, Medicare Charlie surprisingly showed up at the hiking hostel looking ten years younger and healthy. And he had a new attitude – gratitude. He drove to the hiking hostel to talk with us before heading home. This humble man apologized for being so self-righteous towards us. And he expressed gratitude that we helped him. I was surprised by this transformation in Medicare Charlie and accepted his apology. Immediately I felt the residual resentments towards him lessen.

This scripture reminds me that life's journey has stories that connect with one another, but sometimes I don't see the connection until years later. On reflection about these two Trail stories, I realize that I dismissively accepted Medicare Charlie's apology because I saw myself in him when I thought of my attitude towards the women hiking partners. I held onto those resentments for years, never forgiving the "Hiking Partners from Hell". I was ignoring God's presence in that time that was so pivotal in my life. I wanted to blame God for my dilemma. God forgave me for blaming Him and God is daily forgiving me. I wanted to see the story in one dimension – God loves me, but the story was far more complex than I saw it. Through looking at these two stories in my life, I see how God is not in "my box" but is much greater than I will ever grasp. God's forgiveness is beyond measure and full of Grace. I have learned that forgiving others co-exists with accepting my need for God's forgiveness.

Prayer: Merciful Savior, You are patiently ready to forgive me when I come to You, even though I can never earn Your forgiveness. Through my salvation that only You can give, I am renewed with a clean spirit and a pure heart. O Holy Companion, be with me as I seek to be Your messenger to others, sharing Your love and mercy. Help me to ask others for their forgiveness whenever it is the right thing to do. And remind me sweet Jesus, that first, You forgave me. I want to remember this Truth each day and be grateful, for this is joy in life! Amen.

Question to provoke faith journaling: Reflect on grudges or resentments that you have carried over time. How is Christ working in your life today, offering you forgiveness? Are you aware how forgiveness brings you closer to Christ?

Peacemaking

A Step To Faith: May the peace of Christ be with you

Ephesians 4:3-6. *We are all one body, we have the same Spirit, and we have all been called to the same glorious future. There is only one Lord, one faith, one baptism, and there is only one God and Father, who is over all and in us all and living through us all.* NLT

Matthew 5:9. *God blesses those who work for peace, for they will be called the children of God.* NLT

As I neared the last 500 miles to completion of the AT, I began pondering how to openly share God's love when greeting others on the Trail.[85] Reflecting on this urge to share the Good News, I vividly remember how risky and vulnerable it felt to even consider interacting with strangers in this way. I had grown accustomed to proclaiming my faith by wearing the cross necklace and embracing my trail name Spirit when meeting and greeting people. But this new thought was a next step forward in approaching strangers and I did not want to come across offensive in any way.

During previous trips, Smasher inspired me with her shelter journal entries, claiming her message of "new beginning" in life. She punctuated her shelter journal entries with a closing symbol - the Christian image of a new beginning in Jesus Christ – the butterfly. Placing a glittery butterfly sticker next to her journal entry was an eye-catching signal to readers about Jesus' love. Smasher enjoyed sharing this uplifting message and I enjoyed watching her do it.

---

[85] 2014 & 2015 Hiking Trip

People often define peace as the setting where one enjoys "peace and quiet." A primary attraction of the wilderness outdoors is the assurance that we will find refreshing abundance of "peace and quiet." The sound of a mountain stream flowing over rocks as it meanders down the mountain will bring peaceful rest to most.

In Matthew 6, Jesus is speaking to a large crowd of people who were seeking someone to rescue them from the civil unrest and violence throughout the region. Jesus Christ's words to this troubled audience are known as The Sermon on the Mount or also known as the Beatitudes. His teachings focus on the values and beliefs a Christian chooses to practice. The crowd did not want to hear these teachings because Jesus said they must change their outlook on life as well as their ways. They were hoping for "peace and quiet," like most people do. Christ says we must work for peace.

The message of peacemaking came to me as the one to convey to strangers because I had embraced peacemaking through faith for a long time. In 1999, it was the theme that I carried into the new millennium. I chose the theme phrase "Let there be peace on earth and let it begin with me." I convinced the year 2000 high school graduates in my Girl Scout Troop 961 to carry this theme forward into the new millennium with me. Coming to the strong decision of the message God asked me to convey, I moved on to deciding how I could best share the message with strangers who I encountered along the Trail. I found a large quantity of half inch balsawood crafted doves at the hobby craft store. It was the perfect solution. I carried 50 or more doves in my pocket as I hiked. The profoundly deep reactions of some strangers to this tiny gift were far beyond my expectations.

Once on the Trail, I became practiced at smiling boldly as a stranger approached announcing that I had a small gift. When they stopped to listen for more details, I briefly claimed that I was about to complete the AT by the grace of God after many years of Trail section hikes. It was especially important to me that I publicly declared that this enormous success belonged to the glory of God, and not to my personal accomplishments. Then I further stated that I felt called to tell others about the great peace in my life because of faith in God. Then I placed the dove into the stranger's hand and said, "Peace be with you." Quite often, as we stood together in God's Nature and wilderness, strangers passing on the Trail, the vulnerability of our shared human condition surfaced. Our souls united in that moment and an unsaid experience of spiritual beings happened. On several occasions, tears of joy appeared. After initiating that greeting, "Peace be with you," with another person, deepened my trust and obedience to God through the peacemaking ways of God.

One occasion of "passing the peace" particularly stands out in my memories.[86] Smasher and I were hiking southbound towards the Hudson River when we climbed Schaghticoke Mountain near the Connecticut/New York state line. It was there that Smasher and I crossed paths with two young women on the mountain ridge as they were thru-hiking northbound. The women in their 20s had been on the Trail for months enjoying their quest as thru-hikers before settling into post college living in the world of work. On the mountain ridge, we greeted them, and I shared my opening remarks and then handed a dove to each one of the women. They began to tear up with joy and we joined them in tears. The women shared how the special moment with us punctuated the whole of their Trail journey as they embarked into adulthood. Thank you, God, for Your blessings of these peacemaking moments.

---

[86] 2015 Hiking Trip

Near this very mountain top is the home of Franklin and Eleanor Roosevelt. As we toured this historic mansion a few days later, I read the following statement by Eleanor Roosevelt posted there: *"For it is not enough to talk about Peace, one must believe in it. And it isn't enough to believe in it, one must work at it."*

Becoming a peacemaker is to know God's blessings. When we consciously connect with others as a Christian, we are going beyond the culturally defined parameters of insiders and outsiders, we are peacemaking. Christ wants us to be his hands and feet in this world, ever expanding the fellowship of believers wherever we go. This is the Good News to the world!

Whether we are on the AT or a public sidewalk passing someone, let us approach others ready to do peacemaking for God. Let us be peacemaking activists as Jesus called us to be, reaching out to everyone, building the Kingdom of God here on earth.

Prayer: Holy God, send Your Spirit of Wisdom upon us and preserve the good work that You cultivate between people. Help me to understand that You are the Peace Maker. I am blessed to be the hands and feet of Your peacemaking in the sphere of influence You have brought into my life. Guide me to defend the rights of all human beings to worship you God. Make me courageous and strong as I witness to others "the peace of Christ be with you."

Question to provoke faith journaling: Have you recently witnessed Christ's peace in your life?

Encouraging

A Step To Faith: Rely on Jesus' encouraging Word.

Romans 12:8 *If your gift is to encourage others, do it!* NLT

My first impression of "HAD", his Trail name, was his encouraging smile. That first impression was immediately validated by his actions as he introduced his volunteer role, a Trail Angel. My hiking buddy Debra and I were packing the car at the end of the 2010 trip, preparing to drive home to Texas. HAD drove up to the parking lot in his Suburban with North Carolina license plates and offered his help. A retired elementary school teacher with genuine love for people, he promptly offered an encouraging smile. Since we were at the end of our AT trip, I took HAD's contact information and told him I would reach out to him a year later, when I continued through Pennsylvania.

True to his spirit and word, HAD showed up a year later and gave two weeks of support to our 2011 AT hiking excursion.[87] An AT hiker with leg problems keeping him from continuing previous years of hiking and backpacking, HAD did not quit his beloved AT. He encouraged others by supporting their hiking progress, especially in the Pennsylvania section which he knew so well. His time on the AT always included an interest in bird watching, especially the soaring hawks that are prevalent along the Trail ridges of Pennsylvania. As we hiked, HAD frequented observation points to watch the hawks while being ready to help us, just a cell phone call away. HAD shared his Trail experience with us, not as a critic but as a reliable encourager. I especially appreciated his preparatory words about the challenges of the Knife's Edge ridge. Having

---

[87] 2011 September Hiking Trip

my patient attitude in place prior to reaching the slippery dangerous challenge of the ridge allowed for a spirit of adventure to arise within me, rather than an bad attitude of giving up.

The 2011 hiking trip was difficult to face because it was "Rocksylvania." This Trail section filled with grapefruit size rocks made for slow mileage hiking days. Impatience and boredom were constant barriers to finding a good attitude. When you spend the Trail time watching the placement of your feet to avoid turning an ankle or falling, it can make you grumpy! Obviously HAD was not a quitter and with his good spirit, he kept encouraging us to focus on the fun and the adventure of the Trail time.

The challenge of having a good attitude increased. When these thunderstorms and heavy rain began, the rocky Trail became slippery. HAD rescued our depleting spirits with a remedy to escape from the steady rainfall. He led us to the free resource of a park pavilion in Port Clinton, Pa. where we set up our tents and relished a dry base camp inside it. The open air pavilion was our refuge during the multiple days of rain. As we came off the slippery rocky Trail at the end of a tedious day's hike with few miles to show for it, HAD was there at the trailhead with a smile. He surprised us again by being the King of uplifting news.

I joyfully imagine what it was like for elementary kids to be in HAD's classroom. He would have been my favorite teacher.

Smasher and I were so blessed by HAD's presence on the 2011 trip, but he didn't stop caring about our AT progress. When we invited him to the 2015 celebratory party at the Dutch Haus in Virginia, HAD and his wife chose to make the lengthy drive from North Carolina, just to participate in our celebration of finishing the 2000 AT miles.

Though HAD stands out in my memory as the prime example of encouraging others, I was fortunate to hike with Smasher and others who contributed their encouragement to the Trail companionship.

Through typical trials of the Trail — ground bee stings, "turtling" (wearing a backpack while falling), bruises, foot blisters and Smasher's black eye — my hiking buddies exhibited more than a 'don't quit' attitude. We were encouragers to one another. We tried to be bearers of the Good News on the Trail each day.

I strive to be the kind of encourager that HAD was. He demonstrated the discipleship that Jesus wants from us. A changed attitude that comes from salvation. A pastor said something very convicting in his sermon that fits here. He said "Jesus didn't die so we'd be sorry. He died, and was resurrected so we would be changed." To be sorry means that I feel bad about what I said or did. It is a temporary fleeting attitude. To be changed is to be repentant. It is the deep conviction to live corrected and changed. To encourage others is to first hold unto a presence with Jesus, the Way, the Truth, and the Life. Only then are we equipped to be encouraging to others.

Mark 5:1–20, describes how Jesus shocks everyone by healing a mentally ill man when he orders the evil spirits to leave the man's body and then orders the evil spirits to enter the nearby pigs. The pigs, possessed by the evil spirits, run away, and fall off a cliff. The local towns people are scared because they see the new found sanity of the man who had been so crazy. Out of fear, the people tell Jesus and his disciples to leave. The healed and sane man asked Jesus to let him go along in the ministry journey. Jesus says no. Jesus tells the healed man to stay in the area and share with others the wonderful things Jesus has done for him. Later, Jesus returns to this man's community on the eastern side of the Sea of Galilee, where previously the Gentiles and people who lived on the edge of faith communities had rejected him, afraid, and uninterested. When Jesus returns, there are gatherings of believers rejoicing in Jesus' message, the Good News. I believe this one man, who Jesus healed from mental illness, became an encouraging witness to the saving Grace of Christ. This healed man was changed because of faith. And he did not quit sharing the Good News, and the community around him changed because the man was changed. Encouraging others is a gift but it is also an intention that we can choose to convey through our faith, because Jesus loves us.

Prayer: Holy Jesus, only You are the everlasting light in the darkness. Guide me to trust Your patient ways through the barriers on my daily path. Give me the hope that I need to carry on. Teach me to know Your Word that is encouraging me to follow You. Remind me to share Your Word with others, encouraging them to seek Your everlasting light. Amen.

A question to provoke faith journaling – How is Christ consistently encouraging you in specific ways, yet you have missed focusing on this Truth?

Celebrating

A Step To Faith: I am celebrating that it is well with my soul!

Jeremiah 29:10–14 *"The truth is that you will be in Babylon for seventy years. But then I will come and do for you all the good things I have promised, and I will bring you home again. For I know the plans I have for you," says the Lord. "They are plans for good and not for disaster, to give you a future and a hope. In those days when you pray, I will listen. If you look for me in earnest, you will find me when you seek me. I will be found by you," says the Lord.* NLT

What does it mean to celebrate? What is the reason that people enjoy celebrating?

'Celebrating is a ritual that offers opportunities to make meaning from the familiar and the mysterious at the same time.' [88]

The 'familiar' form of celebrating the completion of the AT miles is to stand on Mt. Katahdin behind the mammoth signage and stretch out your arms in victory! A photo of this epoch moment is a declaration that you hiked 2,185 miles. That is the 'familiar' celebration ritual in the AT community. However, the 'familiar' celebration ritual did not have meaning for Smasher and Spirit (me). Our AT section hiking journey found meaning in a different way and we celebrated.[89]

No problem! In Jeremiah we learn that God has a plan for our lives, a plan for good. With God's gracious guidance, a 'mysterious' plan for celebrating the completion of 2,000 hiking miles

---

[88] Evan Imber-Black and Janine Roberts. *Rituals for Our Times*, page 3

[89] 2008 July Hiking Trip, False Summits Reflection Devotional

was unfolding over years of God's good timing. All of this meaning from God was unfolding while we were section hiking the Trail.

As I reflect on the meaning of my life uncovered during the AT hiking trip years, there are three Truths about living that I learned and now I celebrate.

- The journey is more important than the destination.
- Almighty God lives and reigns with Grace and Love over all of life.
- It is well with my soul.

The journey is more important than the destination. Before Smasher and I ever dreamed of climbing Mt. Katahdin to the northern terminus of the AT, God had a plan for 'mysteriously' celebrating our final destination. As we learn from the book of Jeremiah, God promises to be with us throughout the journey while we are learning to see Him. Hopefully we grow to trust Him. God is fully present on our journey of life, and faith is what happens when we begin to depend on that Truth. God knew that I needed a 'mysterious' celebration that forced me to focus on the faith journey itself. God knew how easily I would be distracted by a 'familiar' celebration with a clear finish line.

The 'mysterious' ritual of celebrating the completion of AT miles itself began when Lois Arnold declared that Smasher and I would have the celebration at her home in Monticello, Virginia. Lois made that unquestionable proclamation early in the years of hiking trips. It happened in 2003 when we stayed at the Arnold's AT hiker bunkhouse for shelter during a hurricane. My inner thought reaction to Lois' prophetic words were "that sounds crazy! Where did that notion come from?" Lois somehow knew that Smasher and I would complete the 2,000 AT miles, even though I was clueless at that time to this ending of the journey.

I was content with one section hike at a time. Lois and her husband Earl continued to believe in our AT journey outcome as well as participate in the annual September hiking trips until the end. Their reliable hospitality was a great place for Smasher and I to rendezvous numerous times as we launched our September hikes somewhere along the AT. Year after year, reflections about last year's hiking trip and conversations about the coming trip plan happened at Lois' kitchen table. Lois joined Smasher and me on some of the AT hiking trips. It was many years later that God's plan and 'mysterious' celebration became apparent to me. We would finish the AT miles. Lois and Earl were ready to celebrate when the time came! With open hearts and hearth, our friends and family gathered for a unique celebration at the Dutch Haus, the Arnold's home. That weekend-long celebratory gathering was a love-filled reflection on the journey of life, not the AT journey alone. For me, it was a celebration that connected the 'familiar' with the 'mysterious.'

Almighty God lives and reigns with Grace and Love over all of life. In the Jeremiah passage, the big celebration for me were the words 'I will bring you home again.' My interpretation of this message is that I have left home, I have been on a journey, and I will eventually go home again. Alleluia! The AT journey became a spiritual pilgrimage for me when my faith grew enough to help me grasp that my whole life is a homeward bound journey with God's presence guiding me along the way whenever I listen. I finally let go of a great burden during the AT hiking years, thank you God. I came to realize that God's unconditional Love for me means that I am not responsible for other people accepting that God Is Love. This burden was difficult to turn over to God because the burden was my identity for a long time. I am responsible to God for planting the seeds of God's light.

Our Gracious God shoulders everything else in life. Letting Jesus carry that burden saved me. I accept His Grace and Love each day, and try to pass it on to others.

It is well with my soul. I set out on the Appalachian Trail looking for God's peace to fill the emptiness in my life. I thought that God was done with me because my life purpose as a mother raising children was finished. My nest was empty. What can be more important in life than raising children to become young adults that know who God is? I followed my instincts into God's Nature and slowly filtered out all the worldly distractions of noise that prevented me from hearing my inner thoughts and feelings. These worldly distractions prevented me from hearing God. The Holy Spirit speaks to me in a 'still small voice.' I Kings 19:9. While developing a lifestyle with consistent God time in Nature, my purpose as a living witness to God's Love and Saving Grace became crystal clear, and my soul was filled with Joy.

Being with God in the setting of God's Creation, Nature, is a universal first step in getting to know God. Sure! God works in mysterious ways to bring us Home to God's Love. God pursues us individually and in a unique personable way. But my faith informs me that people seeking God need more time in God's Nature, unplugged from worldly distractions. By doing so, we hear God's presence and more readily dialogue with Him. It is all that we need in life when we can take ownership of the Truth - It is well with my soul!

Prayer: Eternal Gracious God, Your Goodness is evident to me throughout Your Nature and Creation. You are the patient Weaver of my life beginnings intertwined with my life endings. You are the Weaver of my life mysteries intertwined with my life familiarities. I am beginning to understand that my life mysteries have been in Your loving hands all along. Your faithful presence in my life while I wander through life transitions is difficult for me to comprehend. When I am lost, You find me and lead me Home. You are my Resting Place. Teach me to embrace your encouragement on the journey of my life. Help me turn from temptations quickly and turn to You with all my praise and adoration. I celebrate your loving presence in my soul. Amen

Question to provoke faith journaling - What about God's ways or attributes have you come to understand and celebrate?

Living A Spiritual Pilgrimage

A WELL LIT PATH HAS *life direction*

A Well Lit Path Has Life Direction

The traditional spiritual pilgrimage is described as *'a physical journey (which may or may not be long and arduous) to a special destination, accompanied by a particular state of mind and often with the hope of transformation.'*[90]

The Faith Journeys and the Reflection Devotionals illustrate how I, Spirit, was a seeker expecting God to deliver a happy life to replace the burdens of grief and my empty nest life transition. I found the best setting for me to seek a relationship with God was in God's Nature. Going to Nature and into the wilderness to find a relationship with God has deep historical roots; roots that are seen in the Old Testament Bible stories before the times of Christ Jesus. When Jesus began his ministry, his initial step was to go into the wilderness to center on God's presence. Jesus went to the wilderness multiple times to escape the crowds and to turn to God.

In my case, as a faith seeker, I quickly deepened my relationship with God by repeatedly going to the wilderness along the Appalachian Trail. In addition to these immersions with God in Nature, I chose to develop a lifestyle that included months of pre-trip physical conditioning where I was outdoors and alone

---

[90] The Pilgrim Journey, A History of Pilgrimage in the Western World. Page 9.

with God. Eventually the totality of this new lifestyle transformed the hiking trips into faith journeys. Over the years, faith journeys informed and inspired the whole of my life. The Holy Spirit infused the whole of my life, and now I embrace a lifestyle of a spiritual pilgrimage. My destination on this spiritual pilgrimage is Heaven.

But you should ask me, what's next in daily life, now that the AT is completed, and I am on a spiritual pilgrimage? My answer to this question is "Look up child of God!" Living a spiritual pilgrimage means that I am aware that seeking a closer walk with God and relying on His Love to sustain me is my all and all. This is my life's purpose and meaning. Truthfully, I am sometimes confused about the meaning and purpose in daily living. This is a natural human tendency for me and for you, just as it is a natural tendency for a child to need guidance from a Loving Parent.

Spiritual pilgrimages have a long history in human civilization which I found interesting to study.[91] In *The Pilgrim Journey*, James Harpur describes the first Christian pilgrimage as the journey of the Magi to the Christ child. Another example of pilgrimage is evident in the Bible where Abraham was called by God to leave the familiar and go to a new life in the land of Canaan. A third Biblical example of pilgrimage is the exodus of the Children of Israel from bondage in Egypt and their long journey through the wilderness under Moses' leadership.

From my perspective, living a spiritual pilgrimage is more like trailblazing than using an established trail. Trailblazing is the faith seeker's way to center on God so that one's own faith journey can happen. Over time, a spiritual pilgrimage takes root, and the faith seeker transforms into a pilgrim. Notice that I view a spiritual pilgrimage as never outgrowing my desire to continually seek

---

[91] The Pilgrim Journey, A History of Pilgrimage in the Western World, James Harpur

God. When I compare my lengthy experience of Faith Journeys becoming a spiritual pilgrimage with the author Harpur's description of a traveler becoming a pilgrim, I find confirmation of my Faith Journeys transforming me into a pilgrim on a spiritual pilgrimage.

Identifying the tools necessary for staying on the trail of faith growth is essential. If your faith journey approach is like mine, a trailblazer, I found that I need tools to keep me on track and less confused. When I get lost, I need to know how to renew my orientation with God as the center of my life. God is my compass. Learning how to use the tools is helpful but this may take time. It may takes years to transform into a pilgrim on a spiritual pilgrimage. In God's time, not our time!

From these reflection devotionals, you have experienced three essential tools that are important. Those three are attending to Moments of Grace, Moments of Belief, and Moments of Faith. I hope these tools may serve as a guide in blazing your own trail as a believer. Know that there are other essential tools which God gives to us, but I want to remain focused on these three.

Moments of Grace are constantly happening because it is God's Nature to be with you, never ever leaving you, or me. Your awareness of God's loving presence is the hard part since we do not have a natural tendency towards the self-awareness of being a child looking up for the Loving Parent and saying, "Where are you?" Moments of Grace occur in my life when I cultivate this spiritual self-awareness, and hold an expectation that God will answer me. This is true of the first Moments of Grace that we experience as seeds sprouting in the soul and informing us that we are not alone. And additional Moments of Grace occur as faith matures over time into a tree of life, a spiritual pilgrimage.

What you can do:

1. Re-read the Moments of Grace Devotionals for awareness tips about Grace happenings at various times in your own life.
2. In Moments of Grace Devotionals, use the questions that provoke spiritual journaling found at the end of each Devotional.
3. Answering these questions by writing a faith journal will focus assist your awareness that Grace is happening constantly.

Moments of Belief are flowing through your consciousness about your life and about your relationship with God. Unlike the Moments of Grace where you are watching God, here you are tasked with increasing awareness of your beliefs about God, and your beliefs about God's relationship with you and others. Some of those beliefs are old and unexamined by you. We carry beliefs with us from childhood as well as earlier adult years, and these beliefs desperately need dusting off and important examination by your adult maturity. Some beliefs are grounded in what you experience as cognitive thoughts and other beliefs are grounded in what you experience as mixed feelings. You also may hold beliefs where thoughts and feelings are intertwined. God built us with a great capacity for creating beliefs and examining those beliefs. If we do not examine our beliefs for current validity, we are not conscious of the beliefs that we are using. When we do not have validity on our beliefs, the result is misguided decision making. God has given us freewill to make our decisions and learn from the decisions. If we do not spiritually grow in this way, we become lost souls. As travelers in the spiritual wilderness, we cannot survive the life-long journey without frequently examining the spiritual beliefs held within us.

A Well Lit Path Has Life Direction

One common modern-day belief that many faith seekers need to examine is the belief of one's dependence on God. That was a belief confusion at the heart of my empty nest life transition. I was seeking God, but I wanted our relationship on my terms. Being in the AT wilderness really helped me except God's loving ways. Transforming me with a faith-based self-esteem. God understands our humanity. It is our tendency to turn our backs on God's presence, especially when we carry unexamined beliefs about God.

What you can do:

1. Do not live with beliefs of victimhood sustained worry and anxiety. Examine your beliefs. Own your human essential needs such as water, food, shelter, a safe place to sleep. Pray about these needs being met at the level of needs, not wants. Ask God to take away your burdensome worries about your basic needs so that you can hear His guidance in focused problem solving.
2. Re-read the Moments of Beliefs Devotionals for tips on how to identify the beliefs that are inhabiting your unexamined consciousness. In Moments of Beliefs Devotionals, use the questions that provoke spiritual journaling found at the end of each Devotional. Answering these questions by journaling about your beliefs will bring updated informative self-awareness.

Moments of Faith come with greater frequency when I have habitually tuned into my responsibility for awareness about Moments of Grace and Moments of Belief. I cannot predict when you will experience an enduring faith. I can promise that God's relationship with you is better than any other relationship you will experience because of God's unconditional Love for you. Always remember that no human can give unconditional love. I can tell you that God has been and is currently lovingly reaching out to you, wanting you to be in relationship with Him. God sacrificed His Son, Jesus Christ, so that you and I would understand His Love for all.

When your faith falters, and doubting God's presence creeps in, remember that you are a child of God seeking Him. Therefore, go to your Loving Parent privately and ask, "Where are you now God?" And remember to expect an answer. Remember that it is natural to experience Moments of Faith decreasing in times of life transition. I struggled through many life transitions on the faulty belief that I was not worthy of God's holy presence and help. This could be your obstacle as well.

What to do:

1. Find a Bible Study group that encourages you to explore the Word of God and its impact on your life. I did not make the consistent time commitment for Bible Study until I had completed the AT. I honestly did not know what I was missing, and I now wish that I had participated in Bible study earlier in my life. A Bible study with regular group discussion became the cornerstone that I needed for Moments of Faith to become transformative in my life. God's Word helps us see how God has a plan for good in this world, how God wants us to individually join Him in this plan. In a Bible Study group discussion, I hear believers witnessing to God's provision in their lives. And I hear believers asking for prayers because our faith needs that support. I tell others of God's presence in my life as I participate in Bible study

group discussions. I then ask for prayerful support, all of which gives me Holy strength.[92]
2. In Moments of Faith Devotionals, use the questions that provoke spiritual journaling found at the end of each Devotional. Addressing these questions (in writing when helpful) will further build your reliance on faith when you feel the most vulnerable.

When you go to God's Nature, temporarily getting away from the pressures and distractions of life, go to God with expectations that God will refuel and equip you to carry His Light. There are hikers around you on the Trail who do not have an expectation to find God in other parts of life besides their compartmentalized time of being in God's Nature.

Do not put God in the small box. Challenge yourself to know God's presence wherever you are. Do not resign yourself to a hollowness in life, an emptiness of meaning and purpose. Do not turn your back on God's Love that is sometimes easier to experience in God's Nature. God is good and God's Love is everywhere, embracing you the deepest when you need it the most.

In closing, I want to share with you daily life habits that encourage the emergence of a spiritual pilgrimage life:

- Spending regular prayerful conversation time with God.
- Sharing personal experiences of Jesus' mercy and forgiveness with believers who will appreciate your relationship with God.
- Seeking spiritual wisdom about who God is. Noticing that God's Nature is love and we are built to love Him and share His love with others.

---

[92] *Bible Study Fellowship* is my recommendation. An international organization. www.BSF.org

- Telling those who will listen about God's love and His presence in the moment. This means you are spontaneously expressing acknowledgment of a Grace moment when it occurs.
- Discipleship of others. God has put you in a circle of influence to be His presence. Jesus is counting on you.
- Letting Bible study inform you of God's ways and teachings.
- Keep a Faith journal about your walk with Jesus Christ.
- And last, but not least, commit to dedicated quality time immersed in Nature, God's Creation.

By practicing these faith disciplines, conversations with God will find completion, and the roots of a spiritual pilgrimage will take shape. God showed me that He keeps His promises to those who seek Him. It is my hope and my prayer that your faith journey has been enhanced by sharing my faith journeys with you.

Hebrews 12: 1-3 *Let us strip off every weight that slows us down, especially the sin that so easily hinders our progress. And let us run with endurance the race that God has set before us. We do this by keeping our eyes on Jesus, on whom our faith depends, from start to finish.*

Appendices

List of Volunteer Appalachian Maintaining Clubs 1921 - 2021 [93]

Allentown Hiking Club
Appalachian Mountain Club: Western Massachusetts, Connecticut, and Delaware Valley Chapters
Batona Hiking Club
Blue Mountain Eagle Climbing Club
Carolina Mountain Club
Cumberland Valley Appalachian Trail Club
Dartmouth Outing Club
Georgia Appalachian Trail Club
Keystone Trails Association
Maine Appalachian Trail Club
Natural Bridge Appalachian Trail Club
New York – New Jersey Trail Conference
Old Dominion Appalachian Trail Club
Outdoor Club of Virginia Tech
Piedmont Appalachian Trail Hikers
Potomac Appalachian Trail Club
Randolph Mountain Club
Roanoke Appalachian Trail Club
Smoky Mountains Hiking Club
Susquehanna Appalachian Trail Club
Tennessee Eastman Hiking and Canoeing Club
Tidewater Appalachian Trail Club
Wilmington Trail Club
York Hiking Club

---

[93] AT Journeys Magazine, Fall 2021, page 94

List of Abbreviations

NIV: The Holy Bible: New International Version
LNT: New Living Translation
NRSV: The Holy Bible: The New Revised Standard Version
KJV: The Holy Bible: King James Version
AT: Appalachian Trail
SNP: Shenandoah National Park
GSMNP: Great Smoky Mountain National Park

Bibliography

Abel, Beth Eden. *Life Maps Workbook: Lifestyle Goal Setting Journey for Women.* Second Edition. Unpublished. 2013.

Abel, R.W. videographer. "Beth's AT Final Day" https://youtu.be/xrvQkpQCNEg

Adkins, Leonard M. *The Appalachian Trail: A Visitor's Companion.* Birmingham, Alabama: Menasha Ridge Press, 1998.

Bryson, Bill. *A Walk in the Woods, Rediscovering America on the Appalachian Trail.* New York, NY: Broadway Books, 1998.

Chazin, Daniel D. (ed). *Appalachian Trail Data Book 2013.* Harper's Ferry, West Virginia: Appalachian Trail Conservancy, 2012.

Dauphinee, D. *When You Find My Body: The Disappearance of Geraldine Largay on the Appalachian Trail.* Camden, Maine: Down East Books 2019.

Davis, Jennifer Pharr. *Becoming Odyssa: Adventures on the Appalachian Trail.* New York, NY, Beaufort Books, 2010.

Deeds, Jean. *There are Mountains to Climb: An Inspirational Journey.* Indianapolis, Indiana: Silverwood Press, 1996.

Harpur, James. *The Pilgrim Journey: A History of Pilgrimage in the Western World.* Katonah, New York: BlueBridge, 2016.

Holy Bible, The: New International Version. Grand Rapids, Michigan: Zondervan Press 1984.

Homan, Daniel O.S.B. and Lonni Collins Pratt. *Radical Hospitality.* Brewster, Massachusetts: Paraclete Press. 2002.

Imber-Black, Evan and Janine Roberts. *Rituals for Our Times.* New York, NY: Harper Collins 1993.

Irwin, Bill and David McCasland. *Blind Courage*. Waco, Texas: MRS Publishing 1992.

Kubler-Ross, Elisabeth. *On Death & Dying*. New York: Scribner Publishing 1969.

Life Recovery Bible: New Living Translation. Wheaton, Illinois: Tyndale House Publishers, Inc.

Meyer, Kathleen. *How to Shit in the Woods: An Environmentally Sound Approach to a Lost Art*. 4th Edition. New York, Ten Speed Press 2020.

Montgomery, Ben. *Grandma Gatewood's Walk. The Inspirational Story of the Woman who Saved the Appalachian Trail*. Chicago, Illinois: Chicago Revue Press, 2014.

New Oxford Annotated Bible, The: New Revised Standard Version. ed. Bruce M. Metzler and Roland E. Murphy. New York, NY: Oxford University Press 1991.

Orr, Kimberly. *The Upper Room*. Nashville, TN: Upper Room. Bi-Monthly Devotional.

Porter, Winton. *Just Passin' Thru*. Birmingham, Alabama: Menasha Ridge Press, 2009.

Sands, Mary. *Appalachian Trail in Bits and Pieces*. Pittsburg, Pennsylvania: Dorrance Publishing Co., 1992.

Sylvester, Robert ed. *Appalachian Trail Thru-Hiker's Companion 2014*. Harper's Ferry, West Virginia: Appalachian Trail Conservancy, 2013.

CPSIA information can be obtained
at www.ICGtesting.com
Printed in the USA
BVHW020854080522
636308BV00027B/1348